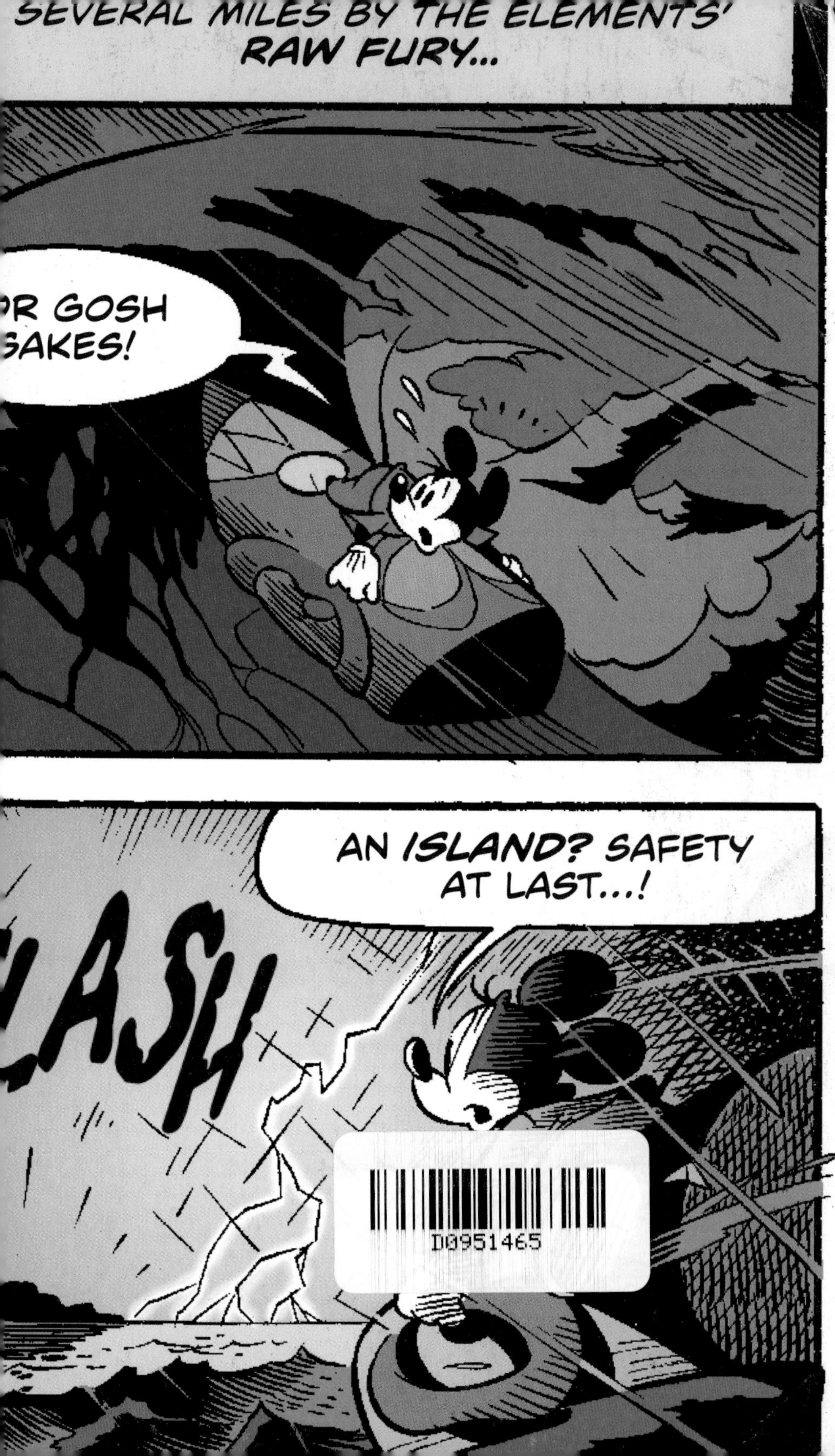
SEVERAL MILES BY THE ELEMENTS' RAW FURY...
R GOSH
AKES!
AN ISLAND? SAFETY AT LAST...!
LASH

MICKEY MOUSE
ON QUANDOMAI ISLAND

Ross Richie - Chief Executive Officer

Mark Waid - Chief Creative Officer

Matt Gagnon - Editor-in-Chief

Adam Fortier - VP-New Business

Wes Harris - VP-Publishing

Lance Kreiter - VP-Licensing & Merchandising

Chip Mosher - Marketing Director

Bryce Carlson - Managing Editor

Ian Brill - Editor

Dafna Pleban - Editor

Christopher Burns - Editor

Christopher Meyer - Editor

Shannon Watters - Assistant Editor

Neil Loughrie - Publishing Coordinator

Travis Beaty - Traffic Coordinator

Ivan Salazar - Marketing Assistant

Kate Hayden - Executive Assistant

Brian Latimer - Graphic Designer

Erika Terriquez - Graphic Designer

MICKEY MOUSE ON QUANDOMAI ISLAND – November 2010 published by BOOM Kids!, a division of Boom Entertainment, Inc. All contents © 2010 Disney Enterprises, Inc. BOOM Kids! and the BOOM Kids! logo are trademarks of Boom Entertainment, Inc., registered in various countries and categories. All rights reserved. Office of publication: 6310 San Vicente Blvd Ste 107, Los Angeles, CA 90048-5457. A catalog record for this book is available from OCLC and on our website www.boom-kids.com on the Librarians page. For information regarding the CPSIA on this printed material call: 203-595-3636 and

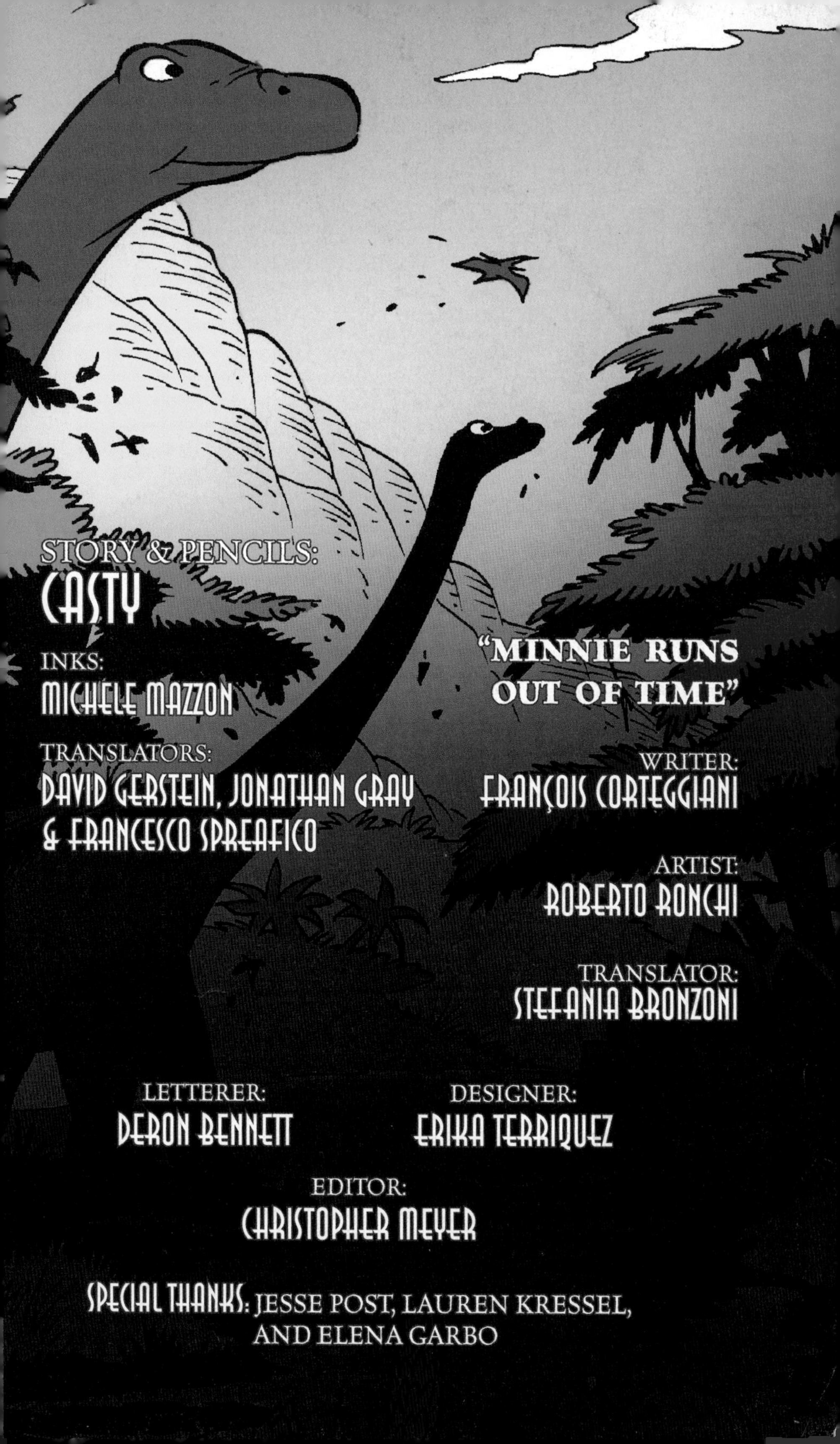

STORY & PENCILS:
CASTY

INKS:
MICHELE MAZZON

TRANSLATORS:
DAVID GERSTEIN, JONATHAN GRAY & FRANCESCO SPREAFICO

"MINNIE RUNS OUT OF TIME"

WRITER:
FRANÇOIS CORTEGGIANI

ARTIST:
ROBERTO RONCHI

TRANSLATOR:
STEFANIA BRONZONI

LETTERER:
DERON BENNETT

DESIGNER:
ERIKA TERRIQUEZ

EDITOR:
CHRISTOPHER MEYER

SPECIAL THANKS: JESSE POST, LAUREN KRESSEL, AND ELENA GARBO

CHAPTER ONE

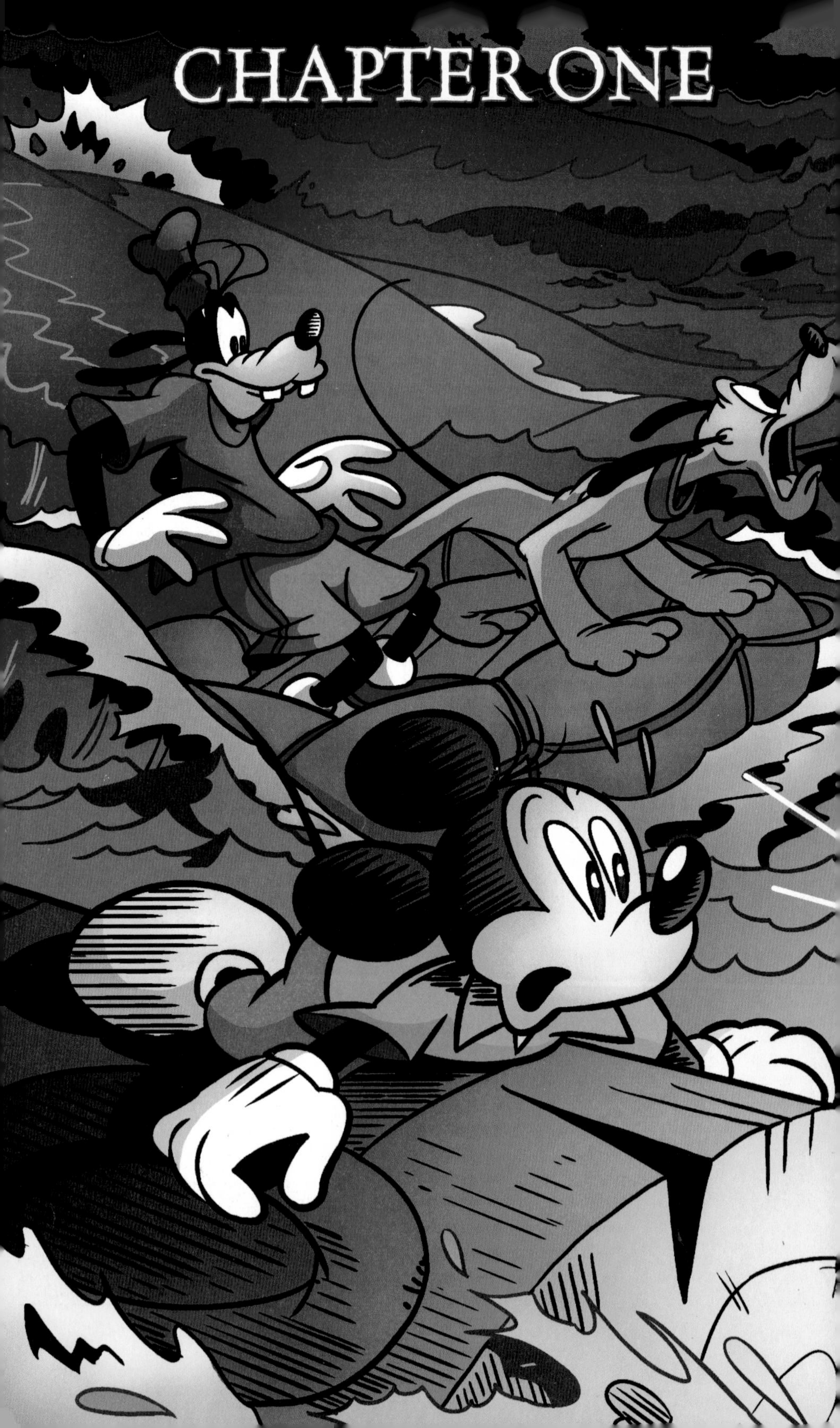

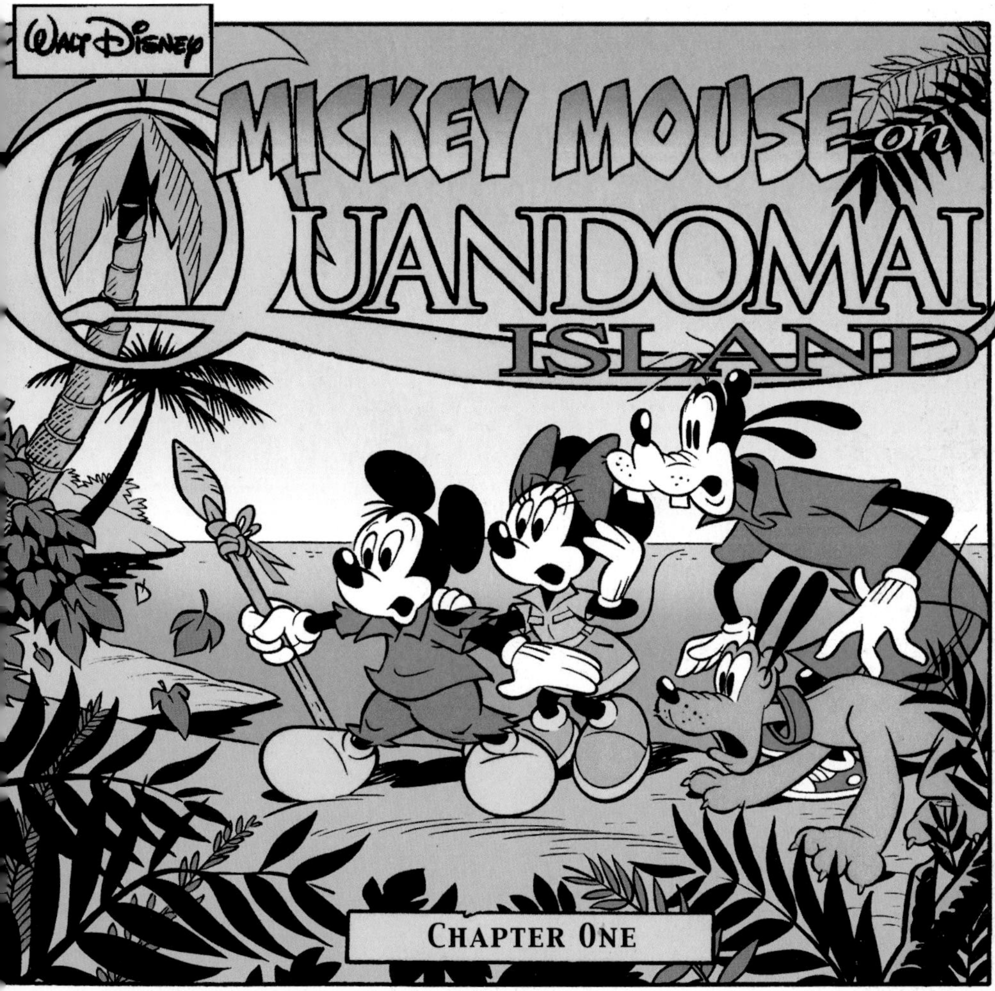
WALT DISNEY
MICKEY MOUSE on
QUANDOMAI
ISLAND
CHAPTER ONE

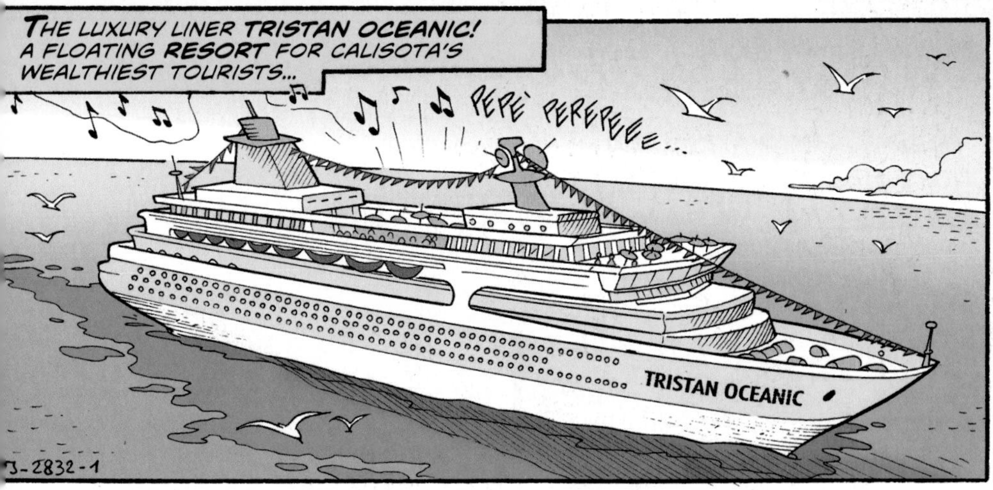
THE LUXURY LINER TRISTAN OCEANIC! A FLOATING RESORT FOR CALISOTA'S WEALTHIEST TOURISTS...
PEPÈ PEREPEEE...
TRISTAN OCEANIC
J-2832-1

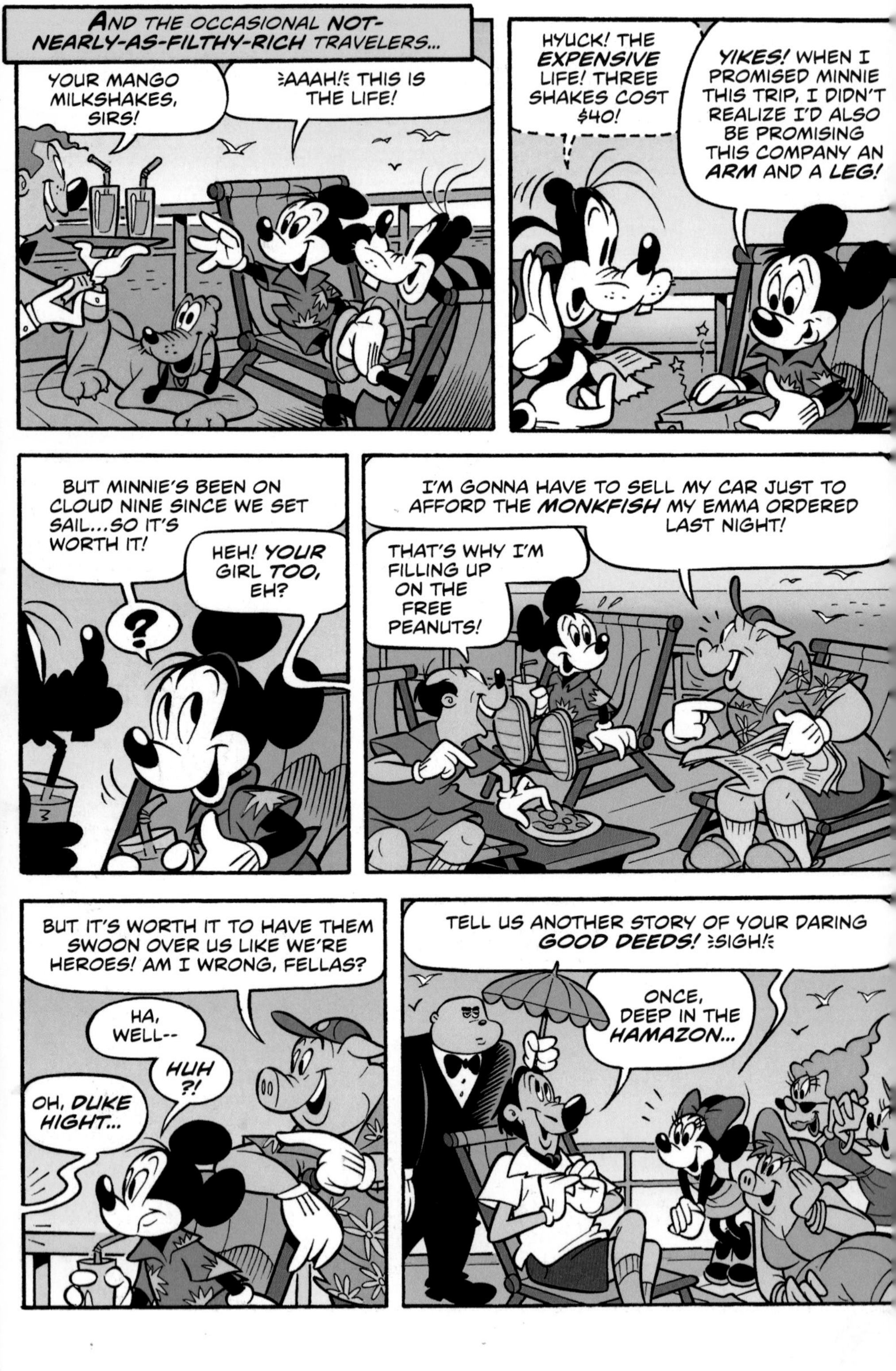
AND THE OCCASIONAL NOT-NEARLY-AS-FILTHY-RICH TRAVELERS...
YOUR MANGO MILKSHAKES, SIRS!
AAAH! THIS IS THE LIFE!
HYUCK! THE EXPENSIVE LIFE! THREE SHAKES COST $40!
YIKES! WHEN I PROMISED MINNIE THIS TRIP, I DIDN'T REALIZE I'D ALSO BE PROMISING THIS COMPANY AN ARM AND A LEG!
BUT MINNIE'S BEEN ON CLOUD NINE SINCE WE SET SAIL...SO IT'S WORTH IT!
HEH! YOUR GIRL TOO, EH?
?
I'M GONNA HAVE TO SELL MY CAR JUST TO AFFORD THE MONKFISH MY EMMA ORDERED LAST NIGHT!
THAT'S WHY I'M FILLING UP ON THE FREE PEANUTS!
BUT IT'S WORTH IT TO HAVE THEM SWOON OVER US LIKE WE'RE HEROES! AM I WRONG, FELLAS?
HA, WELL--
HUH?!
OH, DUKE HIGHT...
TELL US ANOTHER STORY OF YOUR DARING GOOD DEEDS! SIGH!
ONCE, DEEP IN THE HAMAZON...

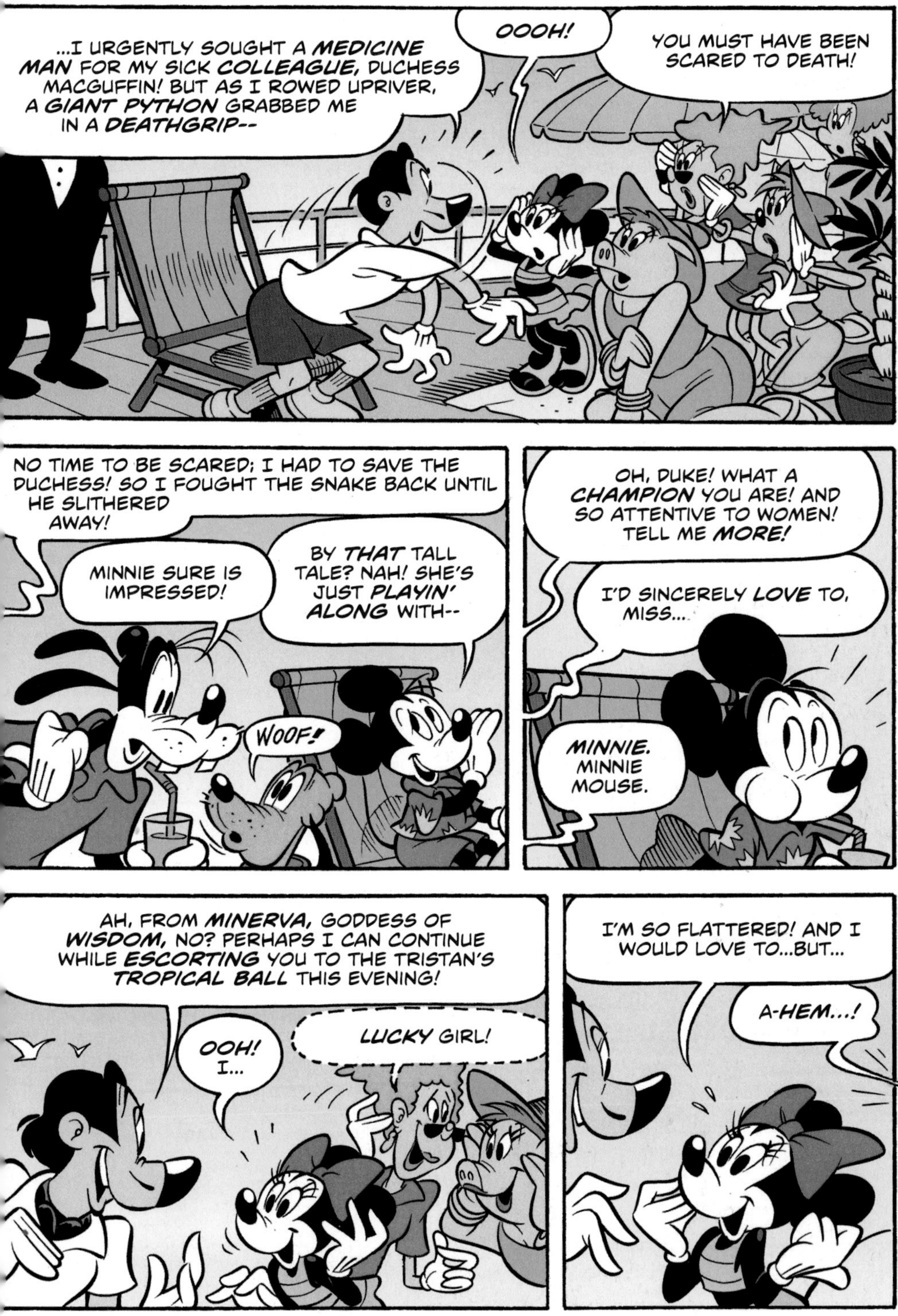
...I URGENTLY SOUGHT A MEDICINE MAN FOR MY SICK COLLEAGUE, DUCHESS MACGUFFIN! BUT AS I ROWED UPRIVER, A GIANT PYTHON GRABBED ME IN A DEATHGRIP--
OOOH!
YOU MUST HAVE BEEN SCARED TO DEATH!
NO TIME TO BE SCARED; I HAD TO SAVE THE DUCHESS! SO I FOUGHT THE SNAKE BACK UNTIL HE SLITHERED AWAY!
MINNIE SURE IS IMPRESSED!
BY THAT TALL TALE? NAH! SHE'S JUST PLAYIN' ALONG WITH--
WOOF!
OH, DUKE! WHAT A CHAMPION YOU ARE! AND SO ATTENTIVE TO WOMEN! TELL ME MORE!
I'D SINCERELY LOVE TO, MISS...
MINNIE. MINNIE MOUSE.
AH, FROM MINERVA, GODDESS OF WISDOM, NO? PERHAPS I CAN CONTINUE WHILE ESCORTING YOU TO THE TRISTAN'S TROPICAL BALL THIS EVENING!
OOH! I...
LUCKY GIRL!
I'M SO FLATTERED! AND I WOULD LOVE TO...BUT...
A-HEM...!

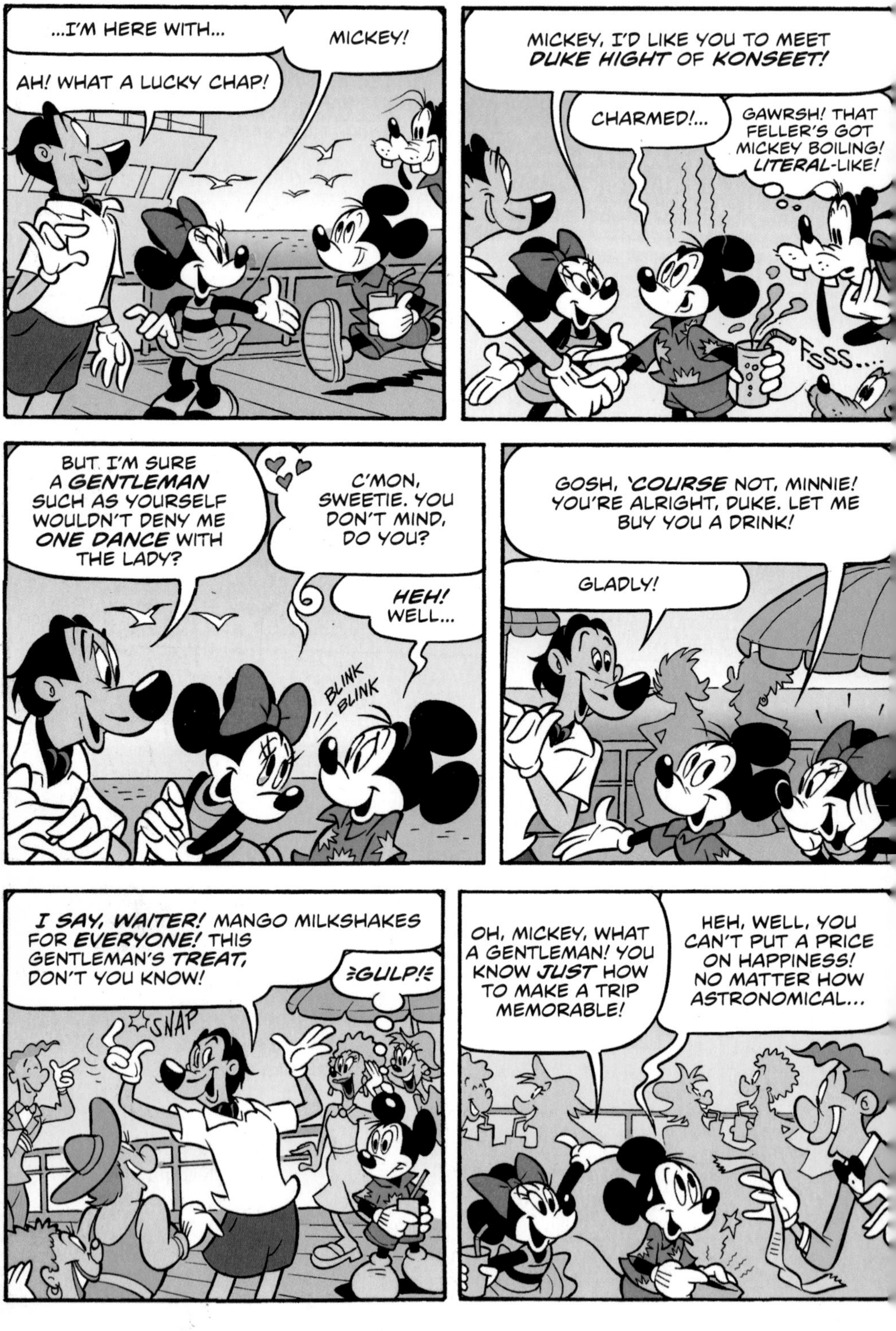
...I'M HERE WITH...
MICKEY!
AH! WHAT A LUCKY CHAP!
MICKEY, I'D LIKE YOU TO MEET DUKE HIGHT OF KONSEET!
CHARMED!...
GAWRSH! THAT FELLER'S GOT MICKEY BOILING! LITERAL-LIKE!
FSSS....
BUT I'M SURE A GENTLEMAN SUCH AS YOURSELF WOULDN'T DENY ME ONE DANCE WITH THE LADY?
C'MON, SWEETIE. YOU DON'T MIND, DO YOU?
HEH! WELL...
BLINK BLINK
GOSH, 'COURSE NOT, MINNIE! YOU'RE ALRIGHT, DUKE. LET ME BUY YOU A DRINK!
GLADLY!
I SAY, WAITER! MANGO MILKSHAKES FOR EVERYONE! THIS GENTLEMAN'S TREAT, DON'T YOU KNOW!
GULP!
SNAP
OH, MICKEY, WHAT A GENTLEMAN! YOU KNOW JUST HOW TO MAKE A TRIP MEMORABLE!
HEH, WELL, YOU CAN'T PUT A PRICE ON HAPPINESS! NO MATTER HOW ASTRONOMICAL...

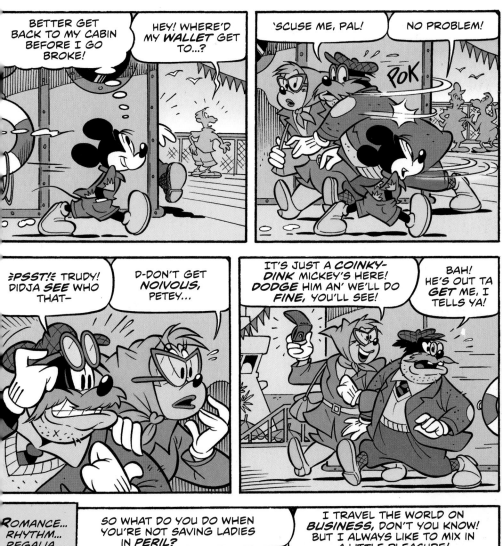

BETTER GET BACK TO MY CABIN BEFORE I GO BROKE!

HEY! WHERE'D MY *WALLET* GET TO...?

'SCUSE ME, PAL!

NO PROBLEM!

POK

≷PSST!≷ TRUDY! DIDJA *SEE* WHO THAT—

D-DON'T GET *NOIVOUS*, PETEY...

IT'S JUST A *COINKY-DINK* MICKEY'S HERE! *DODGE* HIM AN' WE'LL DO *FINE*, YOU'LL SEE!

BAH! HE'S OUT TA *GET* ME, I TELLS YA!

ROMANCE... RHYTHM... REGALIA... IT'S THE TROPICAL BALL!

SO WHAT DO YOU DO WHEN YOU'RE NOT SAVING LADIES IN *PERIL?*

I TRAVEL THE WORLD ON *BUSINESS*, DON'T YOU KNOW! BUT I ALWAYS LIKE TO MIX IN A LITTLE PLEASURE!

PEANUT?

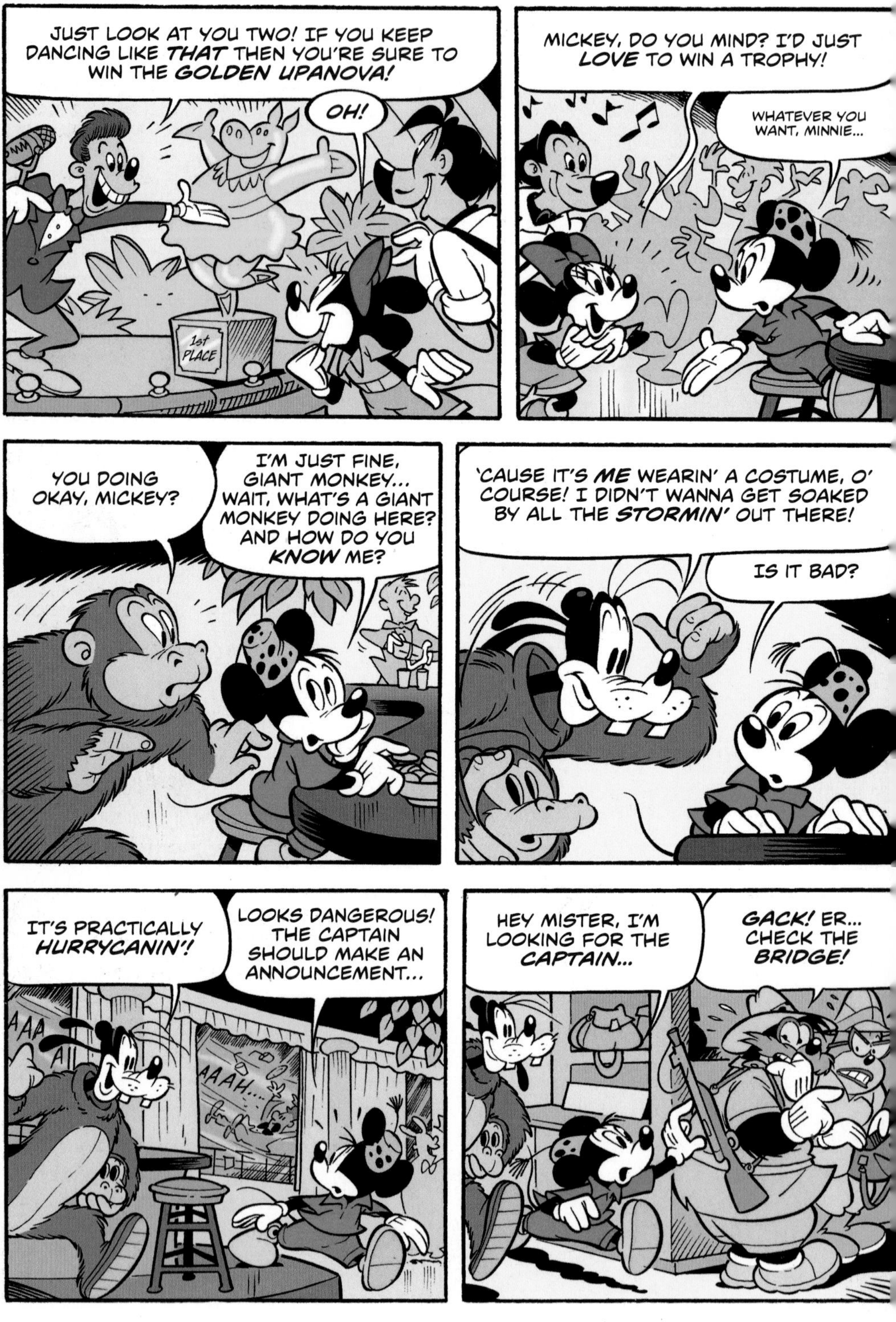
JUST LOOK AT YOU TWO! IF YOU KEEP DANCING LIKE THAT THEN YOU'RE SURE TO WIN THE GOLDEN UPANOVA!
OH!
1st PLACE
MICKEY, DO YOU MIND? I'D JUST LOVE TO WIN A TROPHY!
WHATEVER YOU WANT, MINNIE...
YOU DOING OKAY, MICKEY?
I'M JUST FINE, GIANT MONKEY... WAIT, WHAT'S A GIANT MONKEY DOING HERE? AND HOW DO YOU KNOW ME?
'CAUSE IT'S ME WEARIN' A COSTUME, O' COURSE! I DIDN'T WANNA GET SOAKED BY ALL THE STORMIN' OUT THERE!
IS IT BAD?
IT'S PRACTICALLY HURRYCANIN'!
LOOKS DANGEROUS! THE CAPTAIN SHOULD MAKE AN ANNOUNCEMENT...
AAAH...
HEY MISTER, I'M LOOKING FOR THE CAPTAIN...
GACK! ER... CHECK THE BRIDGE!

CATS AN' *DOGS!*

WOW!

CRACK

EVERYTHING'S UNDER CONTROL! NOTHING TO SEE HERE!

UH...*REALLY?* CAP'N, IF I CAN DO ANYTHING TO HELP...

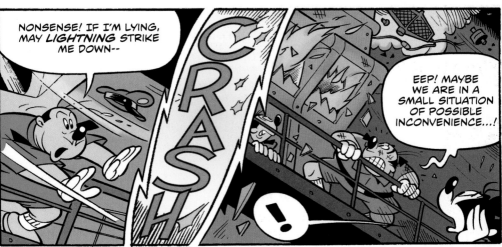

NONSENSE! IF I'M LYING, MAY *LIGHTNING* STRIKE ME DOWN--

CRASH

EEP! MAYBE WE ARE IN A SMALL SITUATION OF POSSIBLE INCONVENIENCE...!

OH DEAR! THE *LIGHTS* WENT OUT!

IS THIS PART OF THE SHOW?

I'M *SCARED!*

ME *TOO!*

STAY CALM, LADIES AND GENTS! WE'RE HAVING A *SMALL* ISSUE WITH THE ELECTRICAL SYSTEM, BUT MY MEN WILL HAVE IT FIXED QUICKLY!

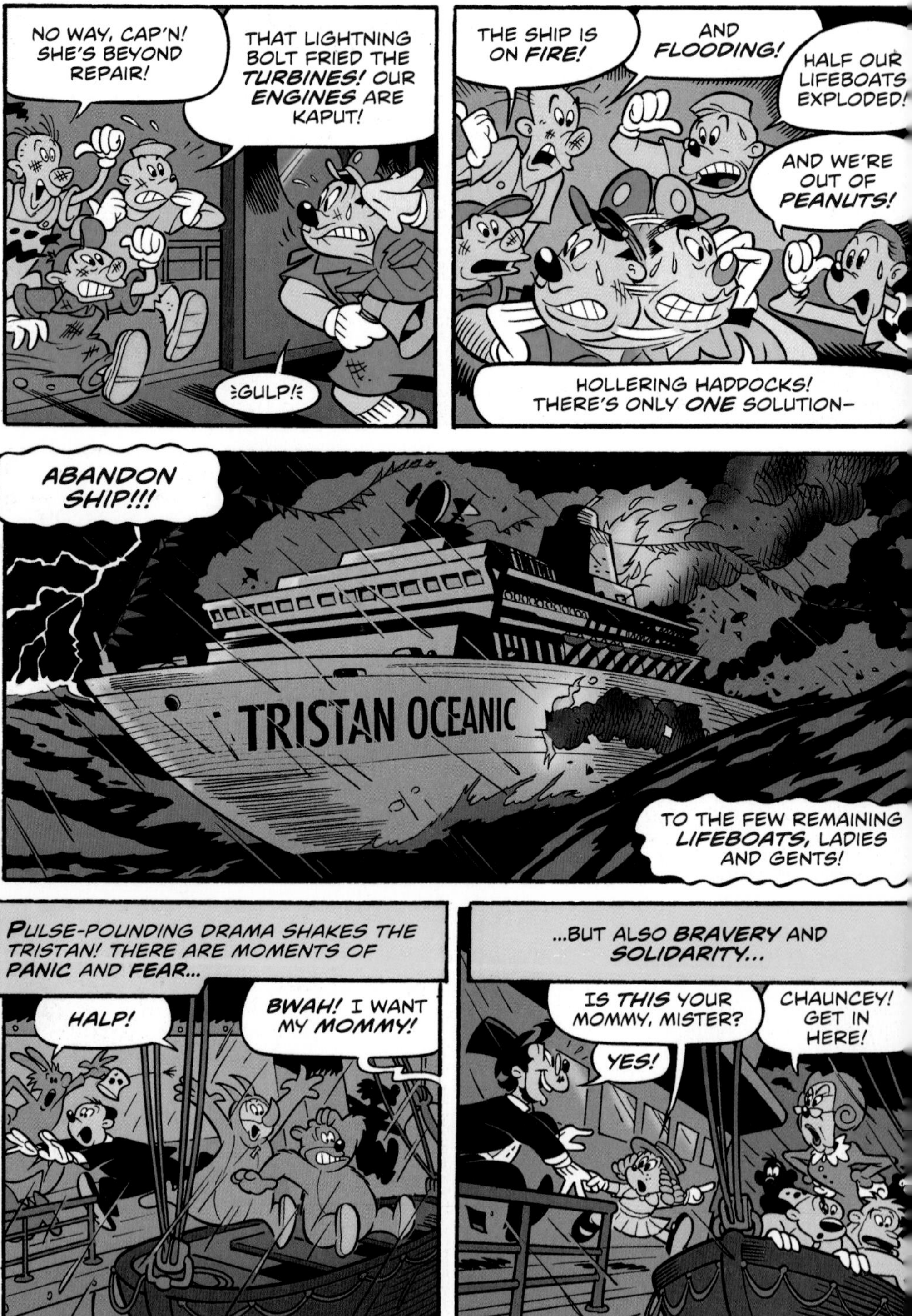
NO WAY, CAP'N! SHE'S BEYOND REPAIR!
THAT LIGHTNING BOLT FRIED THE TURBINES! OUR ENGINES ARE KAPUT!
GULP!
THE SHIP IS ON FIRE!
AND FLOODING!
HALF OUR LIFEBOATS EXPLODED!
AND WE'RE OUT OF PEANUTS!
HOLLERING HADDOCKS! THERE'S ONLY ONE SOLUTION–
ABANDON SHIP!!!
TRISTAN OCEANIC
TO THE FEW REMAINING LIFEBOATS, LADIES AND GENTS!
PULSE-POUNDING DRAMA SHAKES THE TRISTAN! THERE ARE MOMENTS OF PANIC AND FEAR...
HALP!
BWAH! I WANT MY MOMMY!
...BUT ALSO BRAVERY AND SOLIDARITY...
IS THIS YOUR MOMMY, MISTER?
YES!
CHAUNCEY! GET IN HERE!

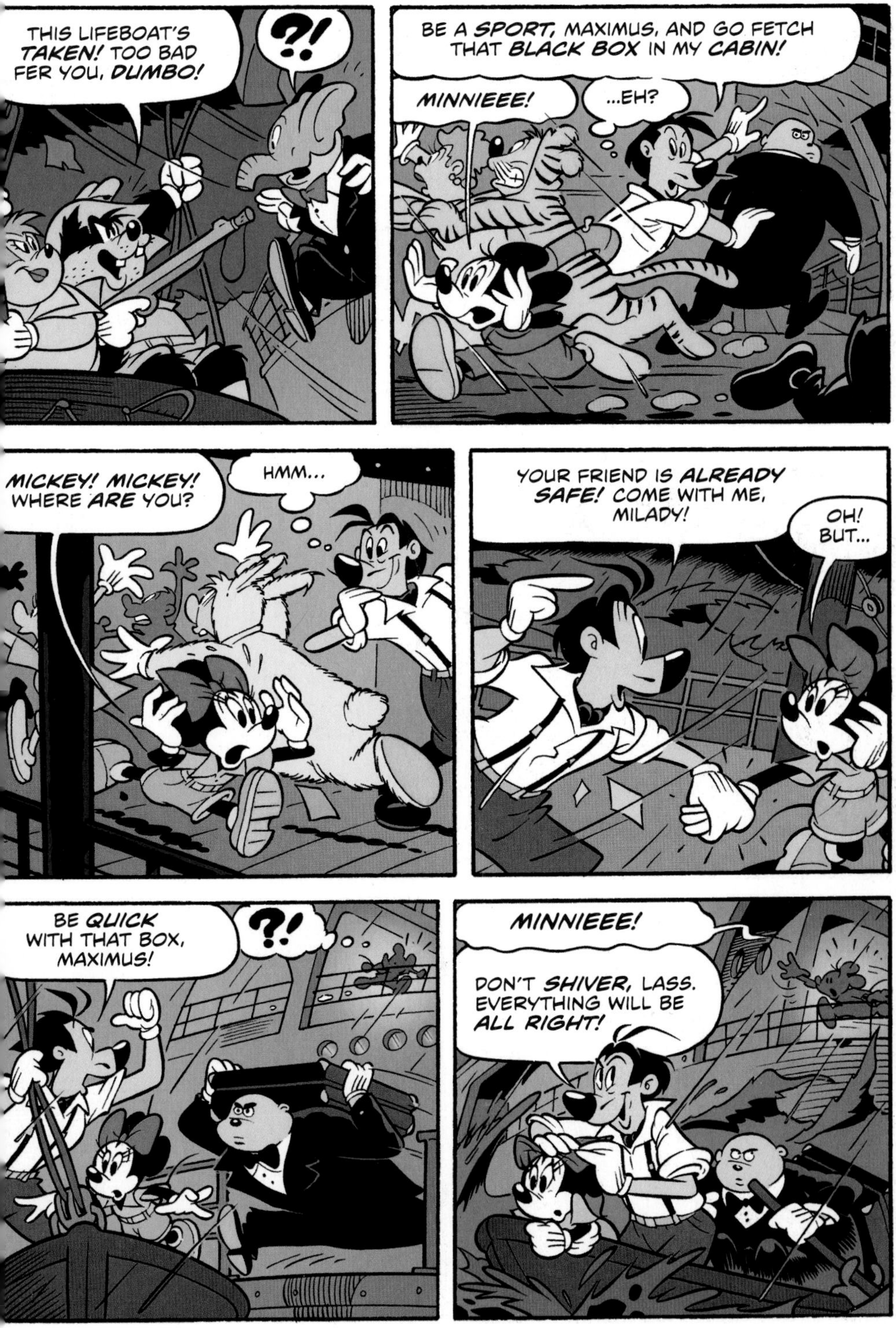
THIS LIFEBOAT'S TAKEN! TOO BAD FER YOU, DUMBO!
?!
BE A SPORT, MAXIMUS, AND GO FETCH THAT BLACK BOX IN MY CABIN!
MINNIEEE!
...EH?
MICKEY! MICKEY! WHERE ARE YOU?
HMM...
YOUR FRIEND IS ALREADY SAFE! COME WITH ME, MILADY!
OH! BUT...
BE QUICK WITH THAT BOX, MAXIMUS!
?!
MINNIEEE!
DON'T SHIVER, LASS. EVERYTHING WILL BE ALL RIGHT!

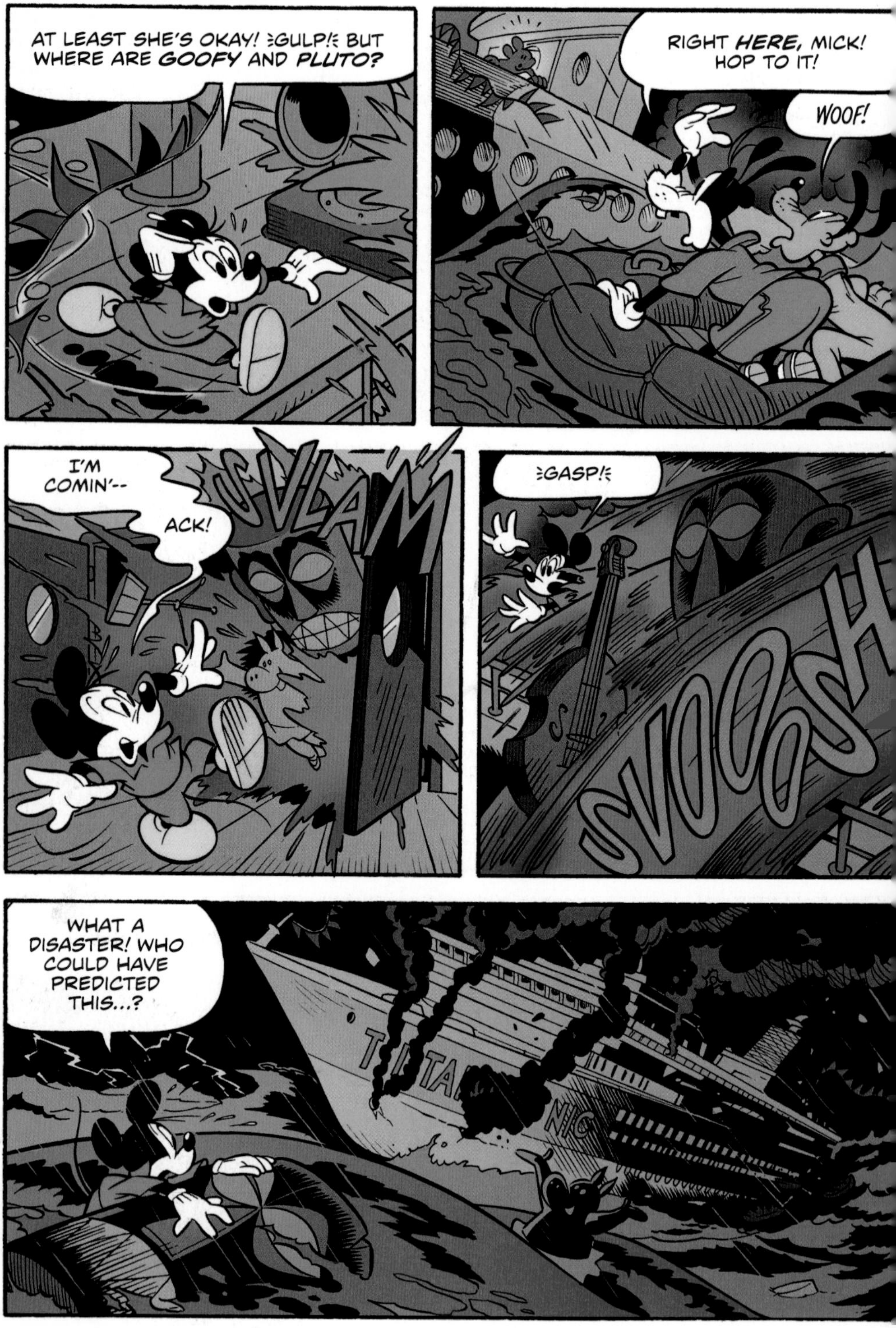
AT LEAST SHE'S OKAY! GULP! BUT WHERE ARE GOOFY AND PLUTO?
RIGHT HERE, MICK! HOP TO IT!
WOOF!
I'M COMIN'--
ACK!
SLAM
GASP!
SVOOOSH
WHAT A DISASTER! WHO COULD HAVE PREDICTED THIS...?

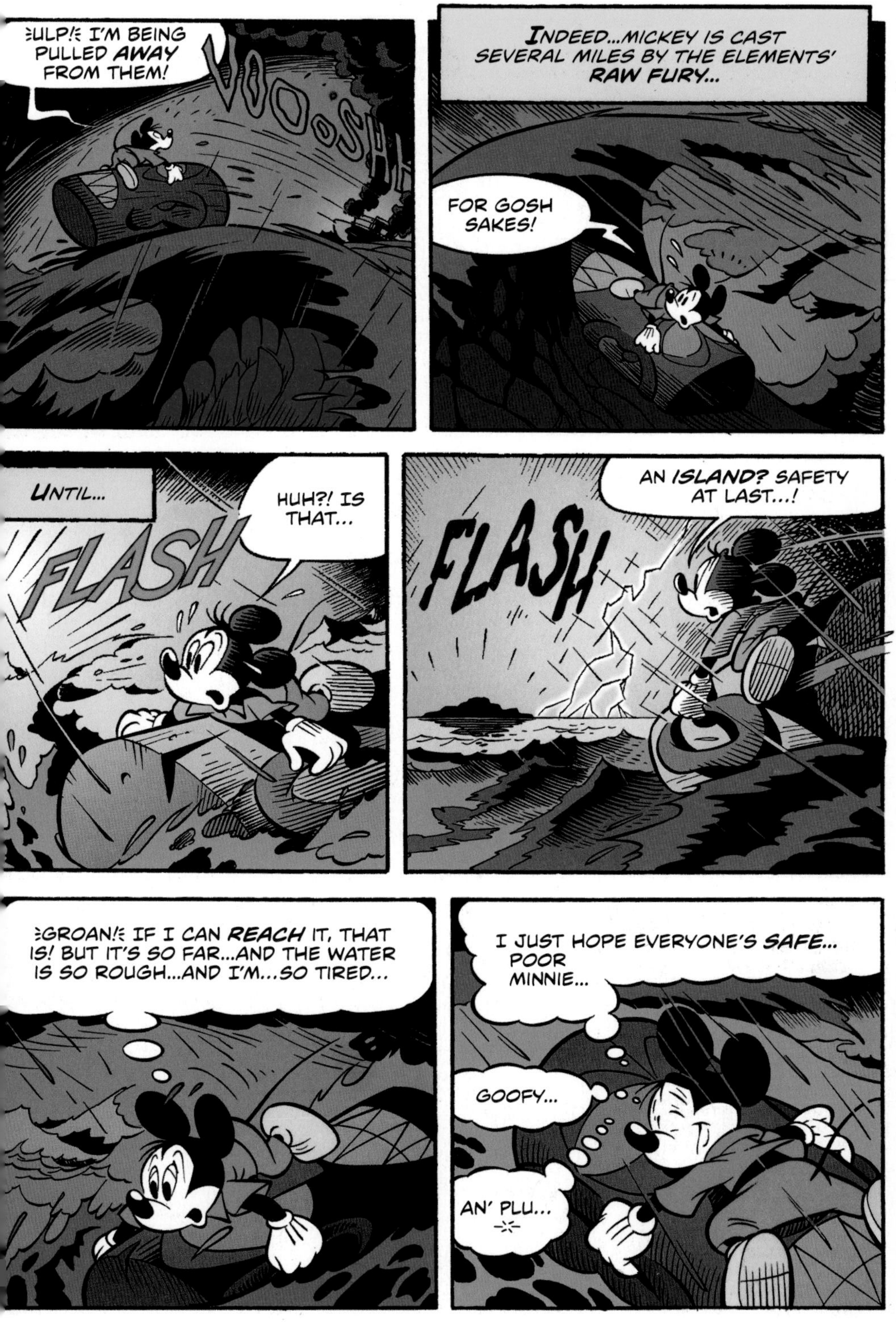

ULP! I'M BEING PULLED AWAY FROM THEM!
VOOOSH
INDEED...MICKEY IS CAST SEVERAL MILES BY THE ELEMENTS' RAW FURY...
FOR GOSH SAKES!
UNTIL...
FLASH
HUH?! IS THAT...
AN ISLAND? SAFETY AT LAST...!
FLASH
GROAN! IF I CAN REACH IT, THAT IS! BUT IT'S SO FAR...AND THE WATER IS SO ROUGH...AND I'M...SO TIRED...
I JUST HOPE EVERYONE'S SAFE... POOR MINNIE...
GOOFY...
AN' PLU...

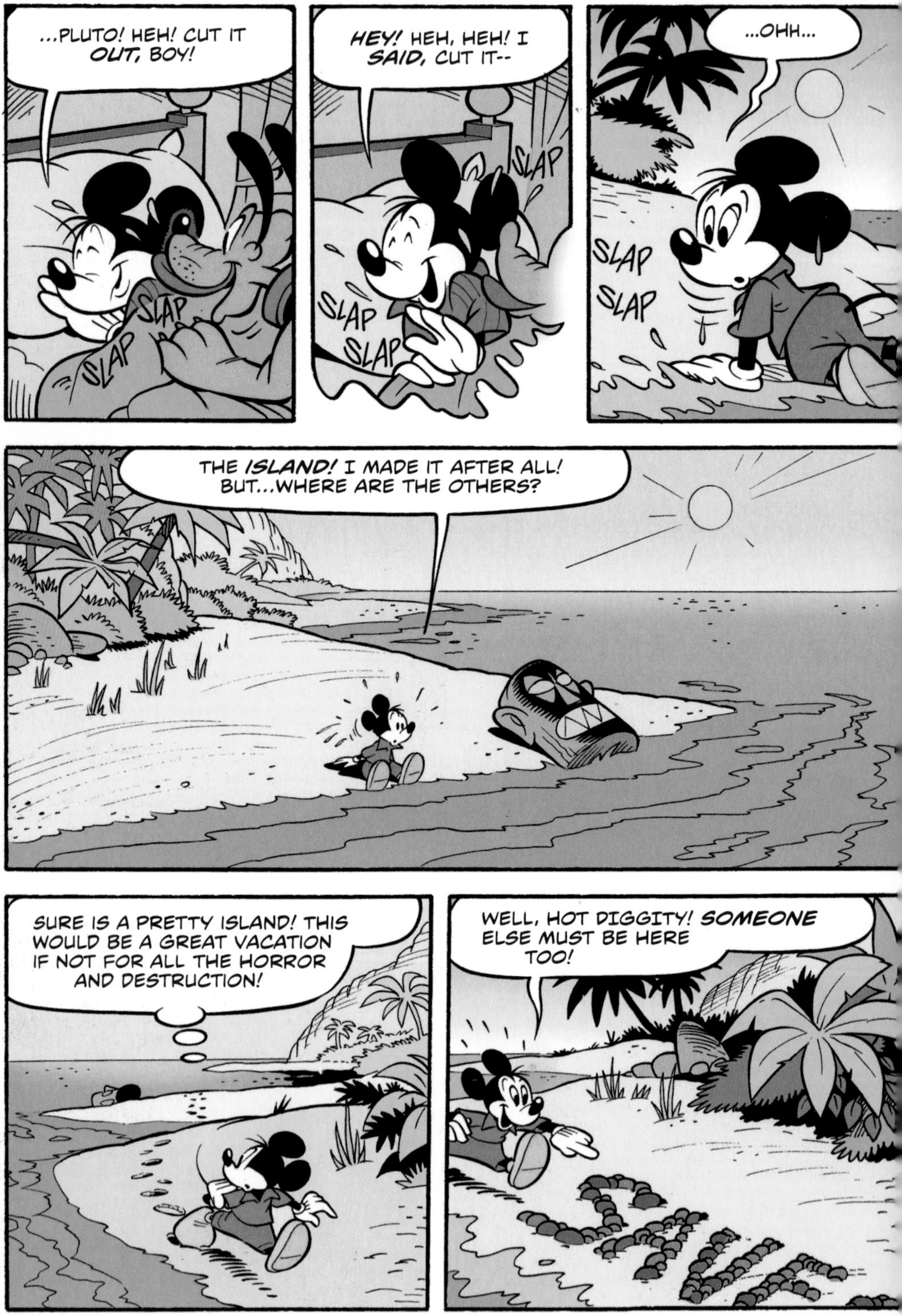
...PLUTO! HEH! CUT IT OUT, BOY!
SLAP
SLAP
HEY! HEH, HEH! I SAID, CUT IT--
SLAP
SLAP
SLAP
...OHH...
SLAP
SLAP
THE ISLAND! I MADE IT AFTER ALL! BUT...WHERE ARE THE OTHERS?
SURE IS A PRETTY ISLAND! THIS WOULD BE A GREAT VACATION IF NOT FOR ALL THE HORROR AND DESTRUCTION!
WELL, HOT DIGGITY! SOMEONE ELSE MUST BE HERE TOO!

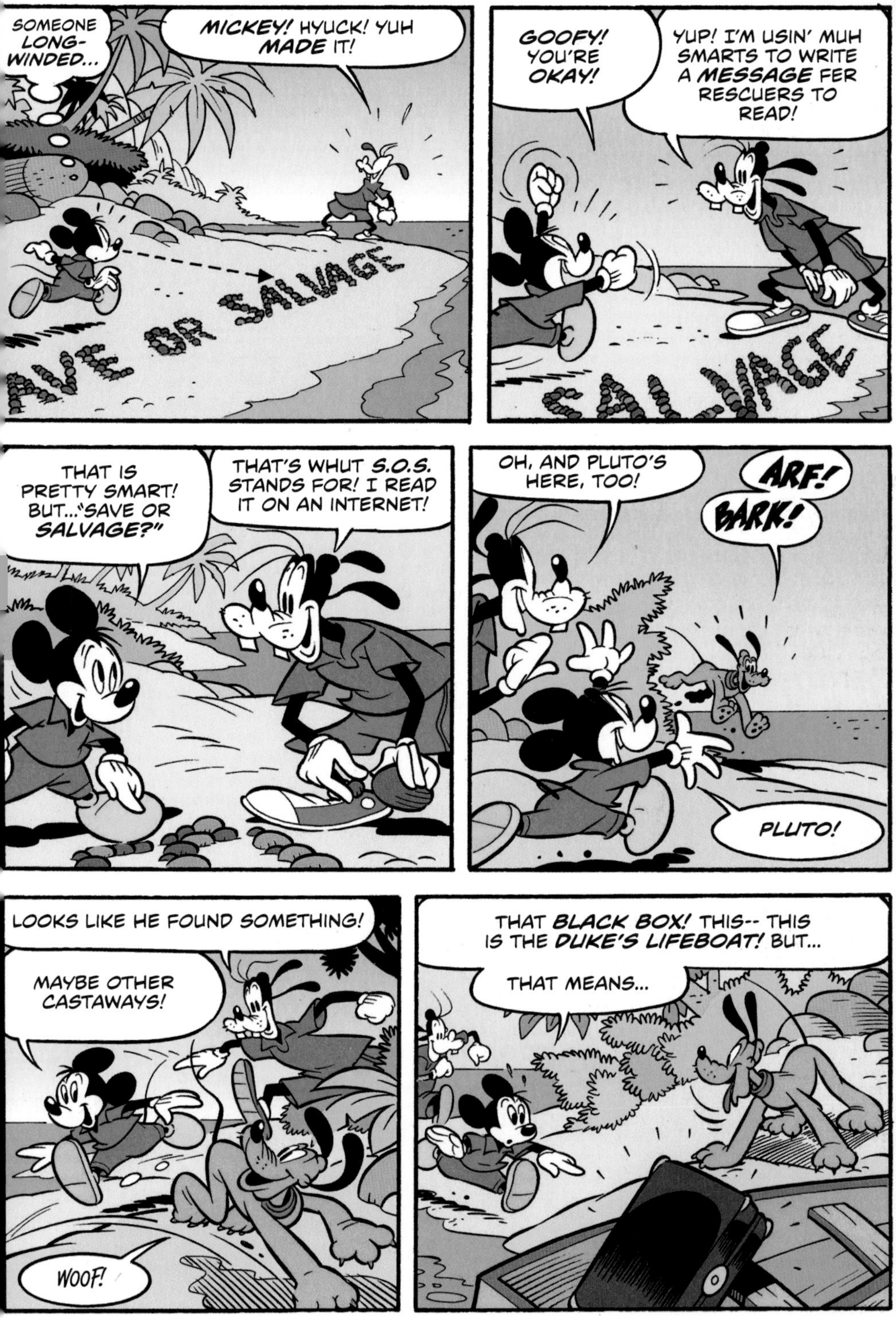
SOMEONE LONG-WINDED...
MICKEY! HYUCK! YUH MADE IT!
AVE OR SALVAGE
GOOFY! YOU'RE OKAY!
YUP! I'M USIN' MUH SMARTS TO WRITE A MESSAGE FER RESCUERS TO READ!
SALVAGE
THAT IS PRETTY SMART! BUT..."SAVE OR SALVAGE?"
THAT'S WHUT S.O.S. STANDS FOR! I READ IT ON AN INTERNET!
OH, AND PLUTO'S HERE, TOO!
ARF!
BARK!
PLUTO!
LOOKS LIKE HE FOUND SOMETHING!
MAYBE OTHER CASTAWAYS!
WOOF!
THAT BLACK BOX! THIS-- THIS IS THE DUKE'S LIFEBOAT! BUT...
THAT MEANS...

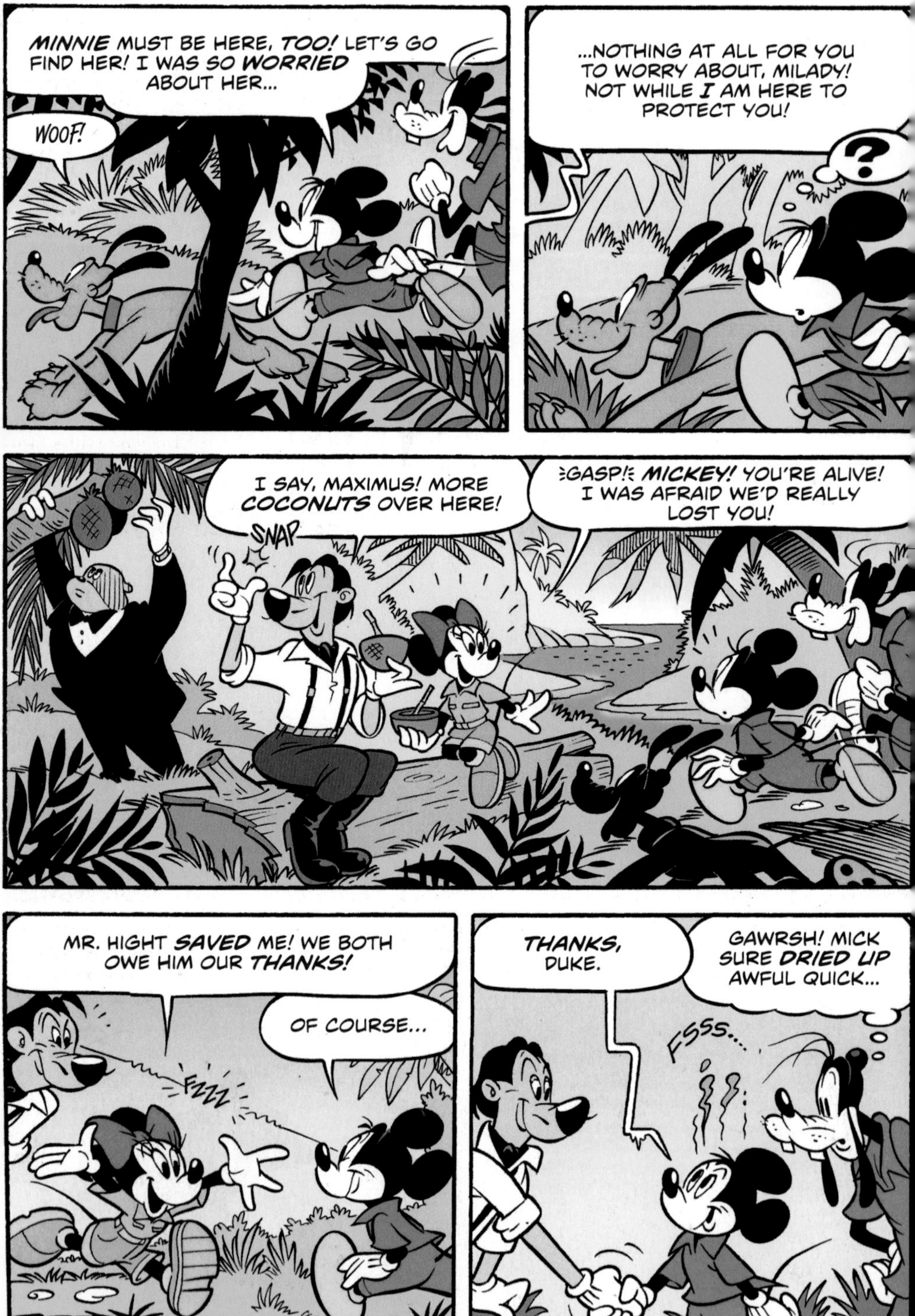
MINNIE MUST BE HERE, TOO! LET'S GO FIND HER! I WAS SO WORRIED ABOUT HER...
WOOF!
...NOTHING AT ALL FOR YOU TO WORRY ABOUT, MILADY! NOT WHILE I AM HERE TO PROTECT YOU!
?
I SAY, MAXIMUS! MORE COCONUTS OVER HERE!
SNAP
GASP! MICKEY! YOU'RE ALIVE! I WAS AFRAID WE'D REALLY LOST YOU!
MR. HIGHT SAVED ME! WE BOTH OWE HIM OUR THANKS!
OF COURSE...
FZZZ
THANKS, DUKE.
GAWRSH! MICK SURE DRIED UP AWFUL QUICK...
FSSS....

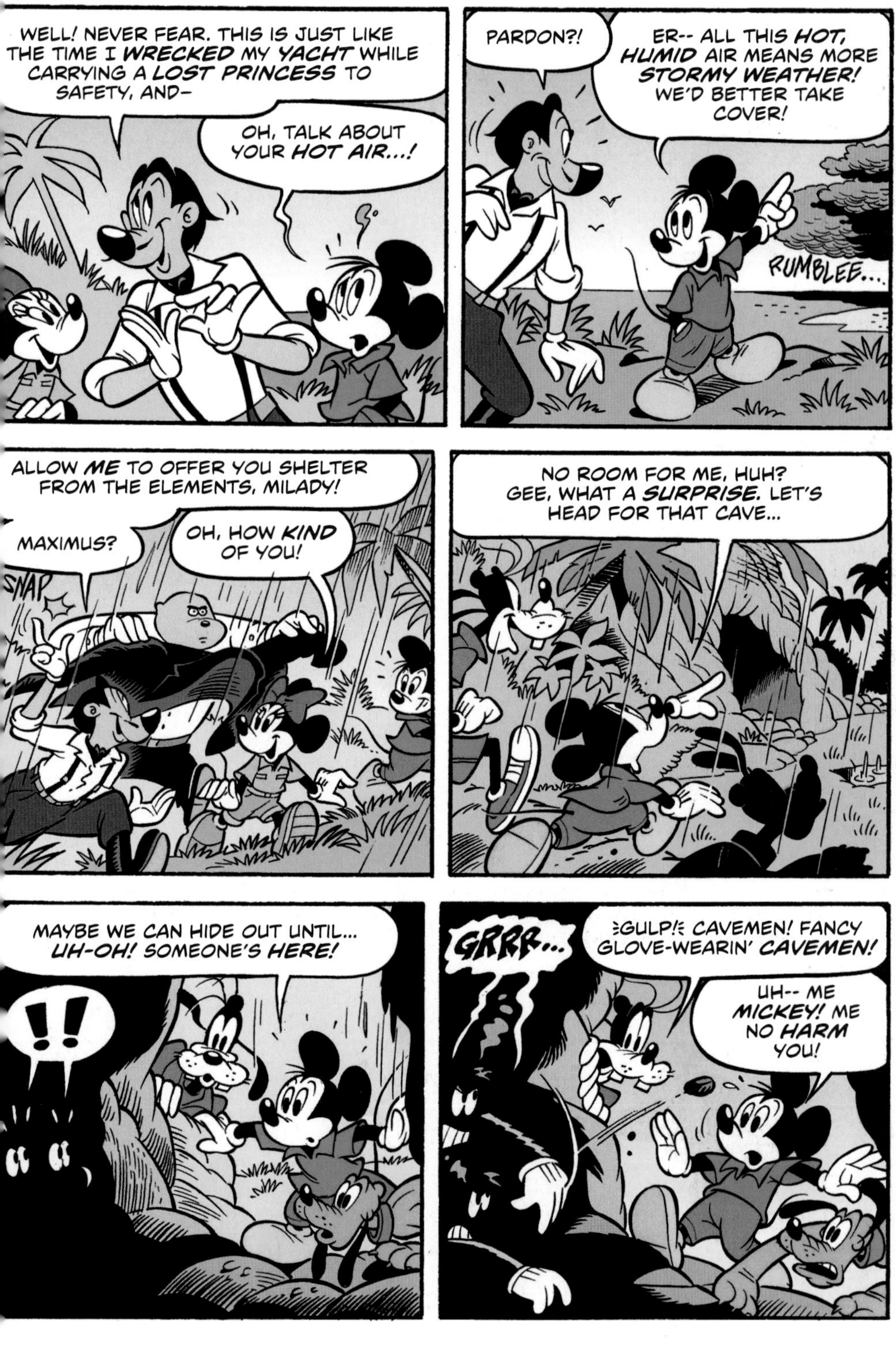
WELL! NEVER FEAR. THIS IS JUST LIKE THE TIME I WRECKED MY YACHT WHILE CARRYING A LOST PRINCESS TO SAFETY, AND—
OH, TALK ABOUT YOUR HOT AIR...!
PARDON?!
ER-- ALL THIS HOT, HUMID AIR MEANS MORE STORMY WEATHER! WE'D BETTER TAKE COVER!
RUMBLEE...
ALLOW ME TO OFFER YOU SHELTER FROM THE ELEMENTS, MILADY!
MAXIMUS?
OH, HOW KIND OF YOU!
SNAP
NO ROOM FOR ME, HUH? GEE, WHAT A SURPRISE. LET'S HEAD FOR THAT CAVE...
MAYBE WE CAN HIDE OUT UNTIL... UH-OH! SOMEONE'S HERE!
!!
GRRR...
GULP! CAVEMEN! FANCY GLOVE-WEARIN' CAVEMEN!
UH-- ME MICKEY! ME NO HARM YOU!

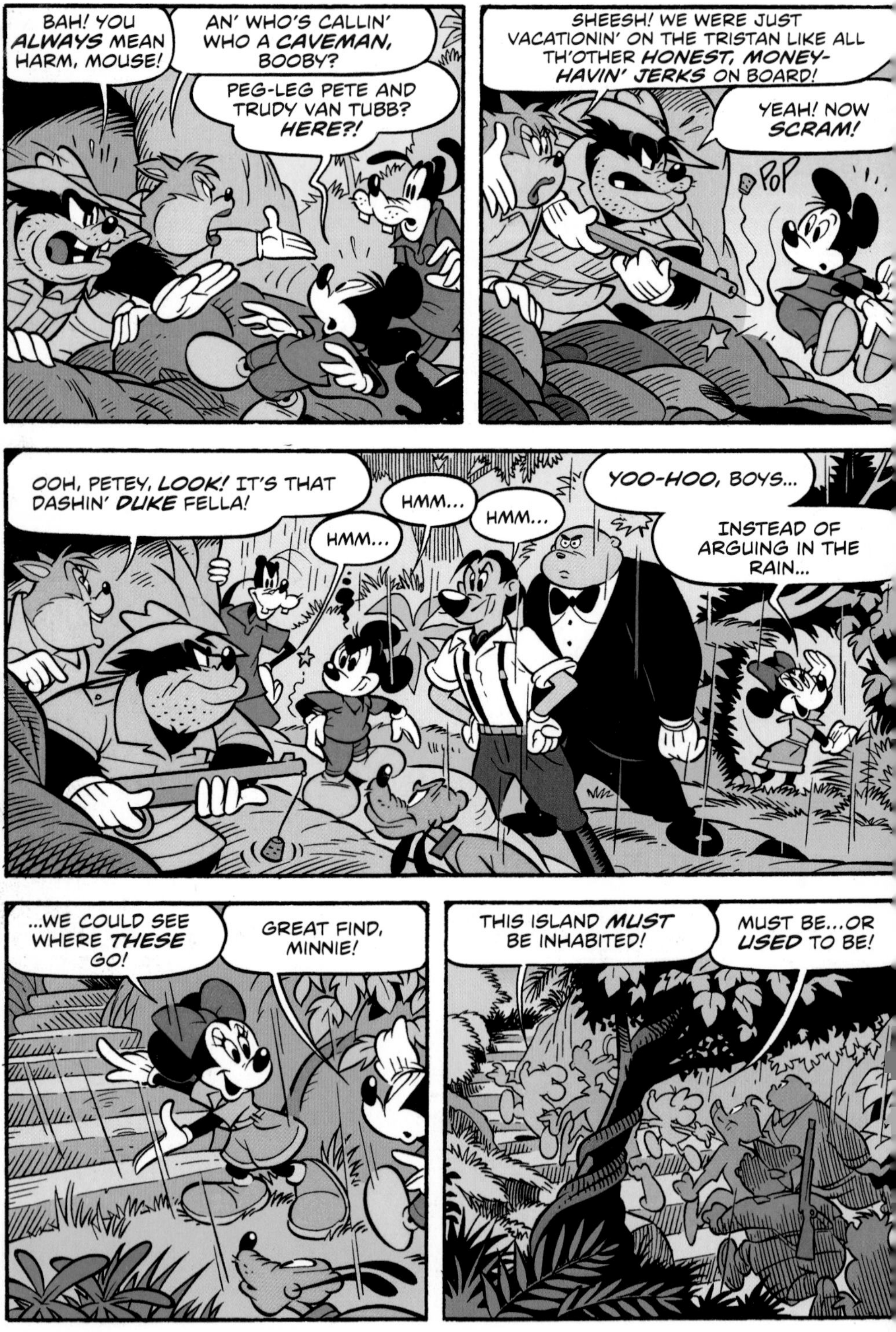
BAH! YOU ALWAYS MEAN HARM, MOUSE!
AN' WHO'S CALLIN' WHO A CAVEMAN, BOOBY?
PEG-LEG PETE AND TRUDY VAN TUBB? HERE?!
SHEESH! WE WERE JUST VACATIONIN' ON THE TRISTAN LIKE ALL TH'OTHER HONEST, MONEY-HAVIN' JERKS ON BOARD!
YEAH! NOW SCRAM!
POP
OOH, PETEY, LOOK! IT'S THAT DASHIN' DUKE FELLA!
HMM...
HMM...
HMM...
YOO-HOO, BOYS...
INSTEAD OF ARGUING IN THE RAIN...
...WE COULD SEE WHERE THESE GO!
GREAT FIND, MINNIE!
THIS ISLAND MUST BE INHABITED!
MUST BE...OR USED TO BE!

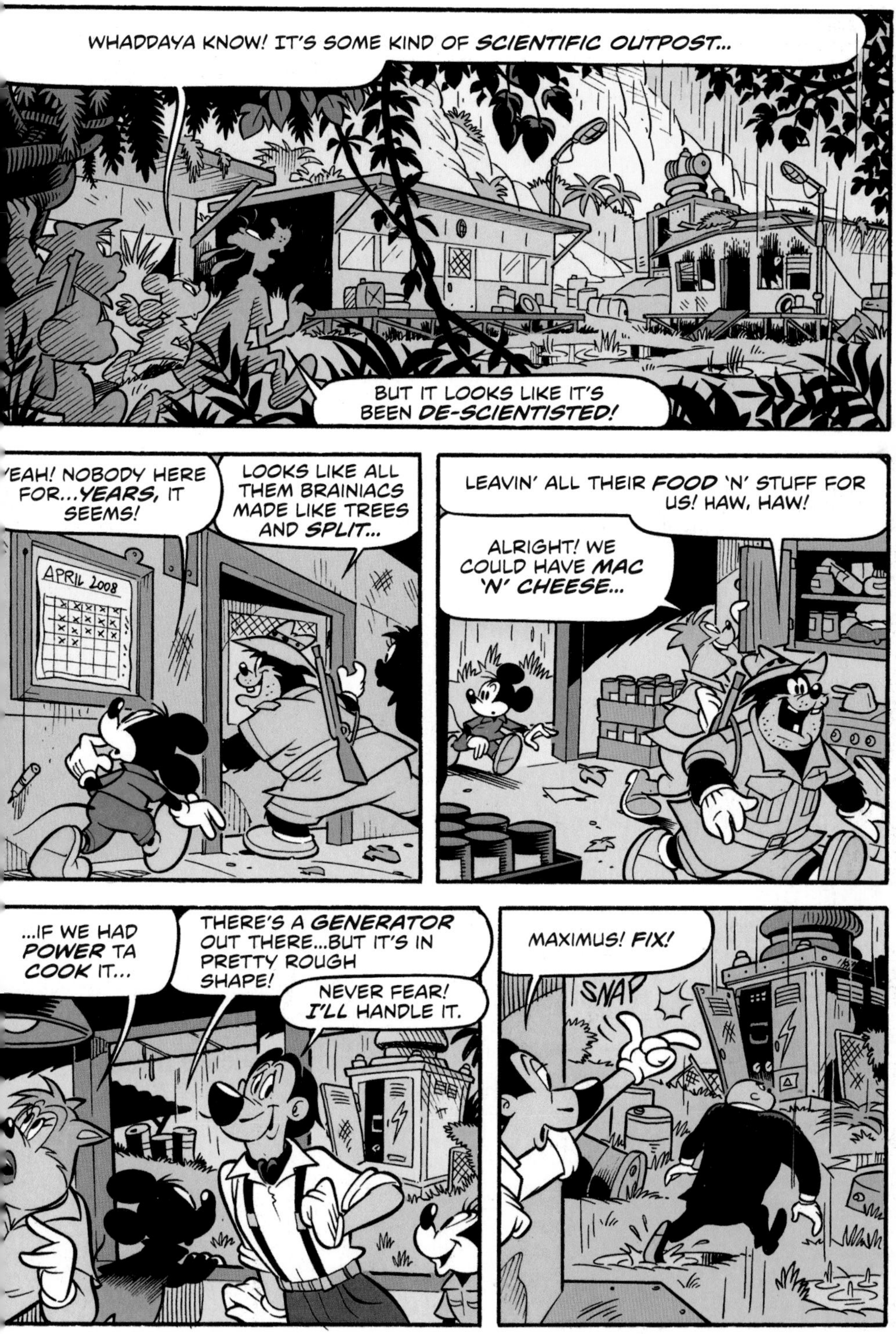
WHADDAYA KNOW! IT'S SOME KIND OF SCIENTIFIC OUTPOST...
BUT IT LOOKS LIKE IT'S BEEN DE-SCIENTISTED!
YEAH! NOBODY HERE FOR...YEARS, IT SEEMS!
APRIL 2008
LOOKS LIKE ALL THEM BRAINIACS MADE LIKE TREES AND SPLIT...
LEAVIN' ALL THEIR FOOD 'N' STUFF FOR US! HAW, HAW!
ALRIGHT! WE COULD HAVE MAC 'N' CHEESE...
...IF WE HAD POWER TA COOK IT...
THERE'S A GENERATOR OUT THERE...BUT IT'S IN PRETTY ROUGH SHAPE!
NEVER FEAR! I'LL HANDLE IT.
MAXIMUS! FIX!
SNAP

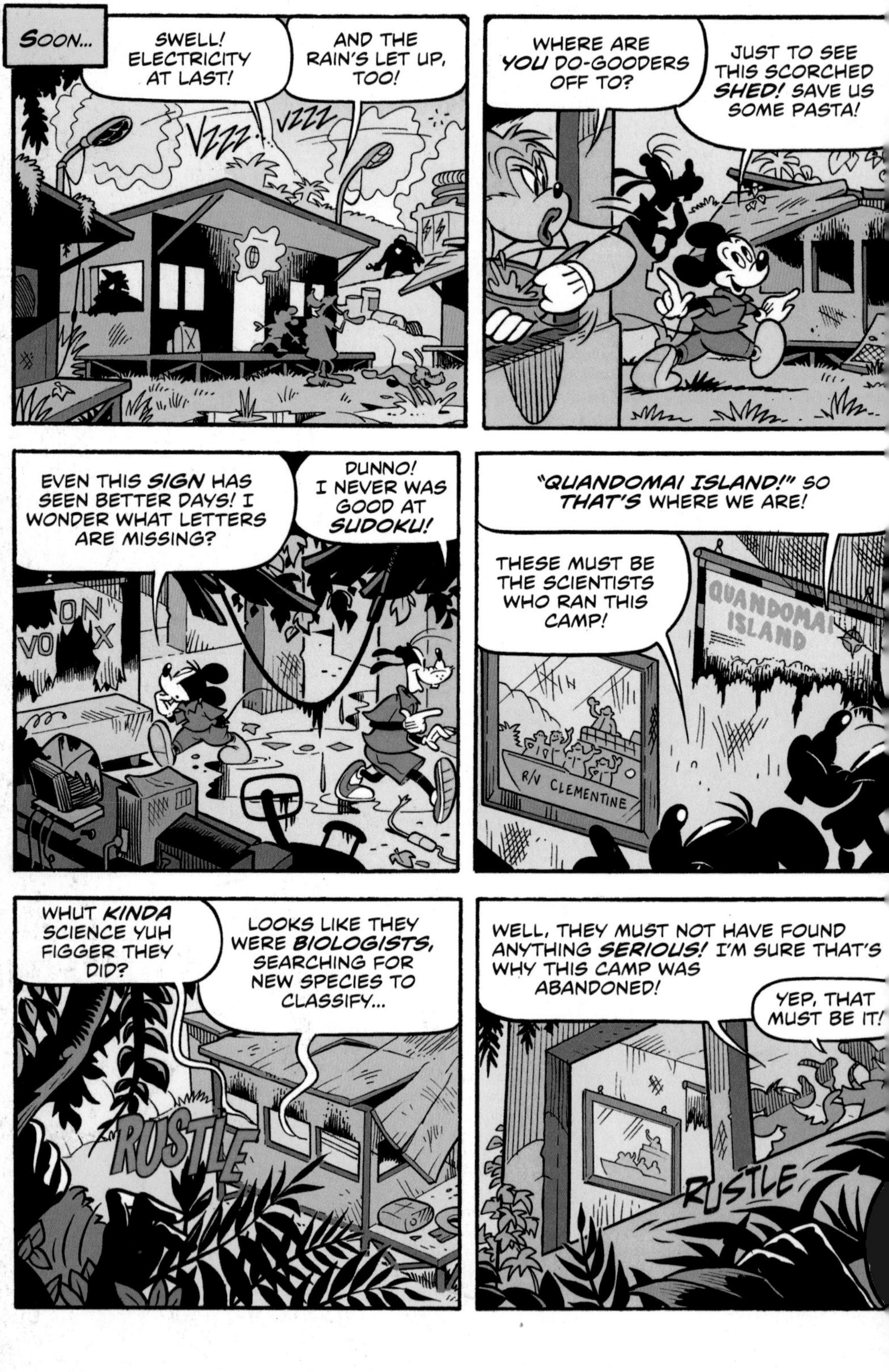
SOON...
SWELL! ELECTRICITY AT LAST!
AND THE RAIN'S LET UP, TOO!
VZZZ
VZZZ
WHERE ARE *YOU* DO-GOODERS OFF TO?
JUST TO SEE THIS SCORCHED *SHED!* SAVE US SOME PASTA!
EVEN THIS *SIGN* HAS SEEN BETTER DAYS! I WONDER WHAT LETTERS ARE MISSING?
DUNNO! I NEVER WAS GOOD AT *SUDOKU!*
VO ON X
"*QUANDOMAI ISLAND!*" SO *THAT'S* WHERE WE ARE!
THESE MUST BE THE SCIENTISTS WHO RAN THIS CAMP!
QUANDOMAI ISLAND
R/V CLEMENTINE
WHUT *KINDA* SCIENCE YUH FIGGER THEY DID?
LOOKS LIKE THEY WERE *BIOLOGISTS,* SEARCHING FOR NEW SPECIES TO CLASSIFY...
RUSTLE
WELL, THEY MUST NOT HAVE FOUND ANYTHING *SERIOUS!* I'M SURE THAT'S WHY THIS CAMP WAS ABANDONED!
YEP, THAT MUST BE IT!
RUSTLE

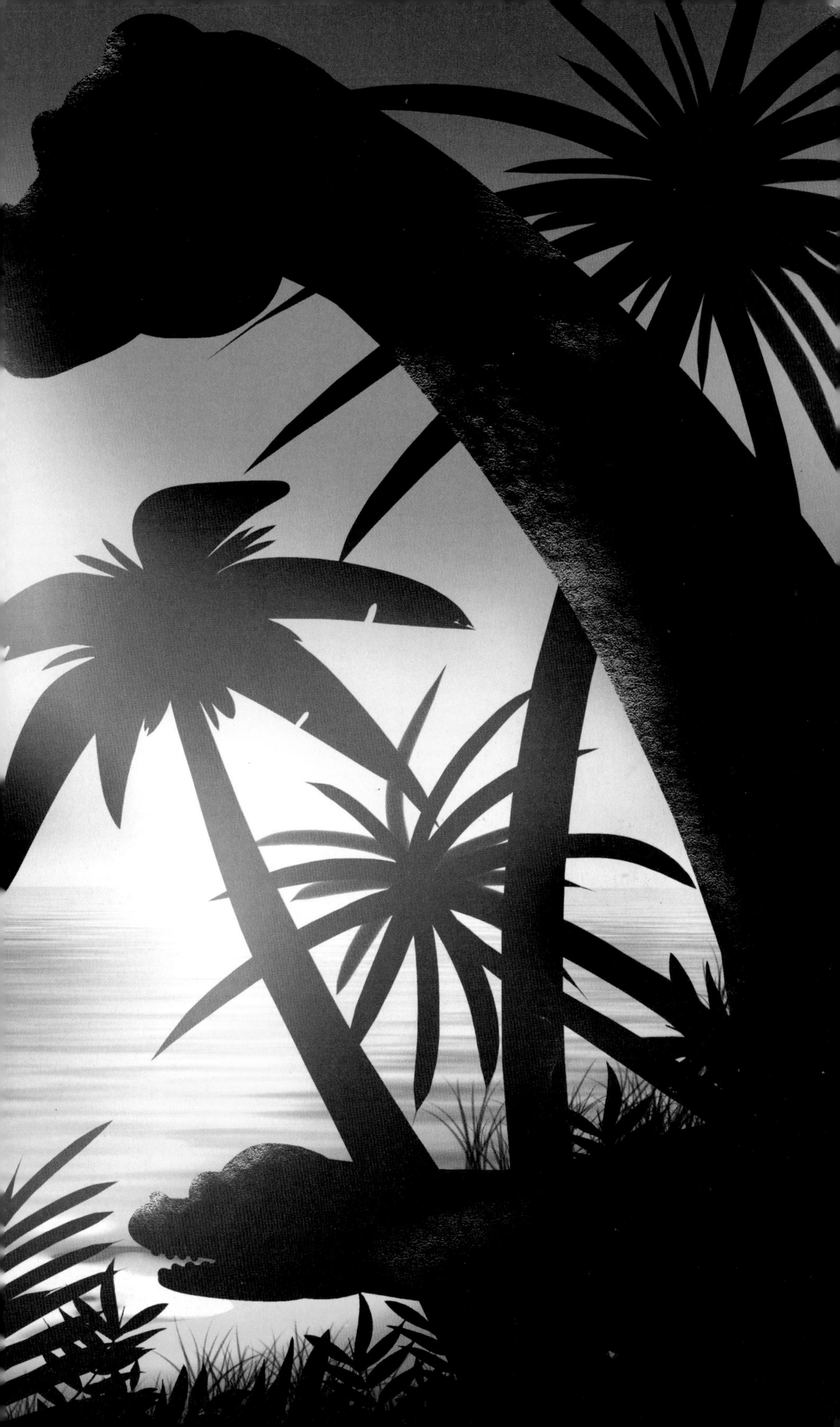

CHAPTER TWO

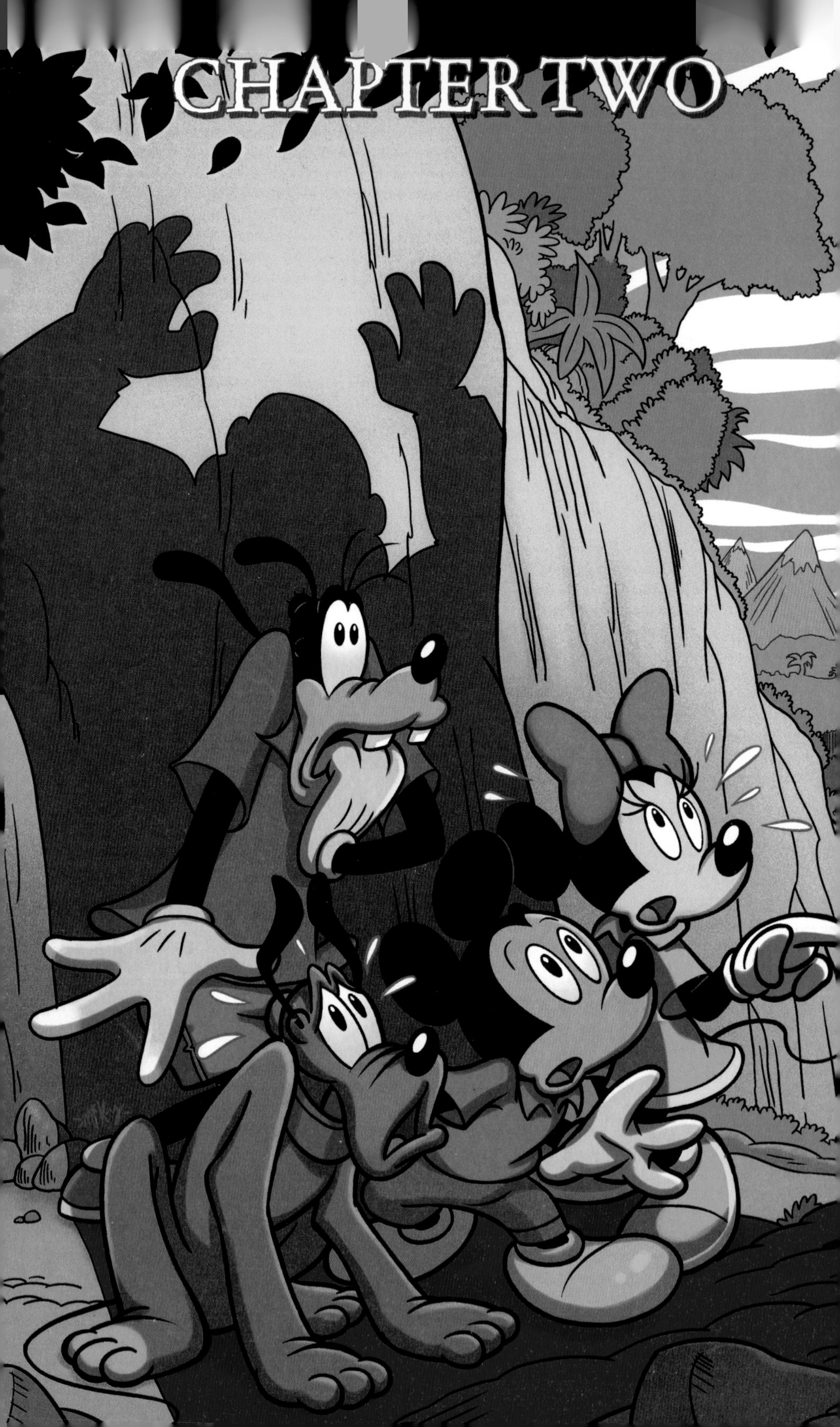

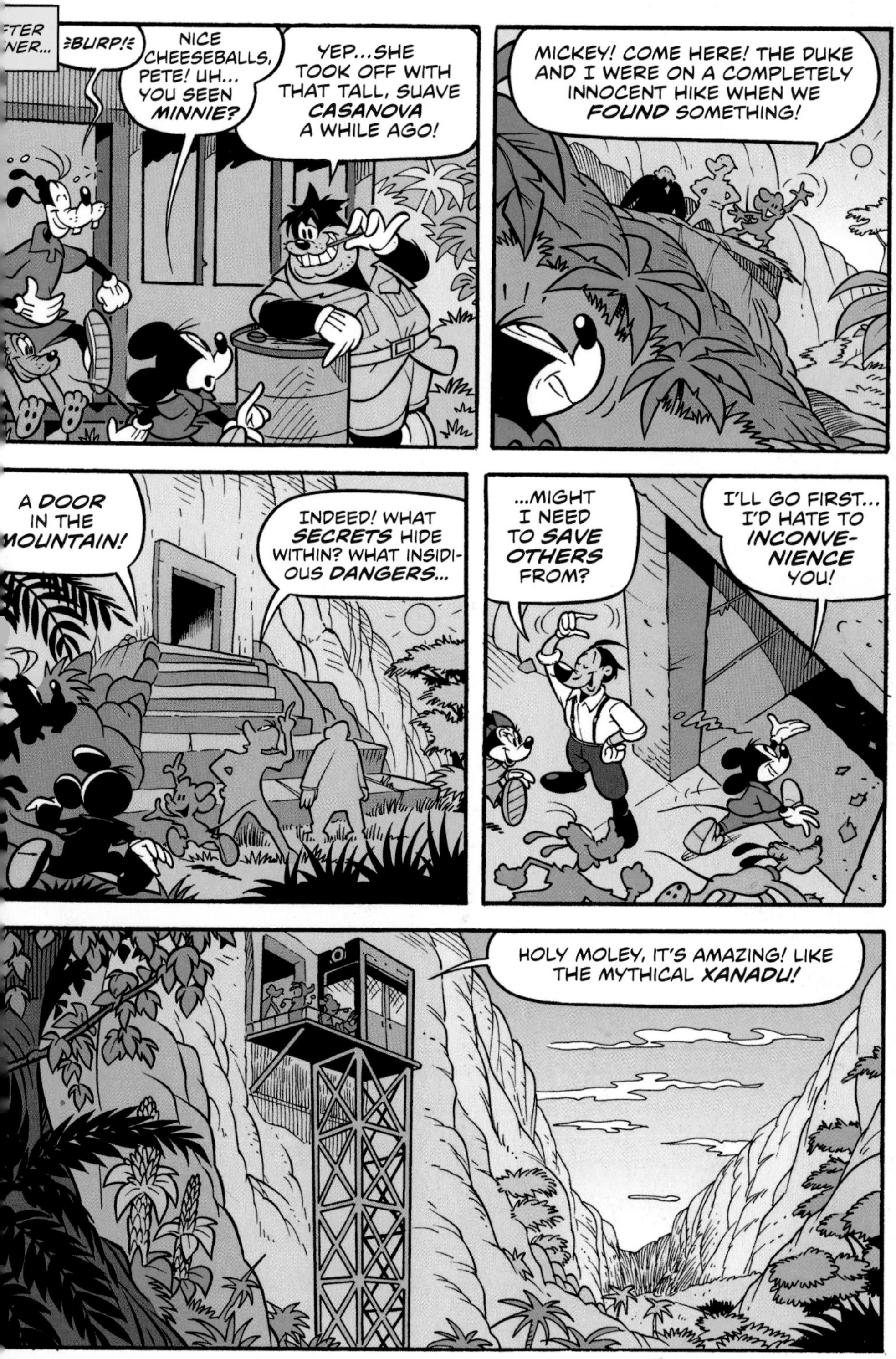

FTER
NER...
BURP!
NICE CHEESEBALLS, PETE! UH... YOU SEEN MINNIE?
YEP...SHE TOOK OFF WITH THAT TALL, SUAVE CASANOVA A WHILE AGO!
MICKEY! COME HERE! THE DUKE AND I WERE ON A COMPLETELY INNOCENT HIKE WHEN WE FOUND SOMETHING!
A DOOR IN THE MOUNTAIN!
INDEED! WHAT SECRETS HIDE WITHIN? WHAT INSIDI-OUS DANGERS...
...MIGHT I NEED TO SAVE OTHERS FROM?
I'LL GO FIRST... I'D HATE TO INCONVE-NIENCE YOU!
HOLY MOLEY, IT'S AMAZING! LIKE THE MYTHICAL XANADU!

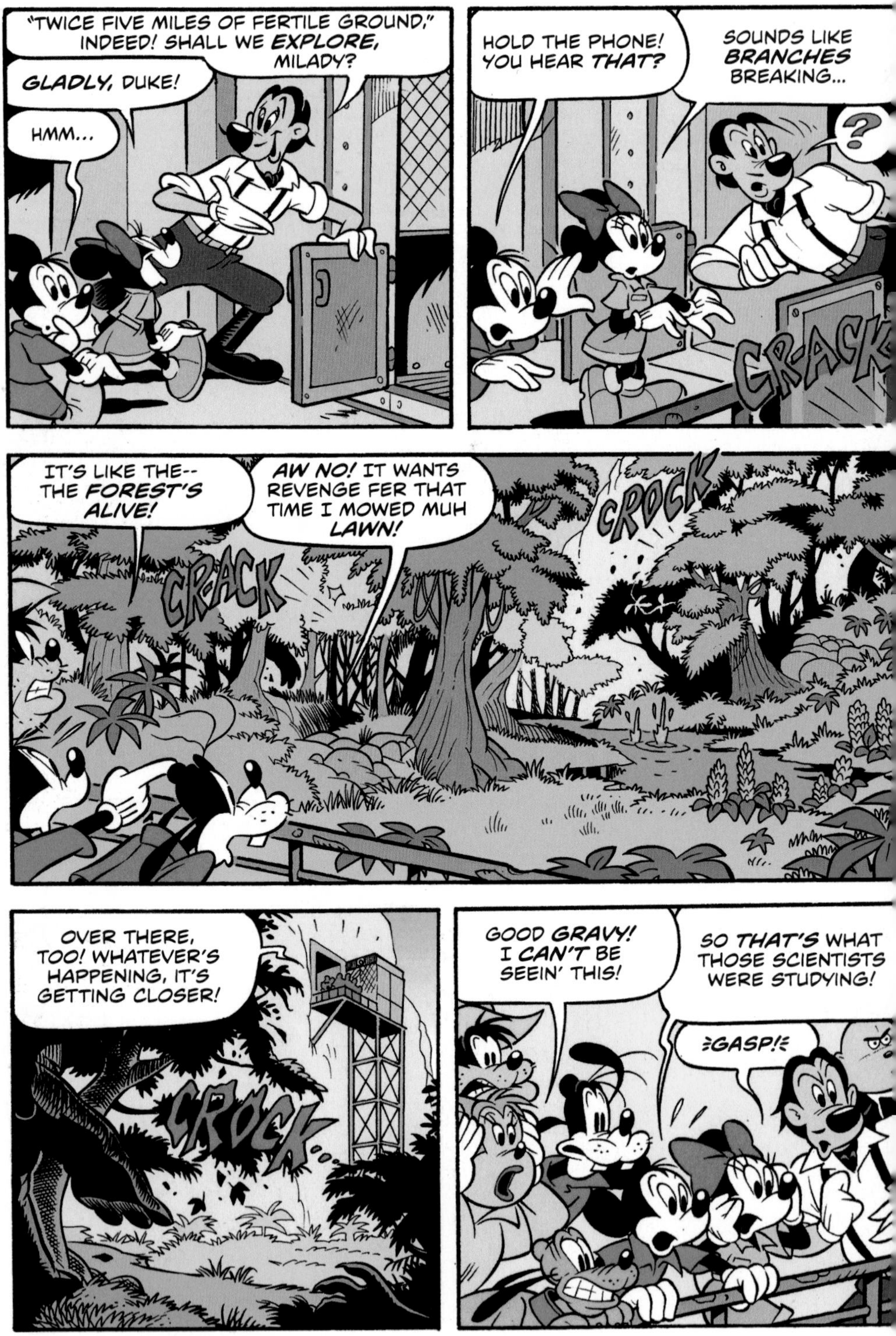
"TWICE FIVE MILES OF FERTILE GROUND," INDEED! SHALL WE EXPLORE, MILADY?
GLADLY, DUKE!
HMM...
HOLD THE PHONE! YOU HEAR THAT?
SOUNDS LIKE BRANCHES BREAKING...
?
CR-ACK
IT'S LIKE THE-- THE FOREST'S ALIVE!
AW NO! IT WANTS REVENGE FER THAT TIME I MOWED MUH LAWN!
CRACK
CROCK
OVER THERE, TOO! WHATEVER'S HAPPENING, IT'S GETTING CLOSER!
CROCK
GOOD GRAVY! I CAN'T BE SEEIN' THIS!
SO THAT'S WHAT THOSE SCIENTISTS WERE STUDYING!
GASP!

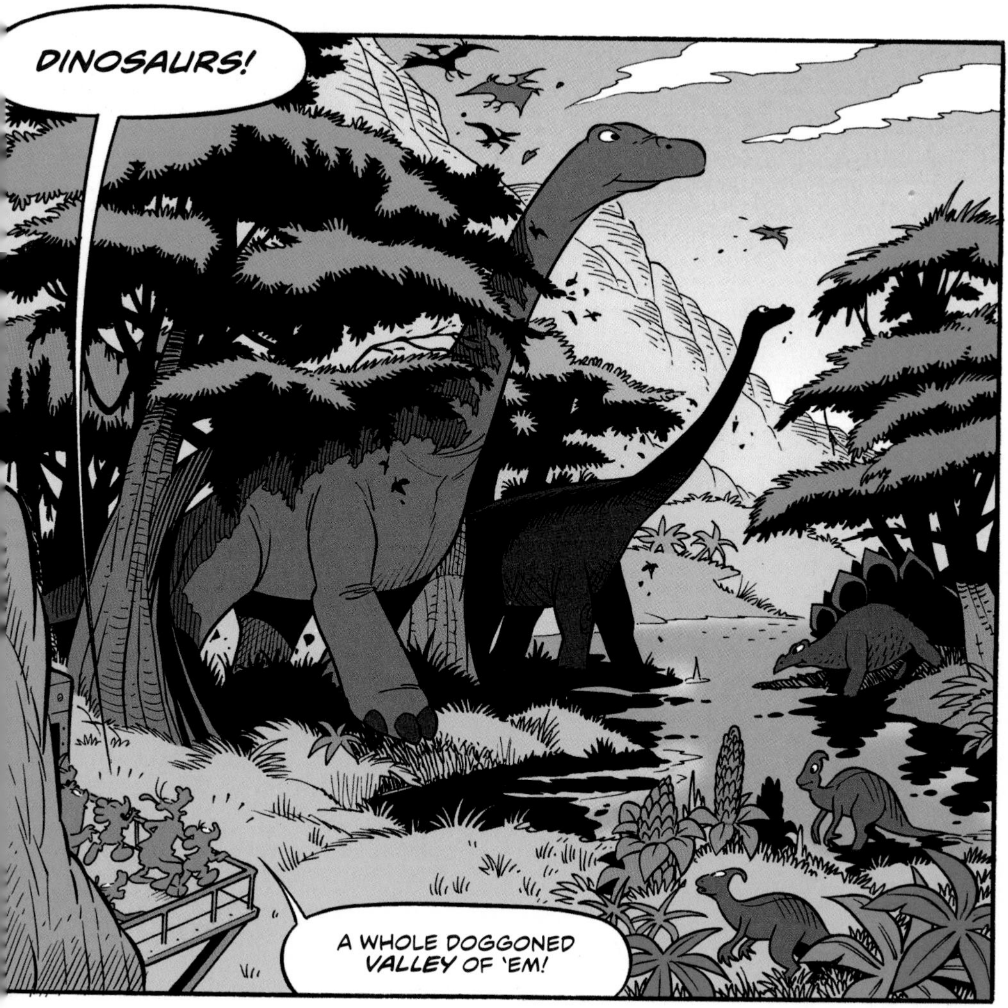
DINOSAURS!
A WHOLE DOGGONED VALLEY OF 'EM!

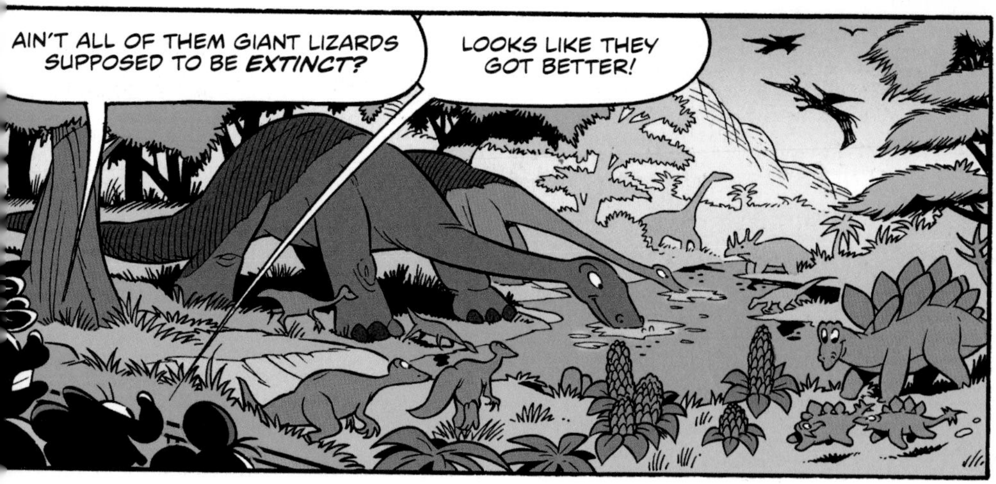
AIN'T ALL OF THEM GIANT LIZARDS SUPPOSED TO BE EXTINCT?
LOOKS LIKE THEY GOT BETTER!

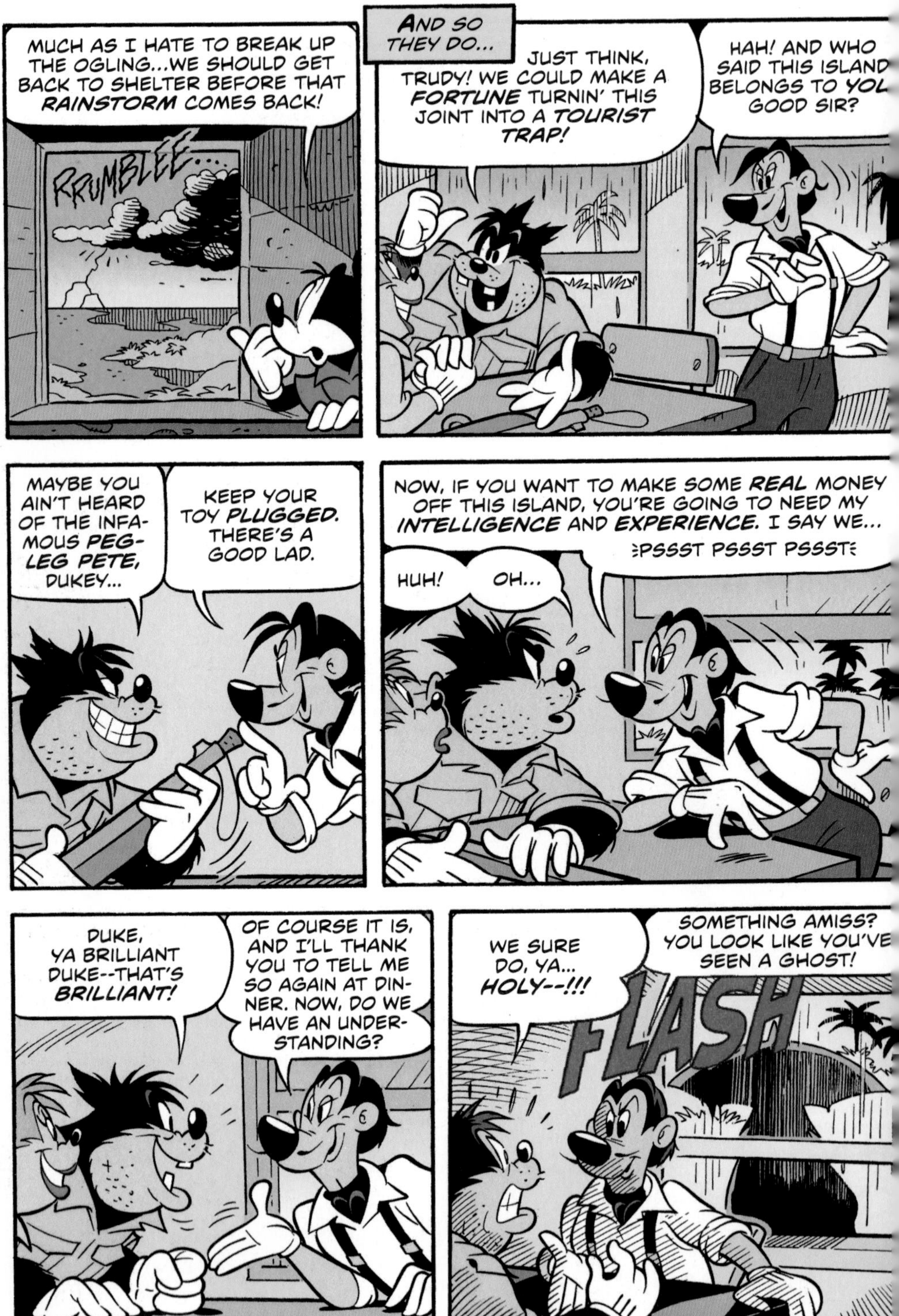
MUCH AS I HATE TO BREAK UP THE OGLING...WE SHOULD GET BACK TO SHELTER BEFORE THAT RAINSTORM COMES BACK!
RRUMBLEE...
AND SO THEY DO...
JUST THINK, TRUDY! WE COULD MAKE A FORTUNE TURNIN' THIS JOINT INTO A TOURIST TRAP!
HAH! AND WHO SAID THIS ISLAND BELONGS TO YOU, GOOD SIR?
MAYBE YOU AIN'T HEARD OF THE INFAMOUS PEG-LEG PETE, DUKEY...
KEEP YOUR TOY PLUGGED. THERE'S A GOOD LAD.
NOW, IF YOU WANT TO MAKE SOME REAL MONEY OFF THIS ISLAND, YOU'RE GOING TO NEED MY INTELLIGENCE AND EXPERIENCE. I SAY WE...
PSSST PSSST PSSST
HUH!
OH...
DUKE, YA BRILLIANT DUKE--THAT'S BRILLIANT!
OF COURSE IT IS, AND I'LL THANK YOU TO TELL ME SO AGAIN AT DINNER. NOW, DO WE HAVE AN UNDERSTANDING?
WE SURE DO, YA... HOLY--!!!
SOMETHING AMISS? YOU LOOK LIKE YOU'VE SEEN A GHOST!
FLASH

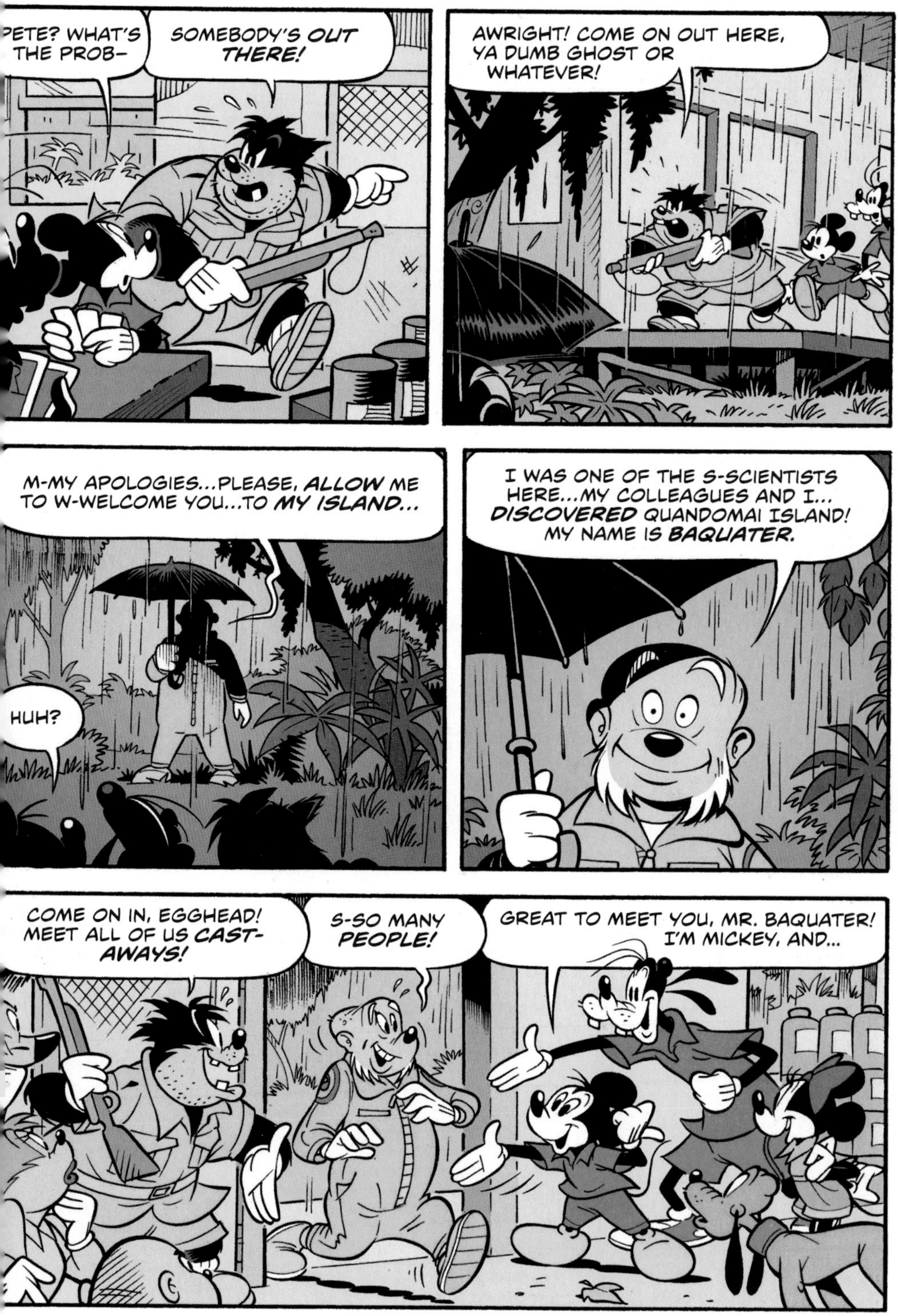
PETE? WHAT'S THE PROB–
SOMEBODY'S OUT THERE!
AWRIGHT! COME ON OUT HERE, YA DUMB GHOST OR WHATEVER!
M-MY APOLOGIES...PLEASE, ALLOW ME TO W-WELCOME YOU...TO MY ISLAND...
HUH?
I WAS ONE OF THE S-SCIENTISTS HERE...MY COLLEAGUES AND I... DISCOVERED QUANDOMAI ISLAND! MY NAME IS BAQUATER.
COME ON IN, EGGHEAD! MEET ALL OF US CAST-AWAYS!
S-SO MANY PEOPLE!
GREAT TO MEET YOU, MR. BAQUATER! I'M MICKEY, AND...

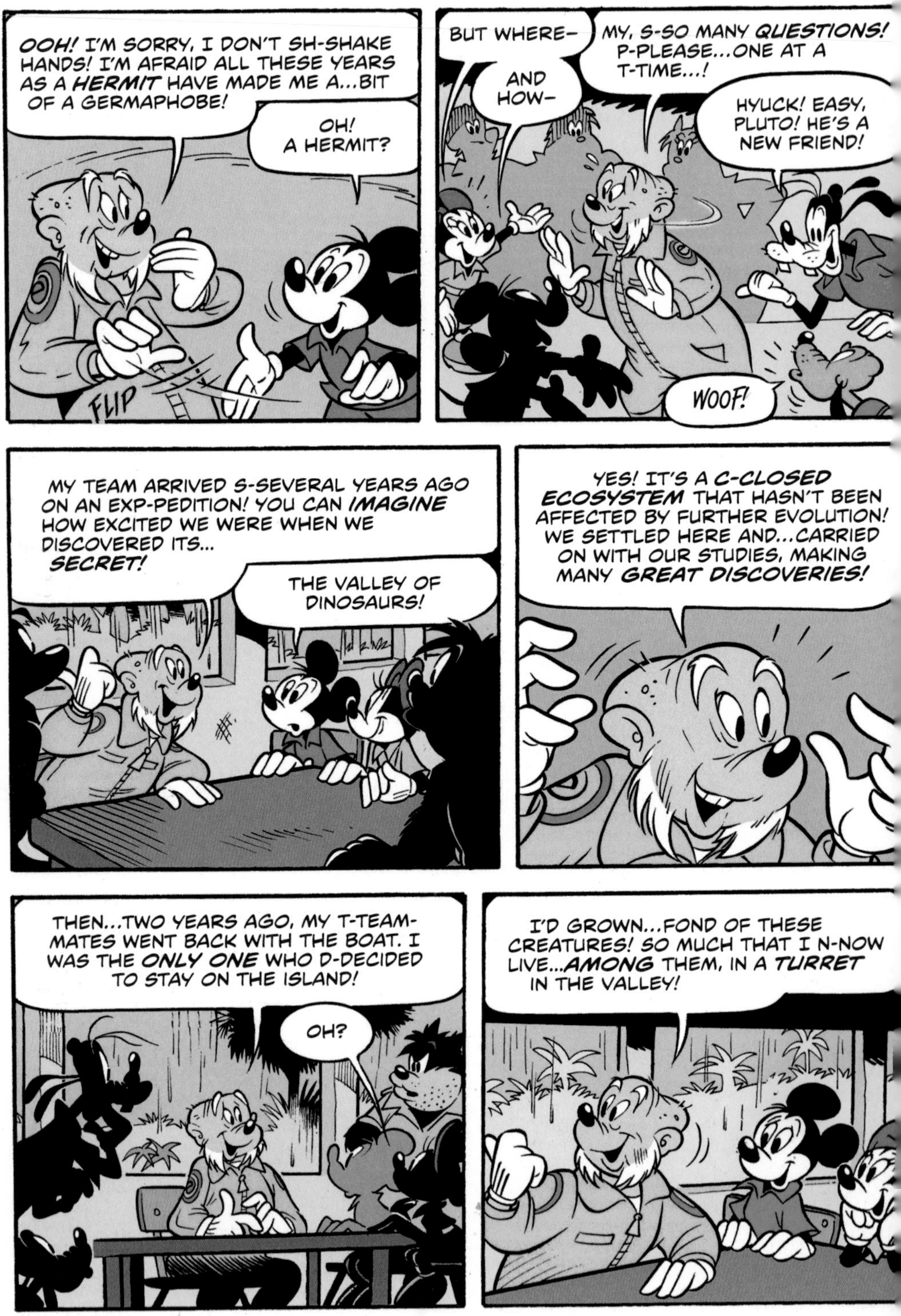
OOH! I'M SORRY, I DON'T SH-SHAKE HANDS! I'M AFRAID ALL THESE YEARS AS A HERMIT HAVE MADE ME A...BIT OF A GERMAPHOBE!
OH! A HERMIT?
FLIP
BUT WHERE–
AND HOW–
MY, S-SO MANY QUESTIONS! P-PLEASE...ONE AT A T-TIME...!
HYUCK! EASY, PLUTO! HE'S A NEW FRIEND!
WOOF!
MY TEAM ARRIVED S-SEVERAL YEARS AGO ON AN EXP-PEDITION! YOU CAN IMAGINE HOW EXCITED WE WERE WHEN WE DISCOVERED ITS... SECRET!
THE VALLEY OF DINOSAURS!
YES! IT'S A C-CLOSED ECOSYSTEM THAT HASN'T BEEN AFFECTED BY FURTHER EVOLUTION! WE SETTLED HERE AND...CARRIED ON WITH OUR STUDIES, MAKING MANY GREAT DISCOVERIES!
THEN...TWO YEARS AGO, MY T-TEAM-MATES WENT BACK WITH THE BOAT. I WAS THE ONLY ONE WHO D-DECIDED TO STAY ON THE ISLAND!
OH?
I'D GROWN...FOND OF THESE CREATURES! SO MUCH THAT I N-NOW LIVE...AMONG THEM, IN A TURRET IN THE VALLEY!

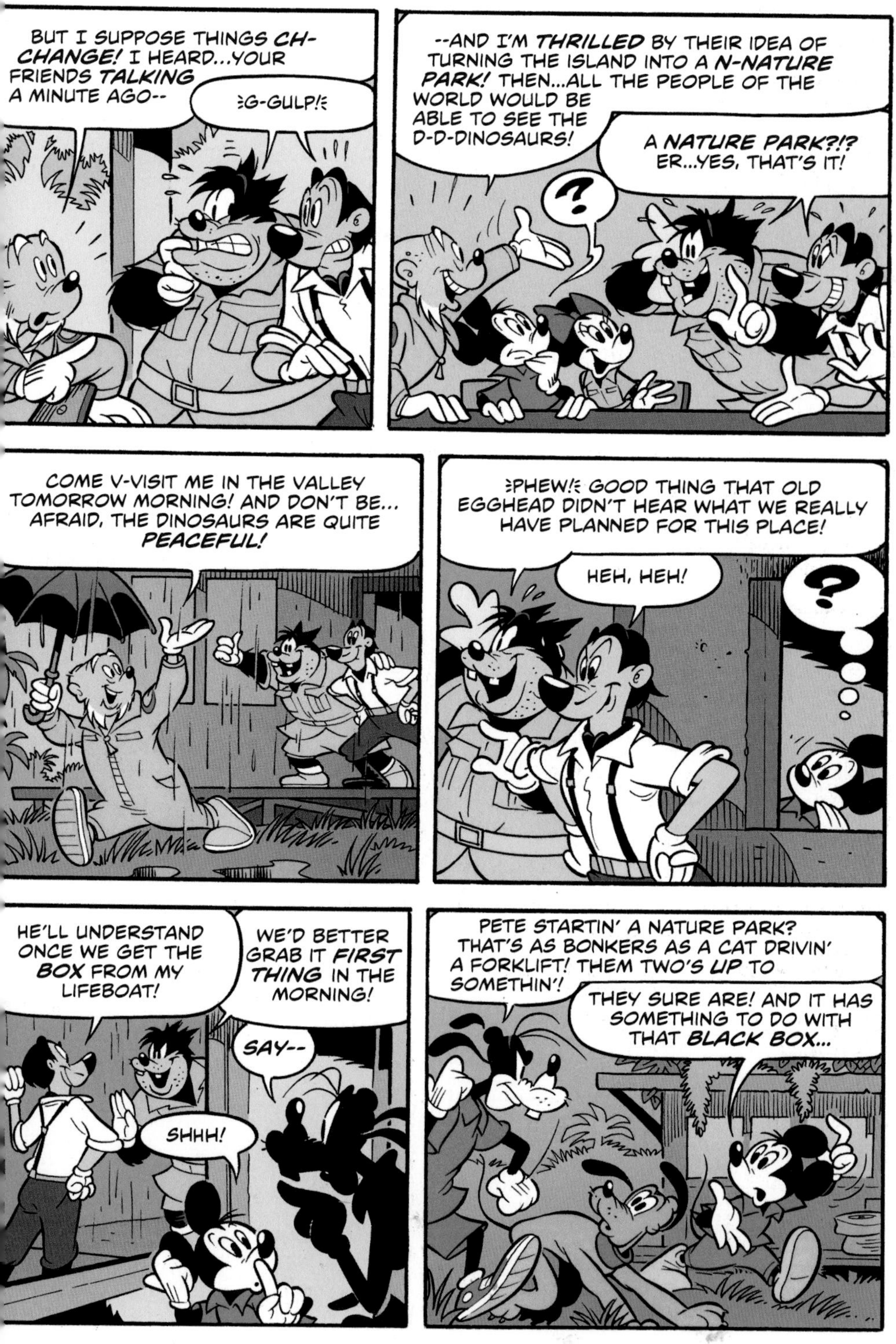
BUT I SUPPOSE THINGS CH-CHANGE! I HEARD...YOUR FRIENDS TALKING A MINUTE AGO--
G-GULP!
--AND I'M THRILLED BY THEIR IDEA OF TURNING THE ISLAND INTO A N-NATURE PARK! THEN...ALL THE PEOPLE OF THE WORLD WOULD BE ABLE TO SEE THE D-D-DINOSAURS!
A NATURE PARK?!? ER...YES, THAT'S IT!
?
COME V-VISIT ME IN THE VALLEY TOMORROW MORNING! AND DON'T BE... AFRAID, THE DINOSAURS ARE QUITE PEACEFUL!
PHEW! GOOD THING THAT OLD EGGHEAD DIDN'T HEAR WHAT WE REALLY HAVE PLANNED FOR THIS PLACE!
HEH, HEH!
?
HE'LL UNDERSTAND ONCE WE GET THE BOX FROM MY LIFEBOAT!
WE'D BETTER GRAB IT FIRST THING IN THE MORNING!
SAY--
SHHH!
PETE STARTIN' A NATURE PARK? THAT'S AS BONKERS AS A CAT DRIVIN' A FORKLIFT! THEM TWO'S UP TO SOMETHIN'!
THEY SURE ARE! AND IT HAS SOMETHING TO DO WITH THAT BLACK BOX...

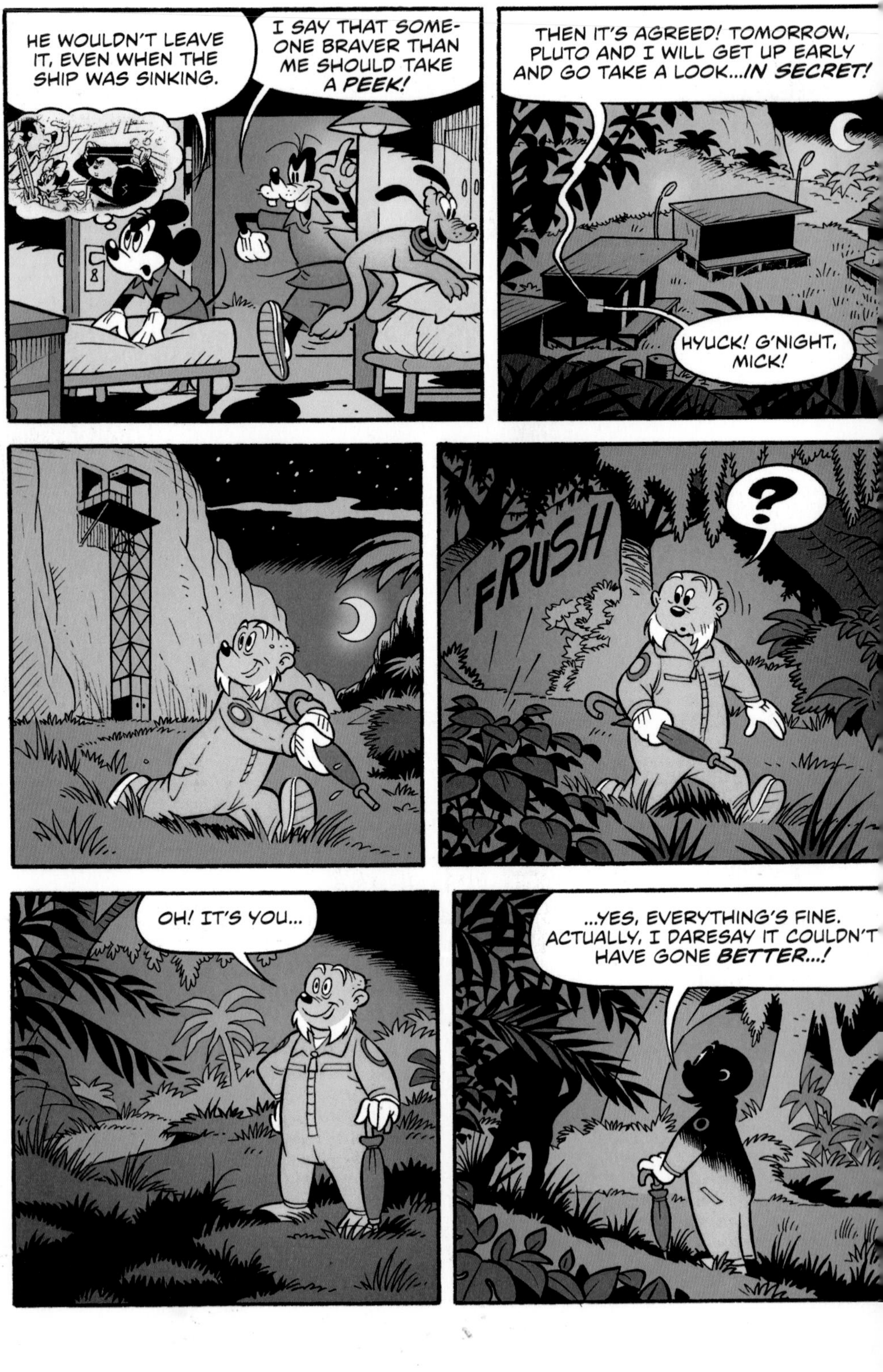
HE WOULDN'T LEAVE IT, EVEN WHEN THE SHIP WAS SINKING.
I SAY THAT SOME-ONE BRAVER THAN ME SHOULD TAKE A *PEEK!*
THEN IT'S AGREED! TOMORROW, PLUTO AND I WILL GET UP EARLY AND GO TAKE A LOOK...*IN SECRET!*
HYUCK! G'NIGHT, MICK!
FRUSH
?
OH! IT'S YOU...
...YES, EVERYTHING'S FINE. ACTUALLY, I DARESAY IT COULDN'T HAVE GONE *BETTER...!*

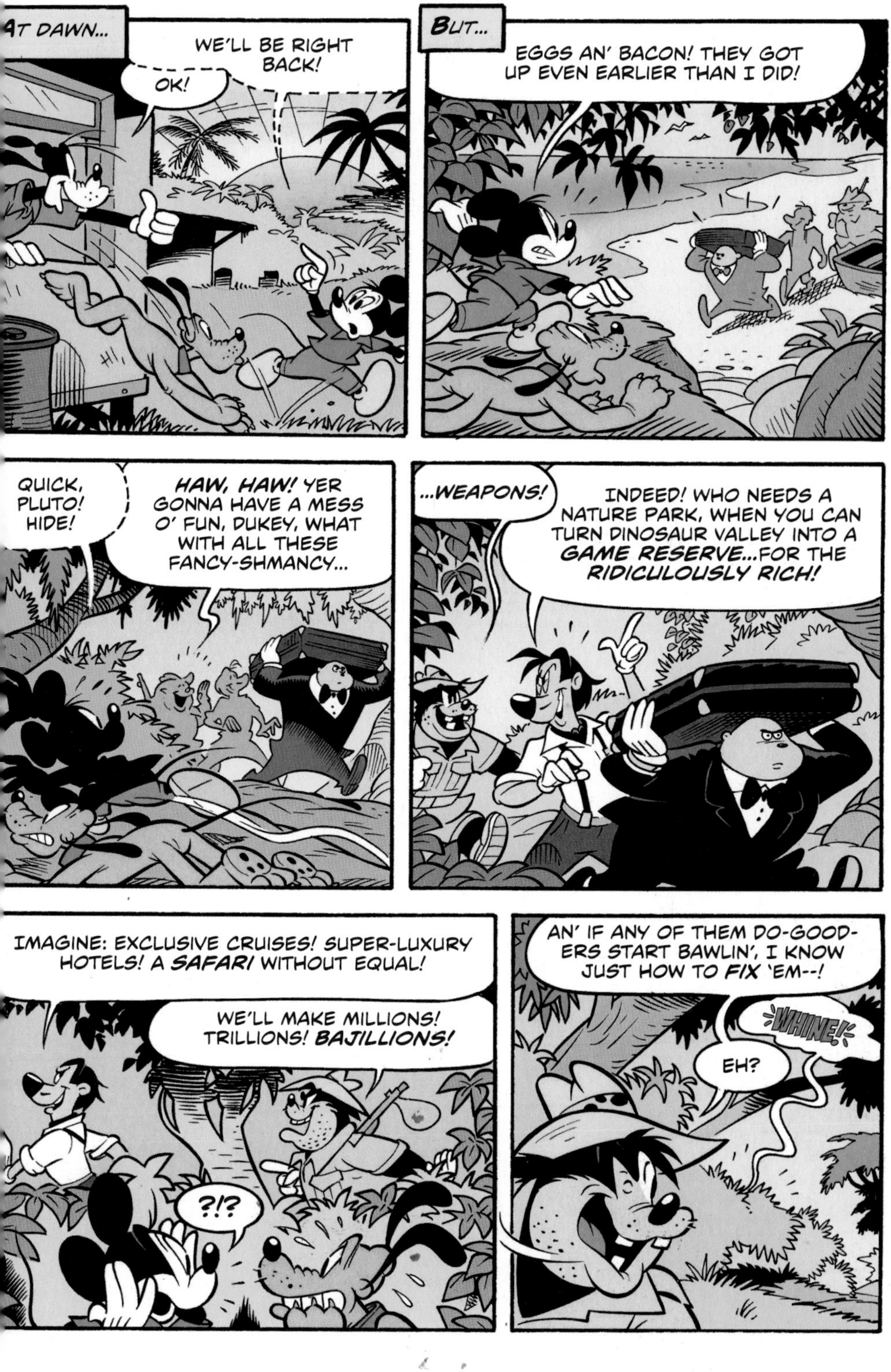
AT DAWN...
WE'LL BE RIGHT BACK!
OK!
BUT...
EGGS AN' BACON! THEY GOT UP EVEN EARLIER THAN I DID!
QUICK, PLUTO! HIDE!
HAW, HAW! YER GONNA HAVE A MESS O' FUN, DUKEY, WHAT WITH ALL THESE FANCY-SHMANCY...
...WEAPONS!
INDEED! WHO NEEDS A NATURE PARK, WHEN YOU CAN TURN DINOSAUR VALLEY INTO A GAME RESERVE...FOR THE RIDICULOUSLY RICH!
IMAGINE: EXCLUSIVE CRUISES! SUPER-LUXURY HOTELS! A SAFARI WITHOUT EQUAL!
WE'LL MAKE MILLIONS! TRILLIONS! BAJILLIONS!
?!?
AN' IF ANY OF THEM DO-GOODERS START BAWLIN', I KNOW JUST HOW TO FIX 'EM--!
WHINE!
EH?

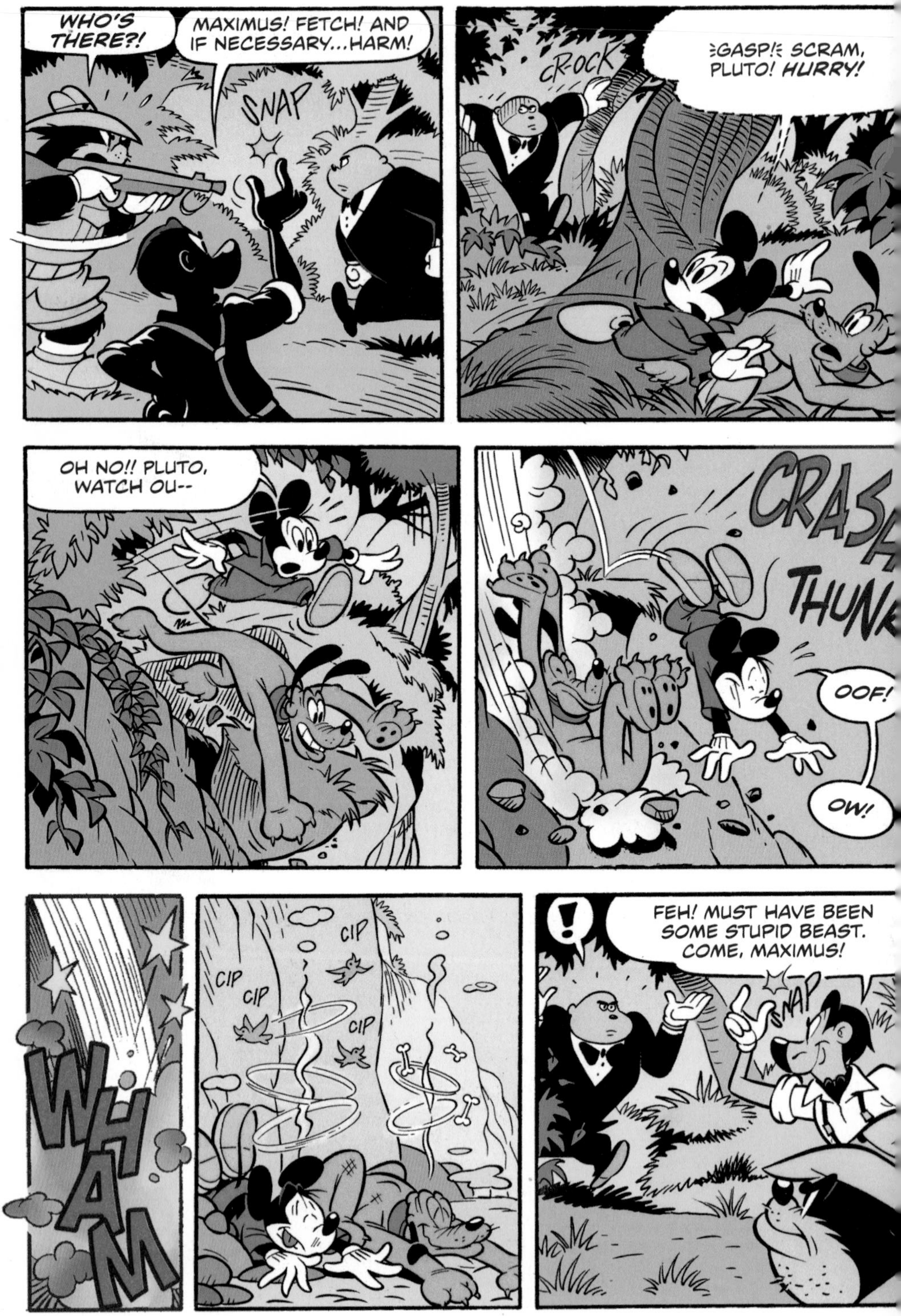

WHO'S THERE?!
MAXIMUS! FETCH! AND IF NECESSARY... HARM!
SNAP
CR-ROCK
GASP! SCRAM, PLUTO! HURRY!
OH NO!! PLUTO, WATCH OU--
CRASH
THUNK
OOF!
OW!
WHAM
CIP
CIP
CIP
CIP
!
FEH! MUST HAVE BEEN SOME STUPID BEAST. COME, MAXIMUS!
SNAP

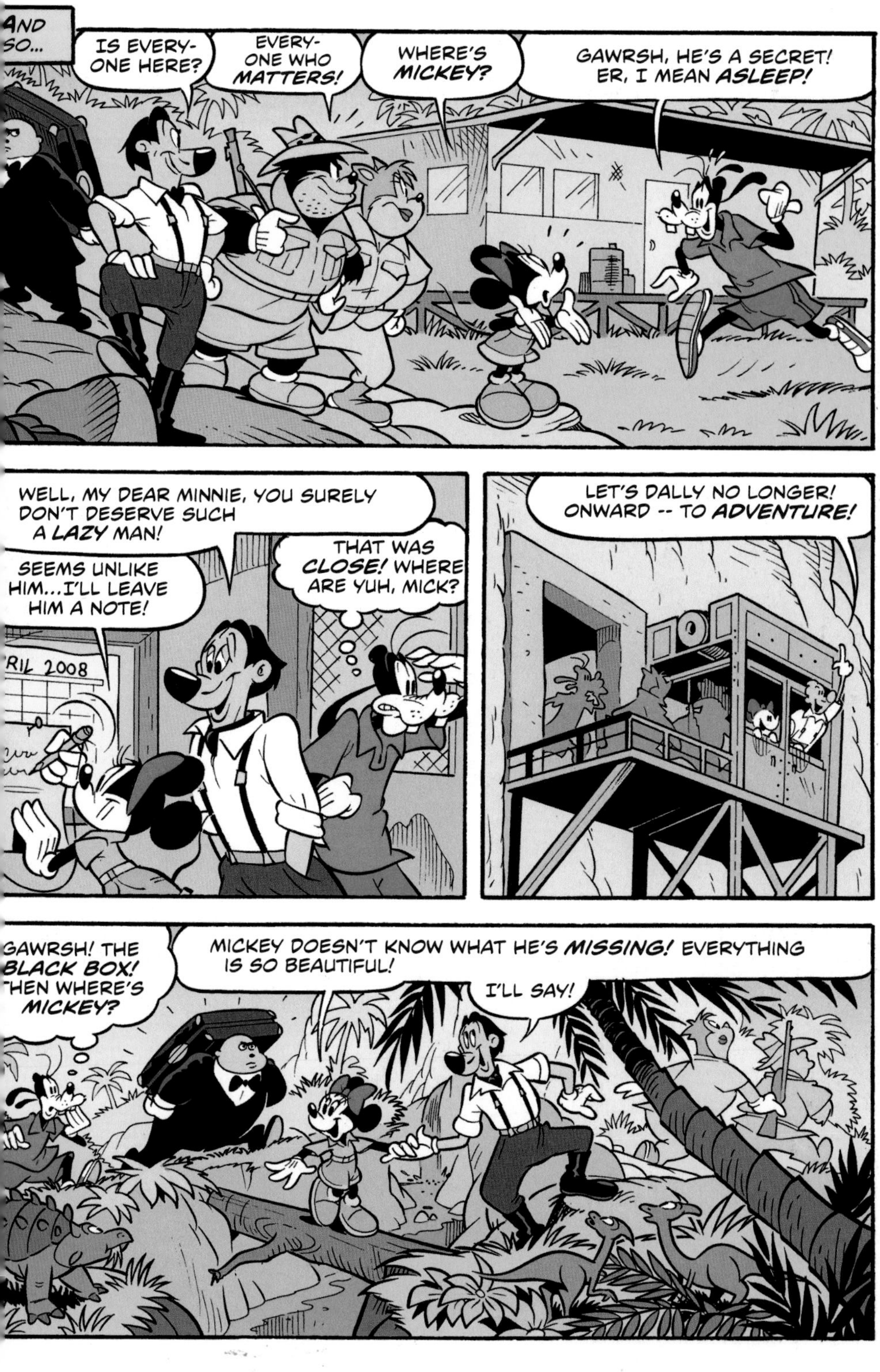
AND SO...
IS EVERY-ONE HERE?
EVERY-ONE WHO MATTERS!
WHERE'S MICKEY?
GAWRSH, HE'S A SECRET! ER, I MEAN ASLEEP!
WELL, MY DEAR MINNIE, YOU SURELY DON'T DESERVE SUCH A LAZY MAN!
SEEMS UNLIKE HIM...I'LL LEAVE HIM A NOTE!
THAT WAS CLOSE! WHERE ARE YUH, MICK?
RIL 2008
LET'S DALLY NO LONGER! ONWARD -- TO ADVENTURE!
GAWRSH! THE BLACK BOX! THEN WHERE'S MICKEY?
MICKEY DOESN'T KNOW WHAT HE'S MISSING! EVERYTHING IS SO BEAUTIFUL!
I'LL SAY!

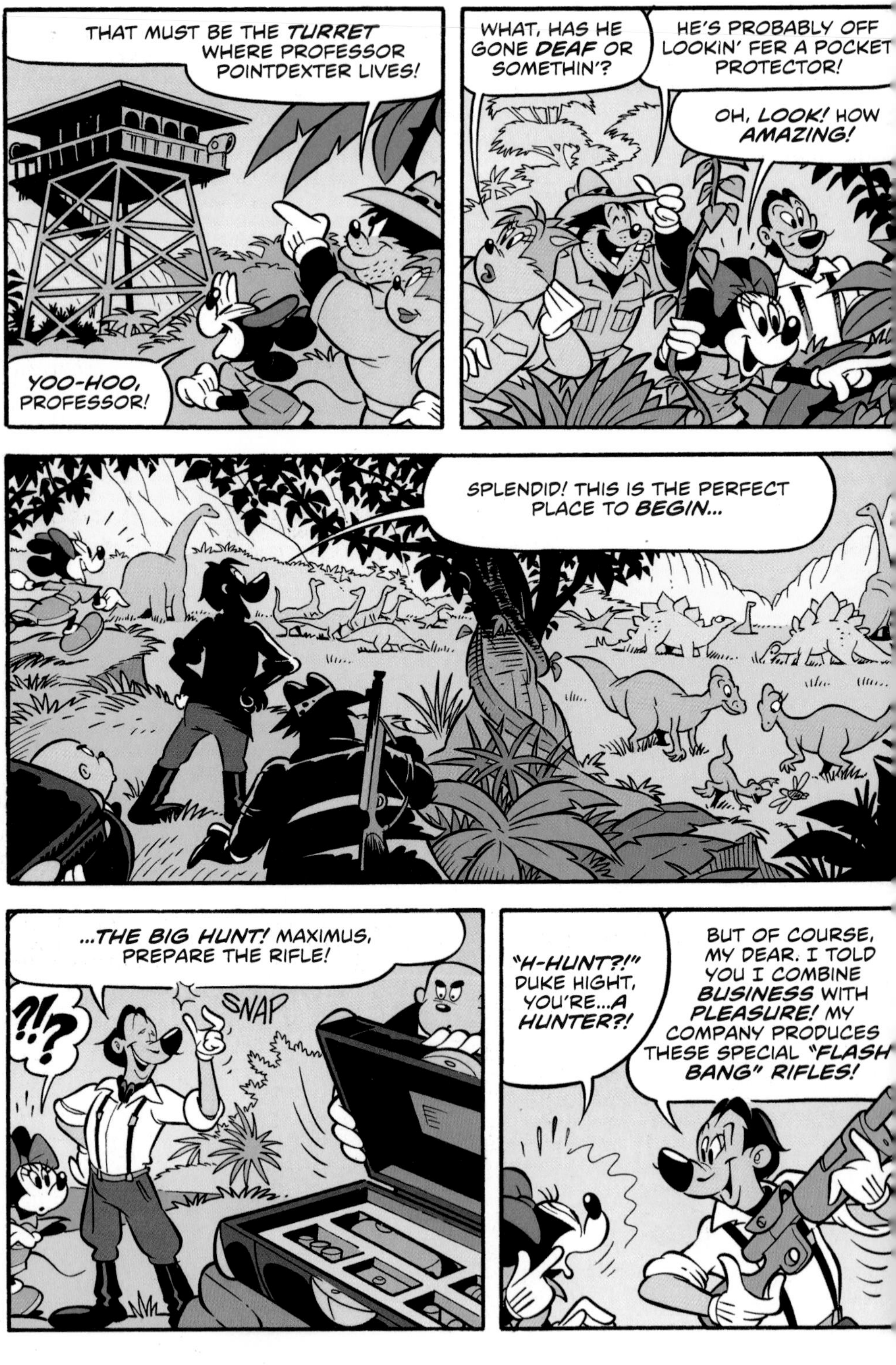
THAT MUST BE THE TURRET WHERE PROFESSOR POINTDEXTER LIVES!
YOO-HOO, PROFESSOR!
WHAT, HAS HE GONE DEAF OR SOMETHIN'?
HE'S PROBABLY OFF LOOKIN' FER A POCKET PROTECTOR!
OH, LOOK! HOW AMAZING!
SPLENDID! THIS IS THE PERFECT PLACE TO BEGIN...
...THE BIG HUNT! MAXIMUS, PREPARE THE RIFLE!
?!?
SNAP
"H-HUNT?!" DUKE HIGHT, YOU'RE...A HUNTER?!
BUT OF COURSE, MY DEAR. I TOLD YOU I COMBINE BUSINESS WITH PLEASURE! MY COMPANY PRODUCES THESE SPECIAL "FLASH BANG" RIFLES!

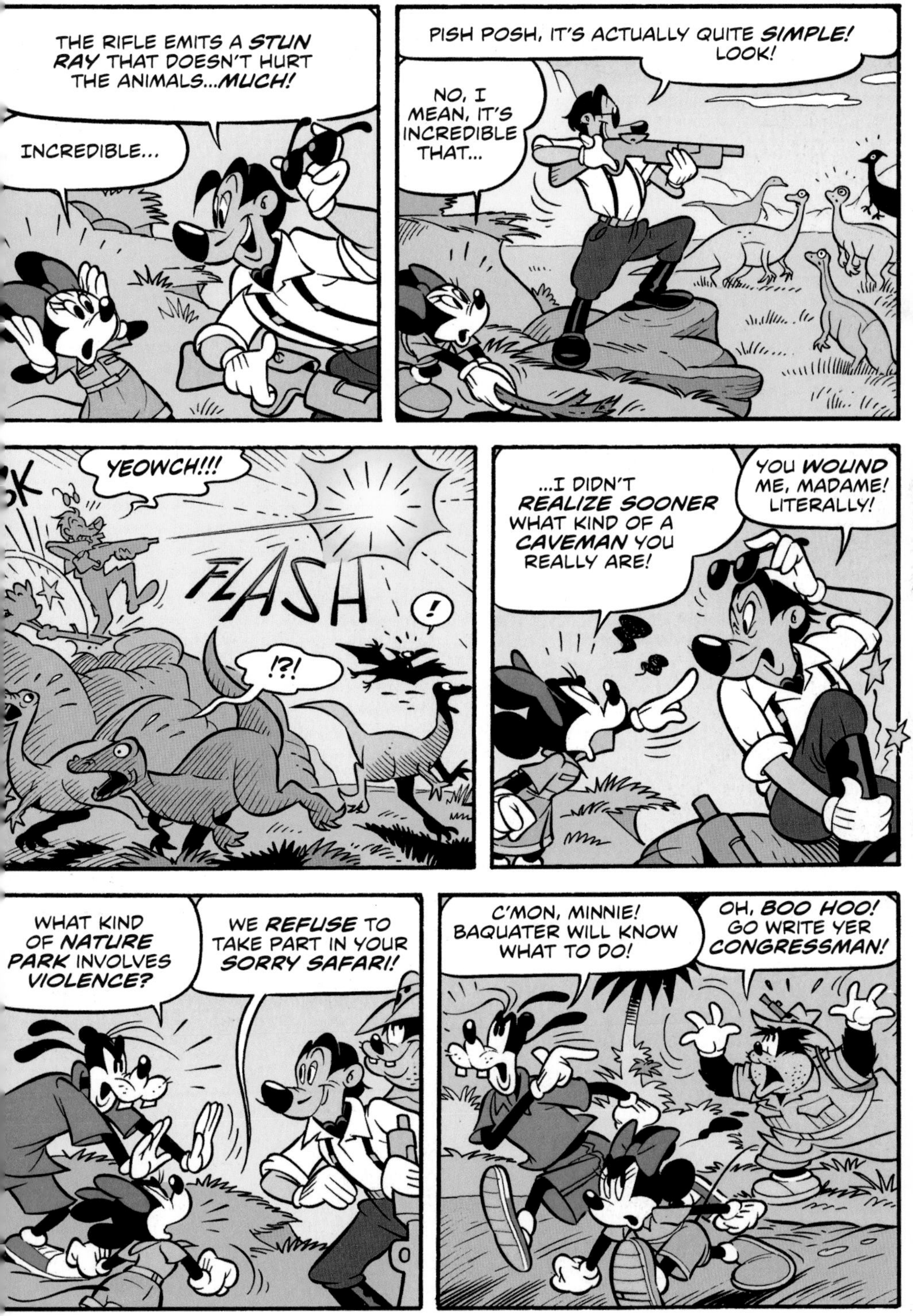
THE RIFLE EMITS A STUN RAY THAT DOESN'T HURT THE ANIMALS...MUCH!
INCREDIBLE...
PISH POSH, IT'S ACTUALLY QUITE SIMPLE! LOOK!
NO, I MEAN, IT'S INCREDIBLE THAT...
YEOWCH!!!
FLASH
!
!?!
...I DIDN'T REALIZE SOONER WHAT KIND OF A CAVEMAN YOU REALLY ARE!
YOU WOUND ME, MADAME! LITERALLY!
WHAT KIND OF NATURE PARK INVOLVES VIOLENCE?
WE REFUSE TO TAKE PART IN YOUR SORRY SAFARI!
C'MON, MINNIE! BAQUATER WILL KNOW WHAT TO DO!
OH, BOO HOO! GO WRITE YER CONGRESSMAN!

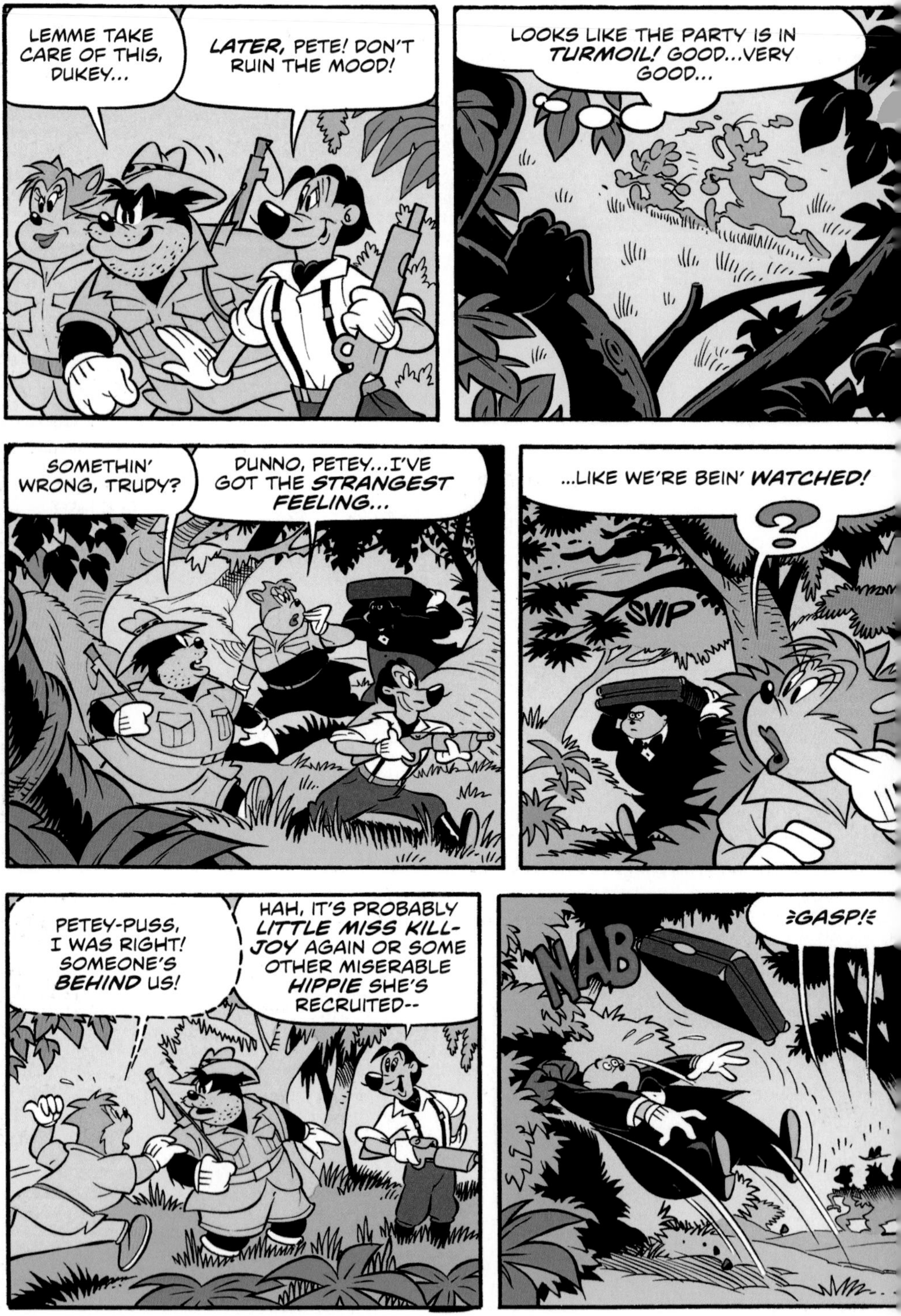
LEMME TAKE CARE OF THIS, DUKEY...
LATER, PETE! DON'T RUIN THE MOOD!
LOOKS LIKE THE PARTY IS IN TURMOIL! GOOD...VERY GOOD...
SOMETHIN' WRONG, TRUDY?
DUNNO, PETEY...I'VE GOT THE STRANGEST FEELING...
...LIKE WE'RE BEIN' WATCHED!
?
SVIP
PETEY-PUSS, I WAS RIGHT! SOMEONE'S BEHIND US!
HAH, IT'S PROBABLY LITTLE MISS KILL-JOY AGAIN OR SOME OTHER MISERABLE HIPPIE SHE'S RECRUITED--
NAB
GASP!

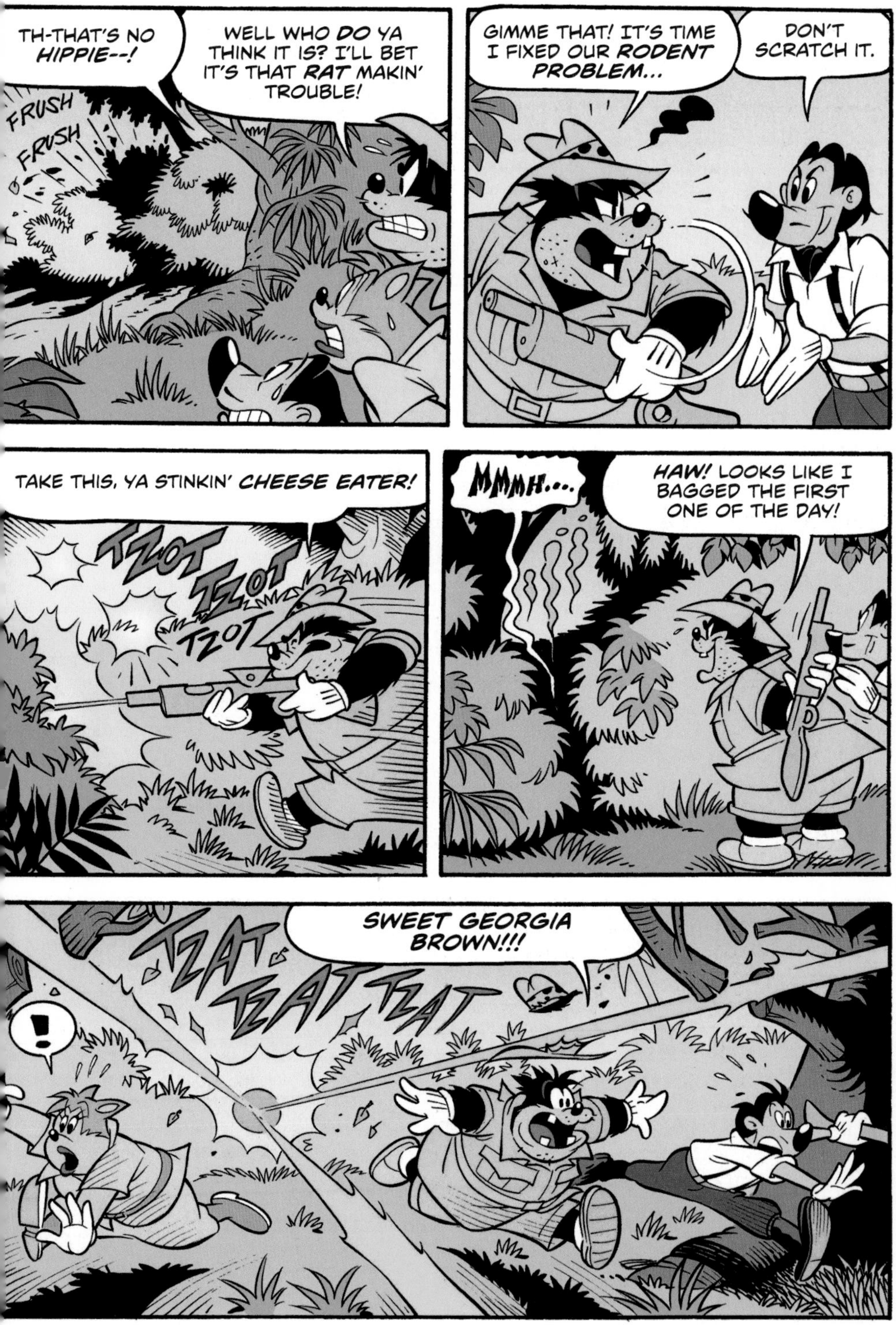

TH-THAT'S NO HIPPIE--!
WELL WHO DO YA THINK IT IS? I'LL BET IT'S THAT RAT MAKIN' TROUBLE!
FRUSH
FRUSH
GIMME THAT! IT'S TIME I FIXED OUR RODENT PROBLEM...
DON'T SCRATCH IT.
TAKE THIS, YA STINKIN' CHEESE EATER!
TZOT
TZOT
TZOT
MMMH....
HAW! LOOKS LIKE I BAGGED THE FIRST ONE OF THE DAY!
SWEET GEORGIA BROWN!!!
TZAT
TZAT
TZAT
!

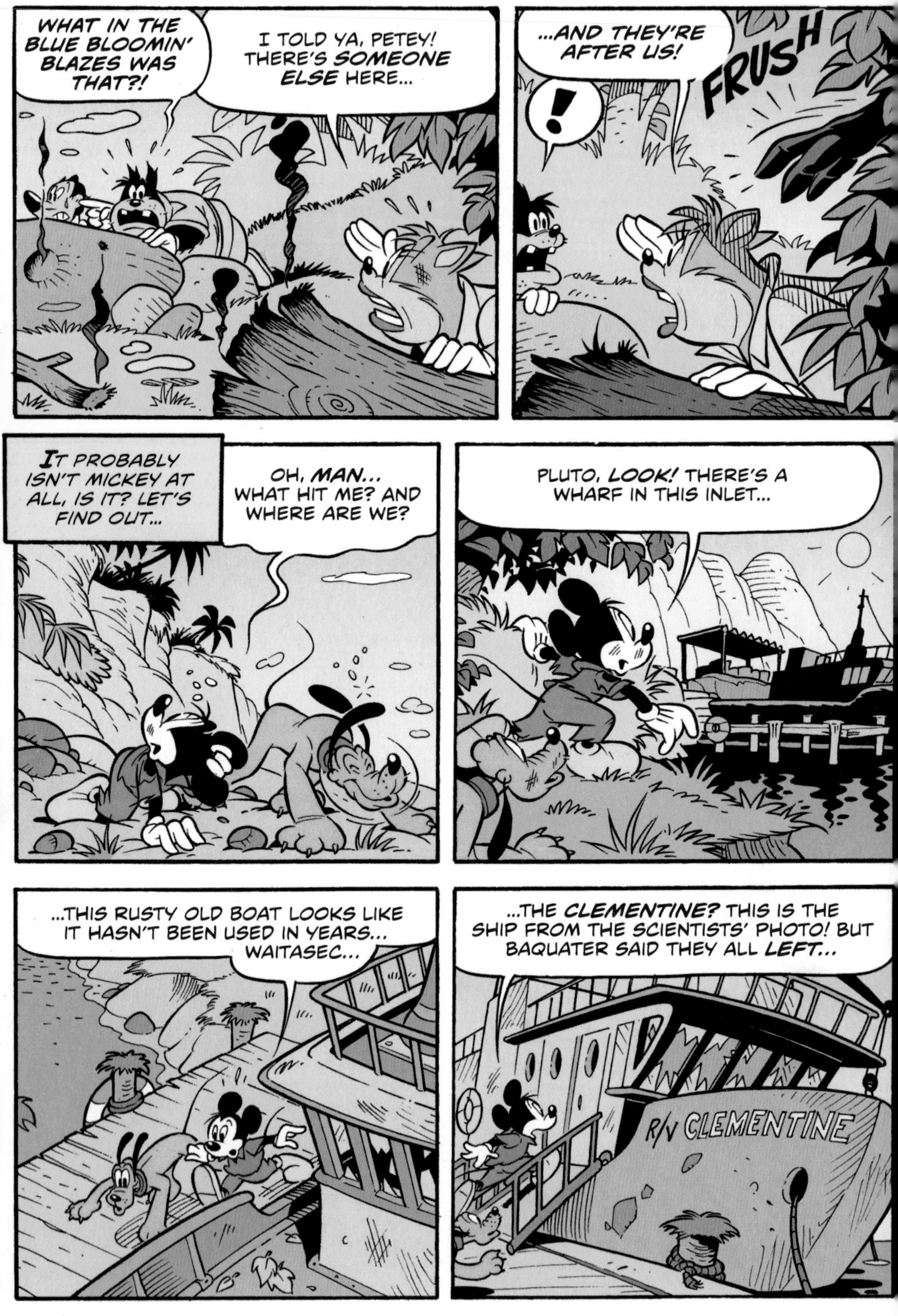
WHAT IN THE BLUE BLOOMIN' BLAZES WAS THAT?!
I TOLD YA, PETEY! THERE'S SOMEONE ELSE HERE...
...AND THEY'RE AFTER US!
!
FRUSH
IT PROBABLY ISN'T MICKEY AT ALL, IS IT? LET'S FIND OUT...
OH, MAN... WHAT HIT ME? AND WHERE ARE WE?
PLUTO, LOOK! THERE'S A WHARF IN THIS INLET...
...THIS RUSTY OLD BOAT LOOKS LIKE IT HASN'T BEEN USED IN YEARS... WAITASEC...
...THE CLEMENTINE? THIS IS THE SHIP FROM THE SCIENTISTS' PHOTO! BUT BAQUATER SAID THEY ALL LEFT...
R/V CLEMENTINE

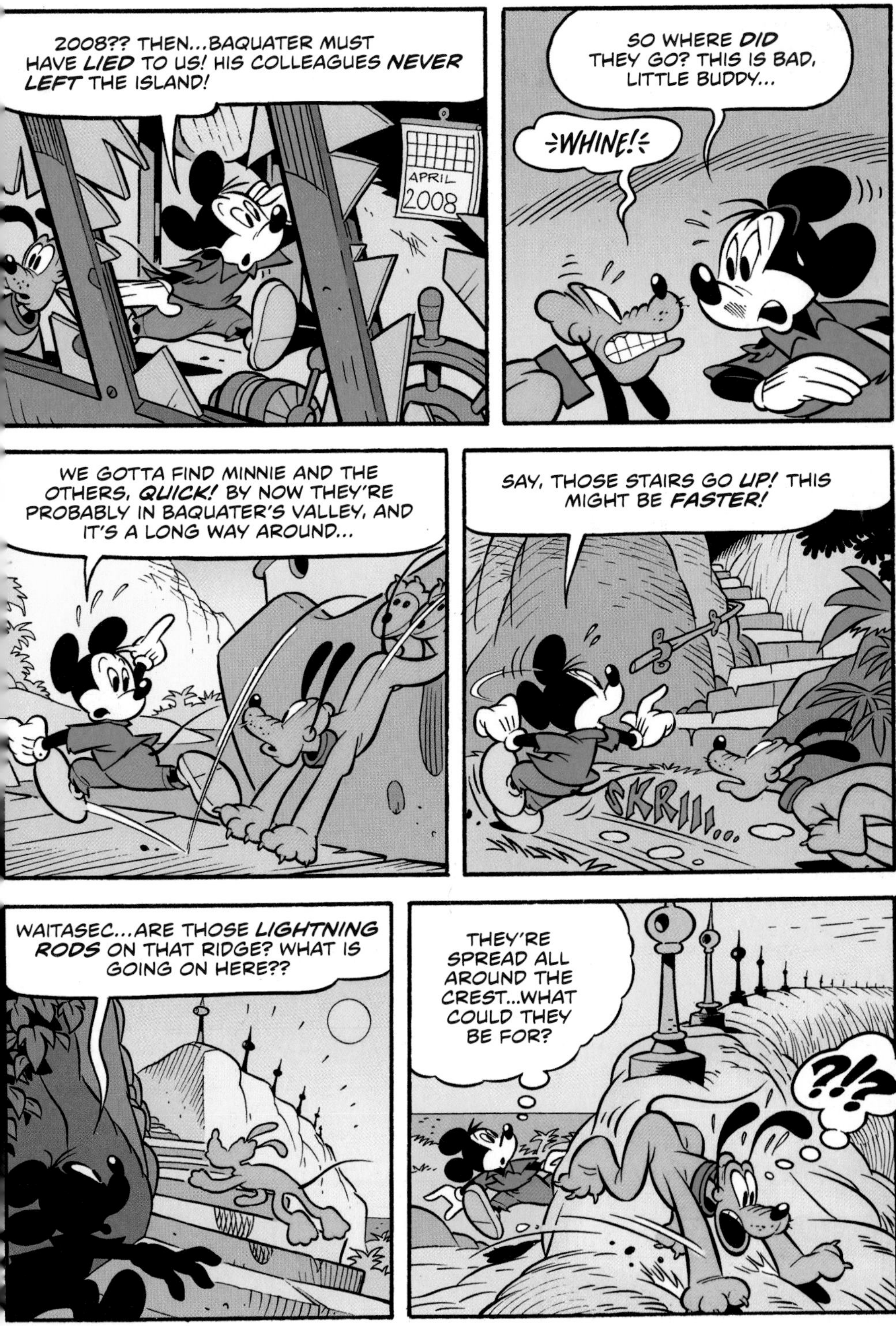
2008?? THEN...BAQUATER MUST HAVE LIED TO US! HIS COLLEAGUES NEVER LEFT THE ISLAND!
APRIL
2008
SO WHERE DID THEY GO? THIS IS BAD, LITTLE BUDDY...
WHINE!
WE GOTTA FIND MINNIE AND THE OTHERS, QUICK! BY NOW THEY'RE PROBABLY IN BAQUATER'S VALLEY, AND IT'S A LONG WAY AROUND...
SAY, THOSE STAIRS GO UP! THIS MIGHT BE FASTER!
SKRIII...
WAITASEC...ARE THOSE LIGHTNING RODS ON THAT RIDGE? WHAT IS GOING ON HERE??
THEY'RE SPREAD ALL AROUND THE CREST...WHAT COULD THEY BE FOR?
?!?

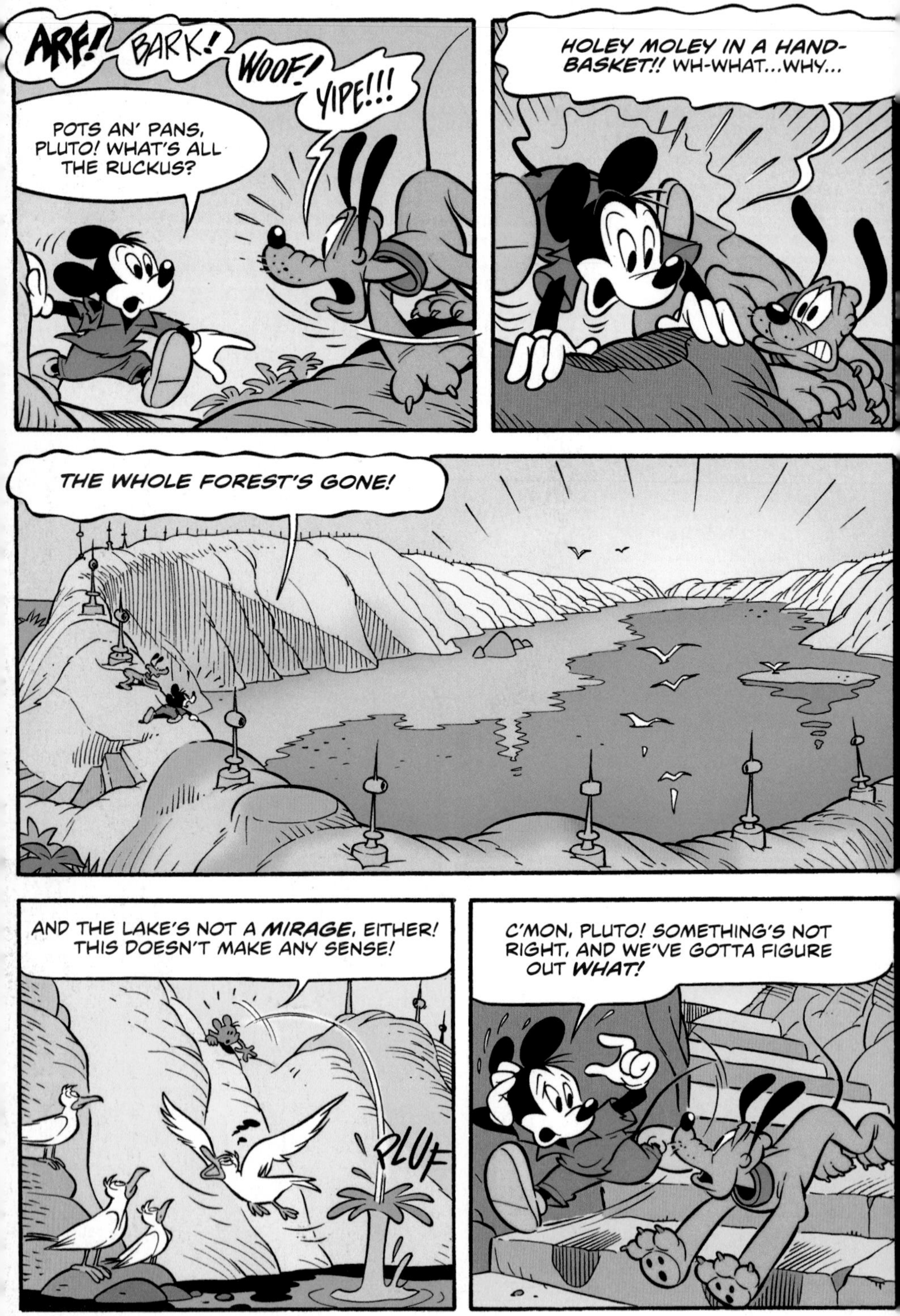
ARF!
BARK!
WOOF!
YIPE!!!
POTS AN' PANS, PLUTO! WHAT'S ALL THE RUCKUS?
HOLEY MOLEY IN A HAND-BASKET!! WH-WHAT...WHY...
THE WHOLE FOREST'S GONE!
AND THE LAKE'S NOT A MIRAGE, EITHER! THIS DOESN'T MAKE ANY SENSE!
PLUF
C'MON, PLUTO! SOMETHING'S NOT RIGHT, AND WE'VE GOTTA FIGURE OUT WHAT!

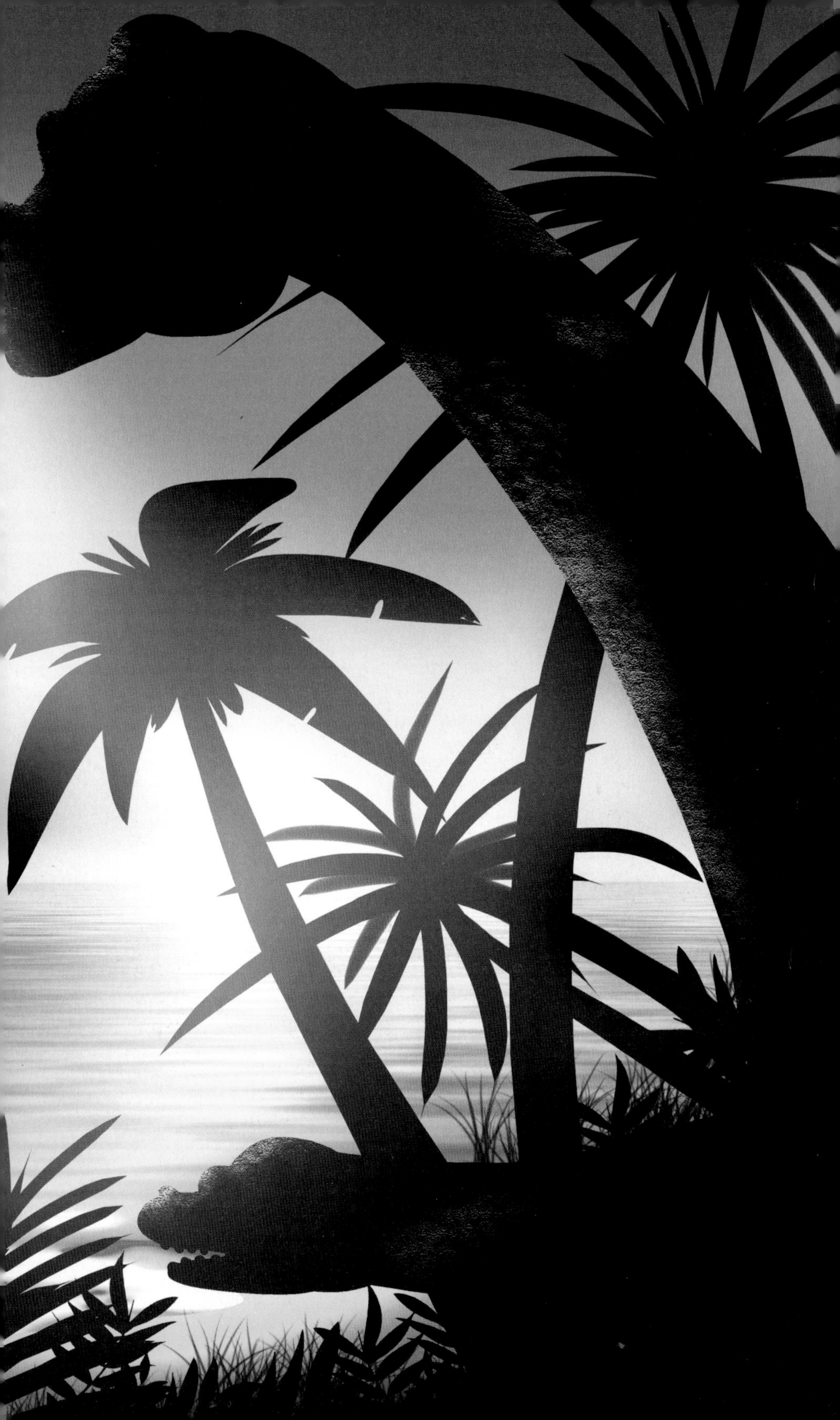

CHAPTER THREE

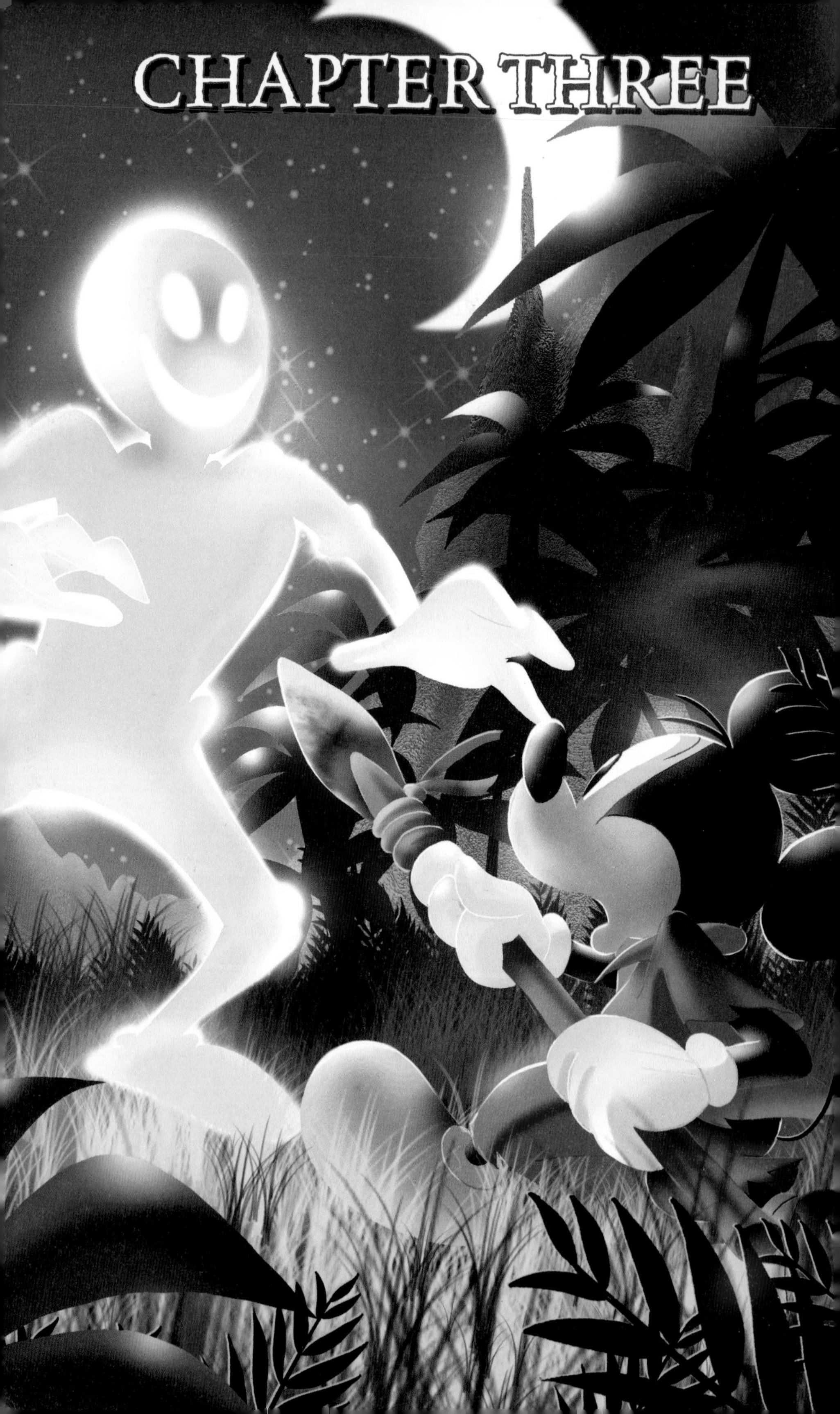

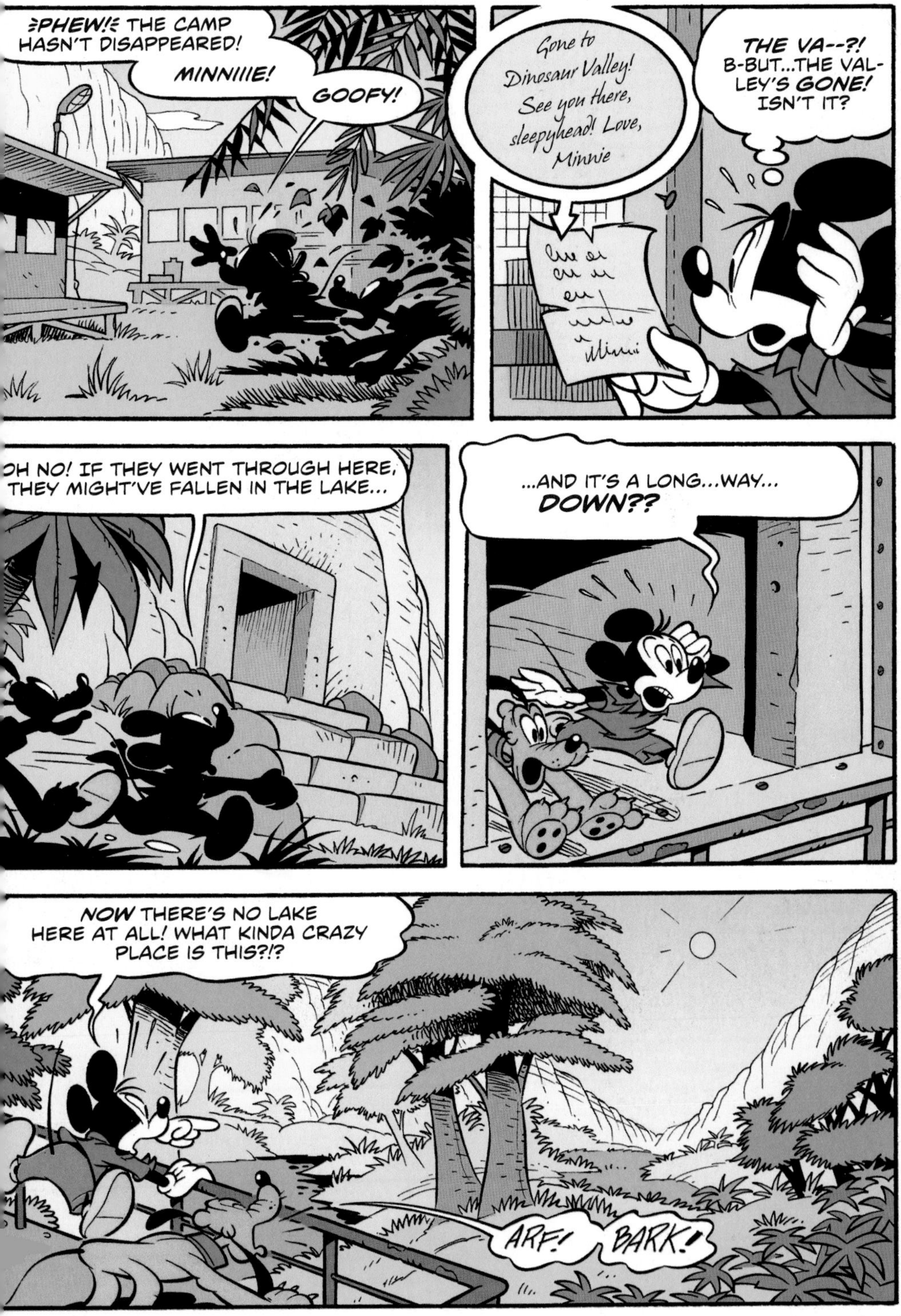

PHEW! THE CAMP HASN'T DISAPPEARED!
MINNIIIE!
GOOFY!
Gone to Dinosaur Valley! See you there, sleepyhead! Love, Minnie
THE VA--?! B-BUT...THE VALLEY'S GONE! ISN'T IT?
OH NO! IF THEY WENT THROUGH HERE, THEY MIGHT'VE FALLEN IN THE LAKE...
...AND IT'S A LONG...WAY... DOWN??
NOW THERE'S NO LAKE HERE AT ALL! WHAT KINDA CRAZY PLACE IS THIS?!?
ARF!
BARK!

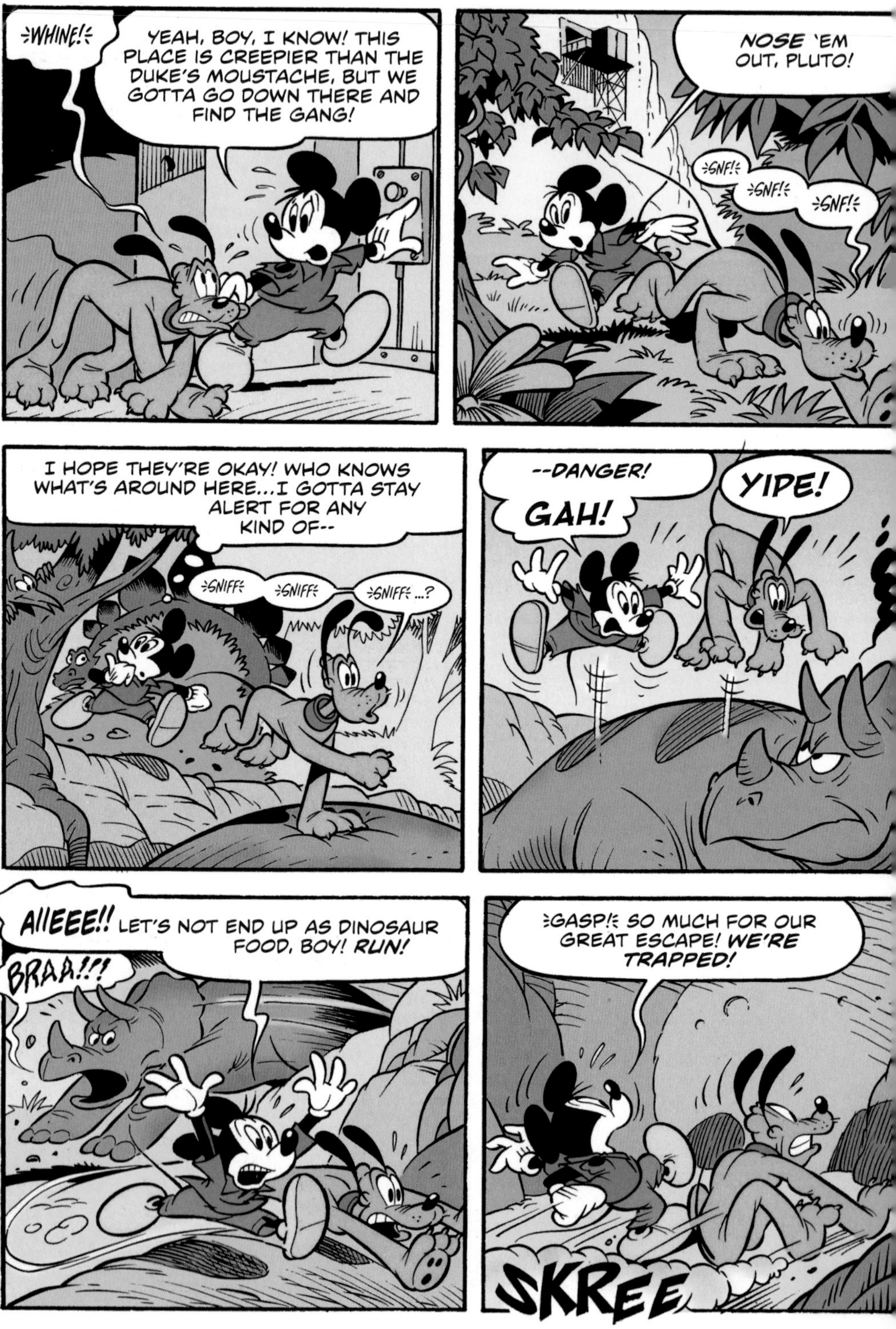

WHINE!
YEAH, BOY, I KNOW! THIS PLACE IS CREEPIER THAN THE DUKE'S MOUSTACHE, BUT WE GOTTA GO DOWN THERE AND FIND THE GANG!
NOSE 'EM OUT, PLUTO!
SNF!
SNF!
SNF!
I HOPE THEY'RE OKAY! WHO KNOWS WHAT'S AROUND HERE...I GOTTA STAY ALERT FOR ANY KIND OF--
SNIFF
SNIFF
SNIFF ...?
--DANGER!
GAH!
YIPE!
AIIEEE!!
LET'S NOT END UP AS DINOSAUR FOOD, BOY! RUN!
BRAA!!!
GASP! SO MUCH FOR OUR GREAT ESCAPE! WE'RE TRAPPED!
SKREE

IT'S BEEN G-GOOD KNOWING YOU, PAL!

RATTLE! RATTLE!

BUT WAIT...!

FIIIII

TRIXIE! DOWN, GIRL!

?!?

SKREEEE

WHO ARE YOU? REVEAL YOUR-SELVES!

"REVEAL OURSELVES?!" WHAT?

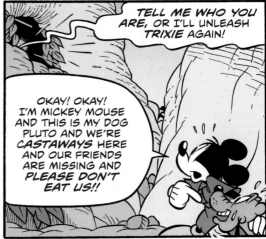

TELL ME WHO YOU ARE, OR I'LL UNLEASH TRIXIE AGAIN!

OKAY! OKAY! I'M MICKEY MOUSE AND THIS IS MY DOG PLUTO AND WE'RE CASTAWAYS HERE AND OUR FRIENDS ARE MISSING AND PLEASE DON'T EAT US!!

I SEE...VERY WELL...

FRUSH

!

I AM THE LONE SURVIVOR OF PROJECT EON VORTEX...MY NAME IS PROFESSOR BENJAMIN BAQUATER!

?!!

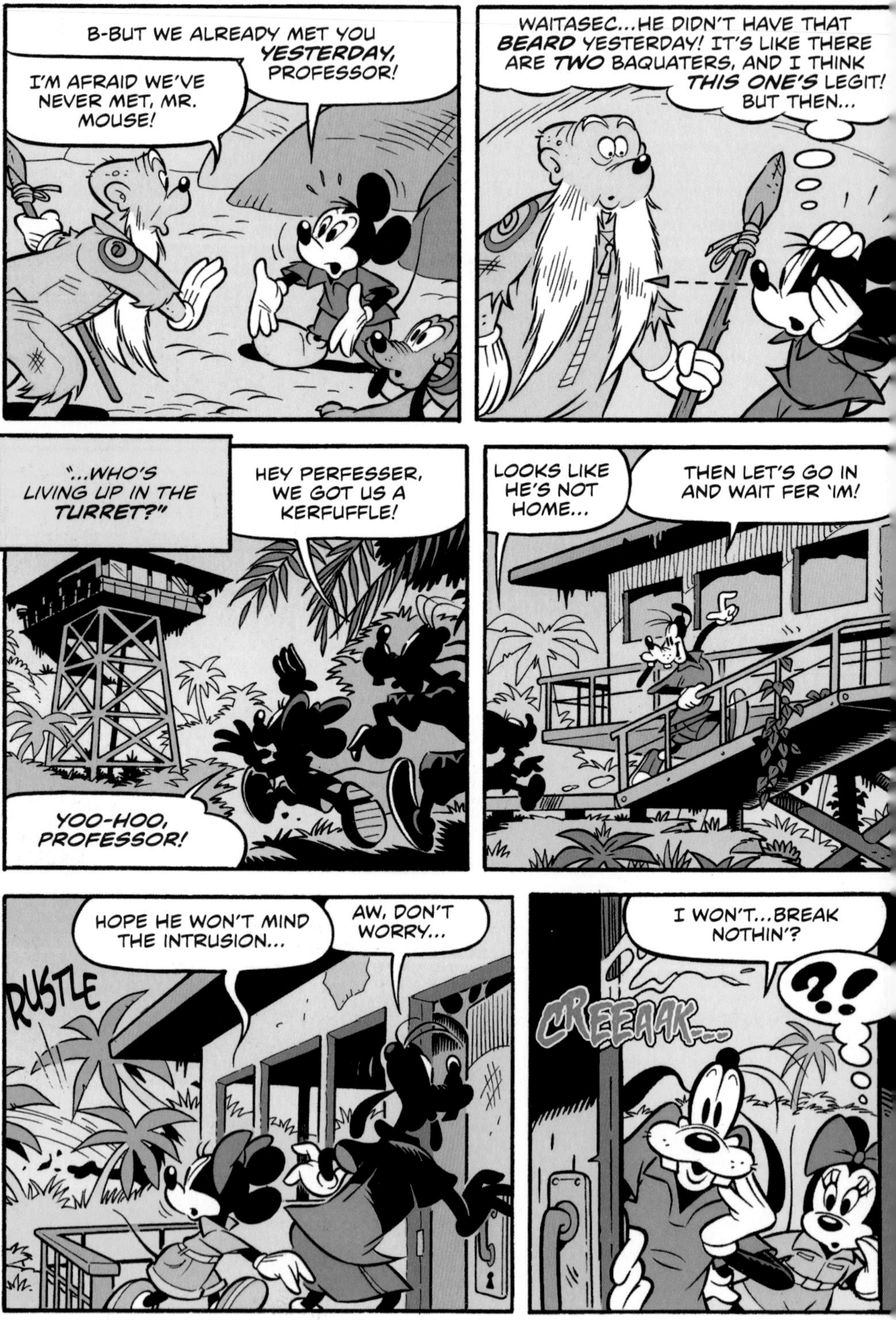
B-BUT WE ALREADY MET YOU YESTERDAY, PROFESSOR!
I'M AFRAID WE'VE NEVER MET, MR. MOUSE!
WAITASEC...HE DIDN'T HAVE THAT BEARD YESTERDAY! IT'S LIKE THERE ARE TWO BAQUATERS, AND I THINK THIS ONE'S LEGIT! BUT THEN...
"...WHO'S LIVING UP IN THE TURRET?"
HEY PERFESSER, WE GOT US A KERFUFFLE!
YOO-HOO, PROFESSOR!
LOOKS LIKE HE'S NOT HOME...
THEN LET'S GO IN AND WAIT FER 'IM!
HOPE HE WON'T MIND THE INTRUSION...
AW, DON'T WORRY...
RUSTLE
I WON'T...BREAK NOTHIN'?
CREEAAK...
?!

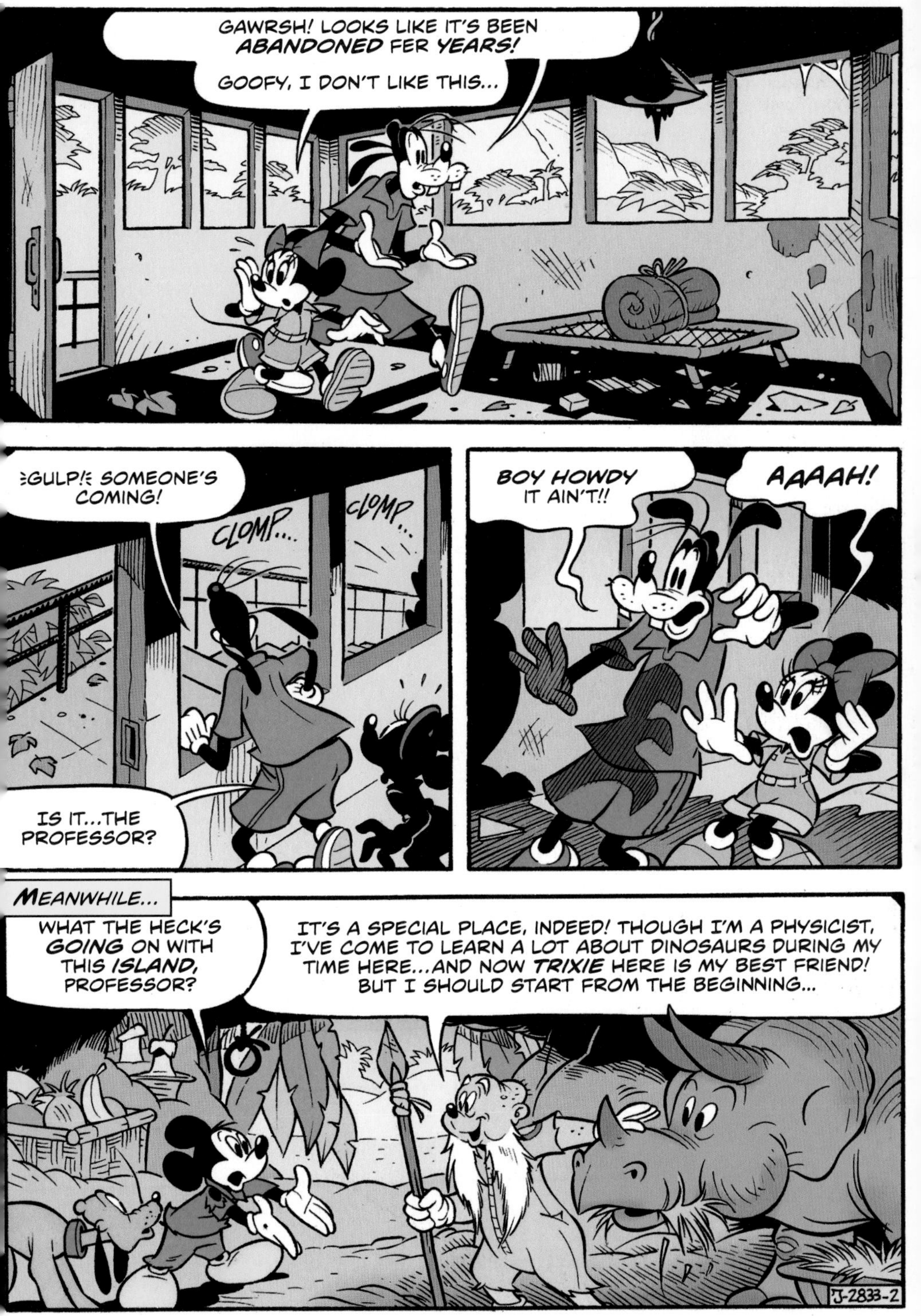

GAWRSH! LOOKS LIKE IT'S BEEN *ABANDONED* FER *YEARS!*
GOOFY, I DON'T LIKE THIS...
⸗GULP!⸗ SOMEONE'S COMING!
CLOMP...
CLOMP...
IS IT...THE PROFESSOR?
BOY HOWDY IT AIN'T!!
AAAAH!
MEANWHILE...
WHAT THE HECK'S *GOING* ON WITH THIS *ISLAND,* PROFESSOR?
IT'S A SPECIAL PLACE, INDEED! THOUGH I'M A PHYSICIST, I'VE COME TO LEARN A LOT ABOUT DINOSAURS DURING MY TIME HERE...AND NOW *TRIXIE* HERE IS MY BEST FRIEND! BUT I SHOULD START FROM THE BEGINNING...
'J-2833-2

FIVE YEARS AGO, A COLLEAGUE IN ROME DISCOVERED THIS ISLAND BY CHANCE. HE NAMED IT *"QUANDOMAI"*--ITALIAN FOR *"WHENEVER"*--BELIEVING IT WOULD BE A PERFECT SPOT FOR OUR AMBITIOUS PROJECT TO GENERATE AN *EON VORTEX!*

CLEMENTINE

A WHAT NOW?

YOU MIGHT HAVE SEEN OUR *CONDUCTORS* ON THE ISLAND'S CREST! THE EON VORTEX IS A FORCE FIELD THAT CAN *ISOLATE TIME!*

IMAGINE IT AS A *CYLINDER* CONTAINING--IN OUR CASE--THE *CRETACEOUS PERIOD!*

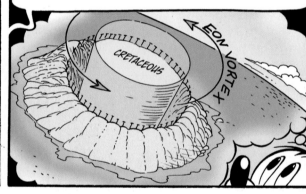

CRETACEOUS

EON VORTEX

TO *ACCESS* THIS AREA--WHICH WE CALLED *"ÜBER-TIME"*--YOU'D JUST NEED TO OPEN A *TUNNEL* IN THE CYLINDER'S SIDE, LIKE THIS...

CRETACEOUS

2010

...AND THEN YOU'D FIND YOURSELF IN THE VALLEY...AS IT EXISTED *130 MILLION YEARS AGO!*

SO *THAT* EXPLAINS WHY WE ONLY SAW A LAKE FROM THE SUMMIT! *I THINK...*

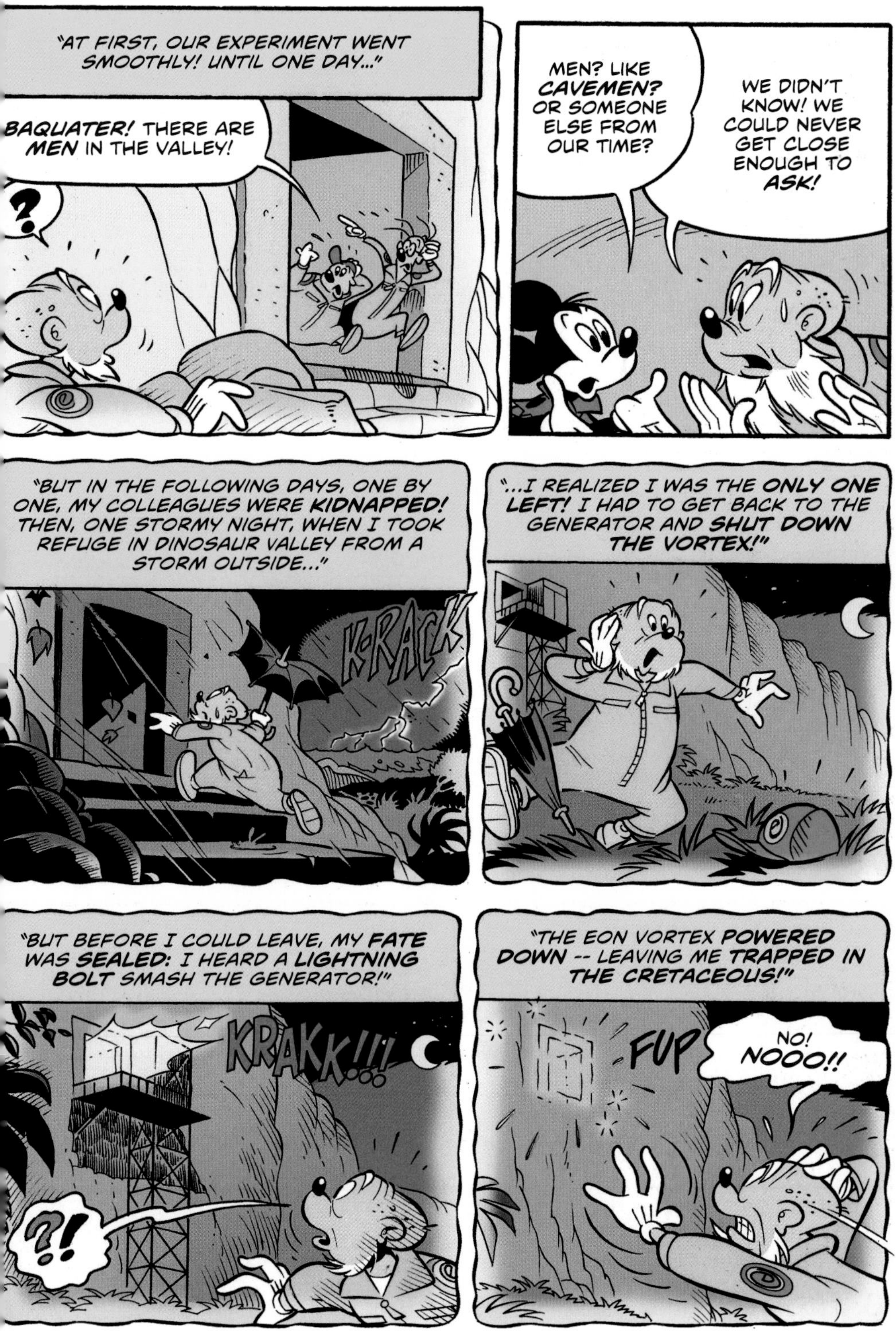
"AT FIRST, OUR EXPERIMENT WENT SMOOTHLY! UNTIL ONE DAY..."
BAQUATER! THERE ARE MEN IN THE VALLEY!
?
MEN? LIKE CAVEMEN? OR SOMEONE ELSE FROM OUR TIME?
WE DIDN'T KNOW! WE COULD NEVER GET CLOSE ENOUGH TO ASK!
"BUT IN THE FOLLOWING DAYS, ONE BY ONE, MY COLLEAGUES WERE KIDNAPPED! THEN, ONE STORMY NIGHT, WHEN I TOOK REFUGE IN DINOSAUR VALLEY FROM A STORM OUTSIDE..."
K-RACK
"...I REALIZED I WAS THE ONLY ONE LEFT! I HAD TO GET BACK TO THE GENERATOR AND SHUT DOWN THE VORTEX!"
"BUT BEFORE I COULD LEAVE, MY FATE WAS SEALED: I HEARD A LIGHTNING BOLT SMASH THE GENERATOR!"
KRAKK!!!
?!
"THE EON VORTEX POWERED DOWN -- LEAVING ME TRAPPED IN THE CRETACEOUS!"
FUP
NO! NOOO!!

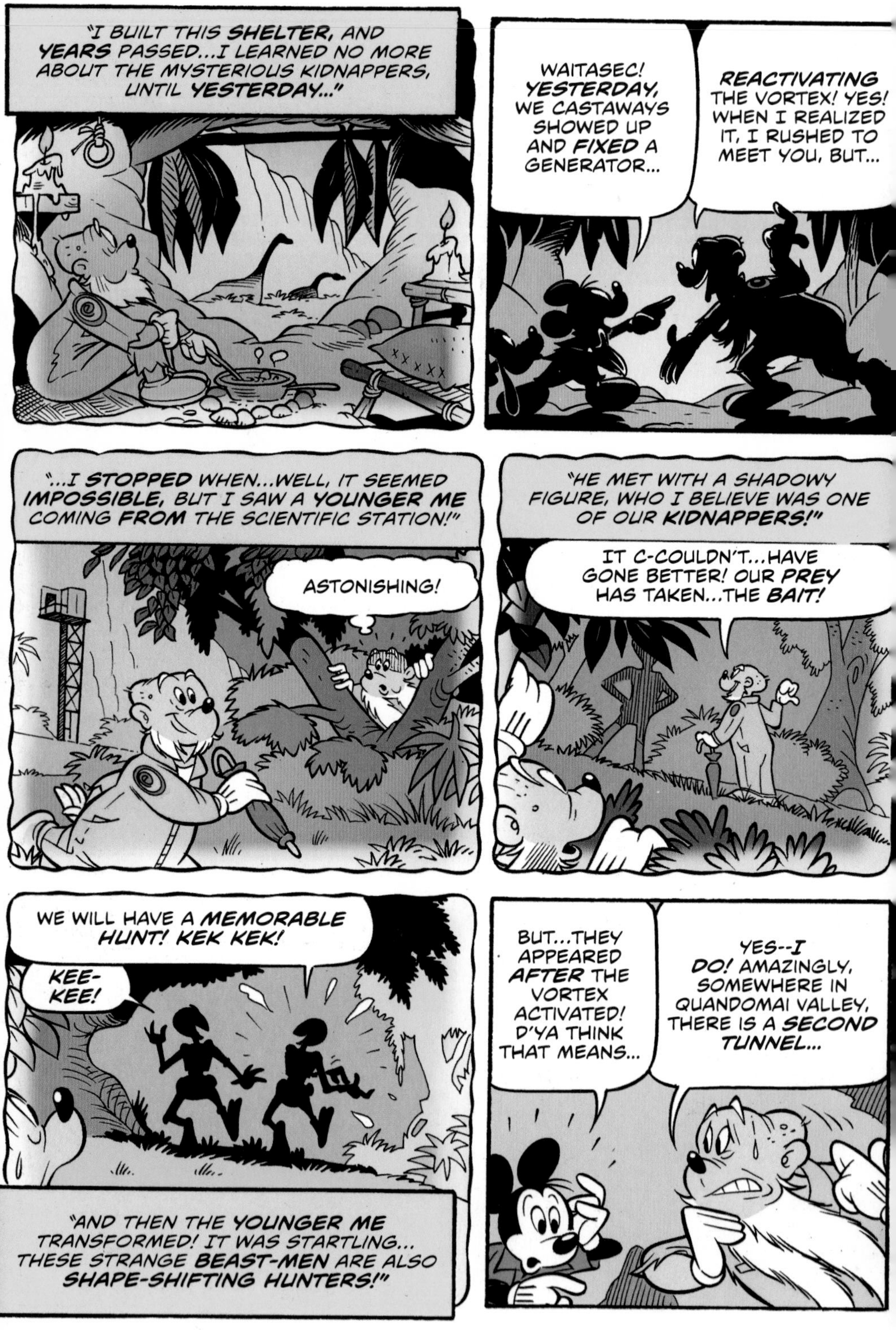
"I BUILT THIS SHELTER, AND YEARS PASSED...I LEARNED NO MORE ABOUT THE MYSTERIOUS KIDNAPPERS, UNTIL YESTERDAY..."
WAITASEC! YESTERDAY, WE CASTAWAYS SHOWED UP AND FIXED A GENERATOR...
REACTIVATING THE VORTEX! YES! WHEN I REALIZED IT, I RUSHED TO MEET YOU, BUT...
"...I STOPPED WHEN...WELL, IT SEEMED IMPOSSIBLE, BUT I SAW A YOUNGER ME COMING FROM THE SCIENTIFIC STATION!"
ASTONISHING!
"HE MET WITH A SHADOWY FIGURE, WHO I BELIEVE WAS ONE OF OUR KIDNAPPERS!"
IT C-COULDN'T...HAVE GONE BETTER! OUR PREY HAS TAKEN...THE BAIT!
WE WILL HAVE A MEMORABLE HUNT! KEK KEK!
KEE-KEE!
"AND THEN THE YOUNGER ME TRANSFORMED! IT WAS STARTLING... THESE STRANGE BEAST-MEN ARE ALSO SHAPE-SHIFTING HUNTERS!"
BUT...THEY APPEARED AFTER THE VORTEX ACTIVATED! D'YA THINK THAT MEANS...
YES--I DO! AMAZINGLY, SOMEWHERE IN QUANDOMAI VALLEY, THERE IS A SECOND TUNNEL...

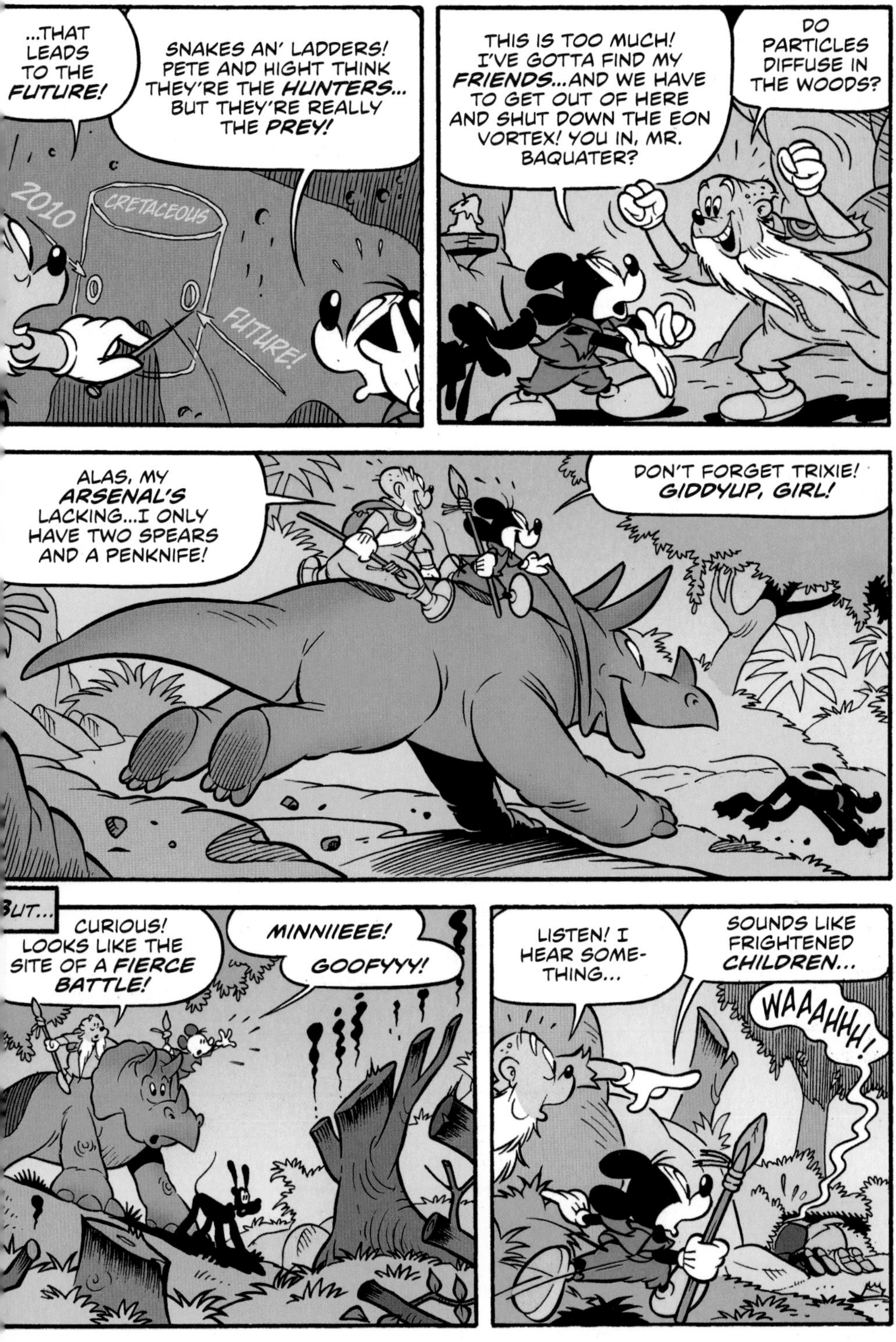
...THAT LEADS TO THE FUTURE!
SNAKES AN' LADDERS! PETE AND HIGHT THINK THEY'RE THE HUNTERS... BUT THEY'RE REALLY THE PREY!
2010
CRETACEOUS
FUTURE!
THIS IS TOO MUCH! I'VE GOTTA FIND MY FRIENDS...AND WE HAVE TO GET OUT OF HERE AND SHUT DOWN THE EON VORTEX! YOU IN, MR. BAQUATER?
DO PARTICLES DIFFUSE IN THE WOODS?
ALAS, MY ARSENAL'S LACKING...I ONLY HAVE TWO SPEARS AND A PENKNIFE!
DON'T FORGET TRIXIE! GIDDYUP, GIRL!
BUT...
CURIOUS! LOOKS LIKE THE SITE OF A FIERCE BATTLE!
MINNIIEEE!
GOOFYYY!
LISTEN! I HEAR SOME-THING...
SOUNDS LIKE FRIGHTENED CHILDREN...
WAAAHHH!

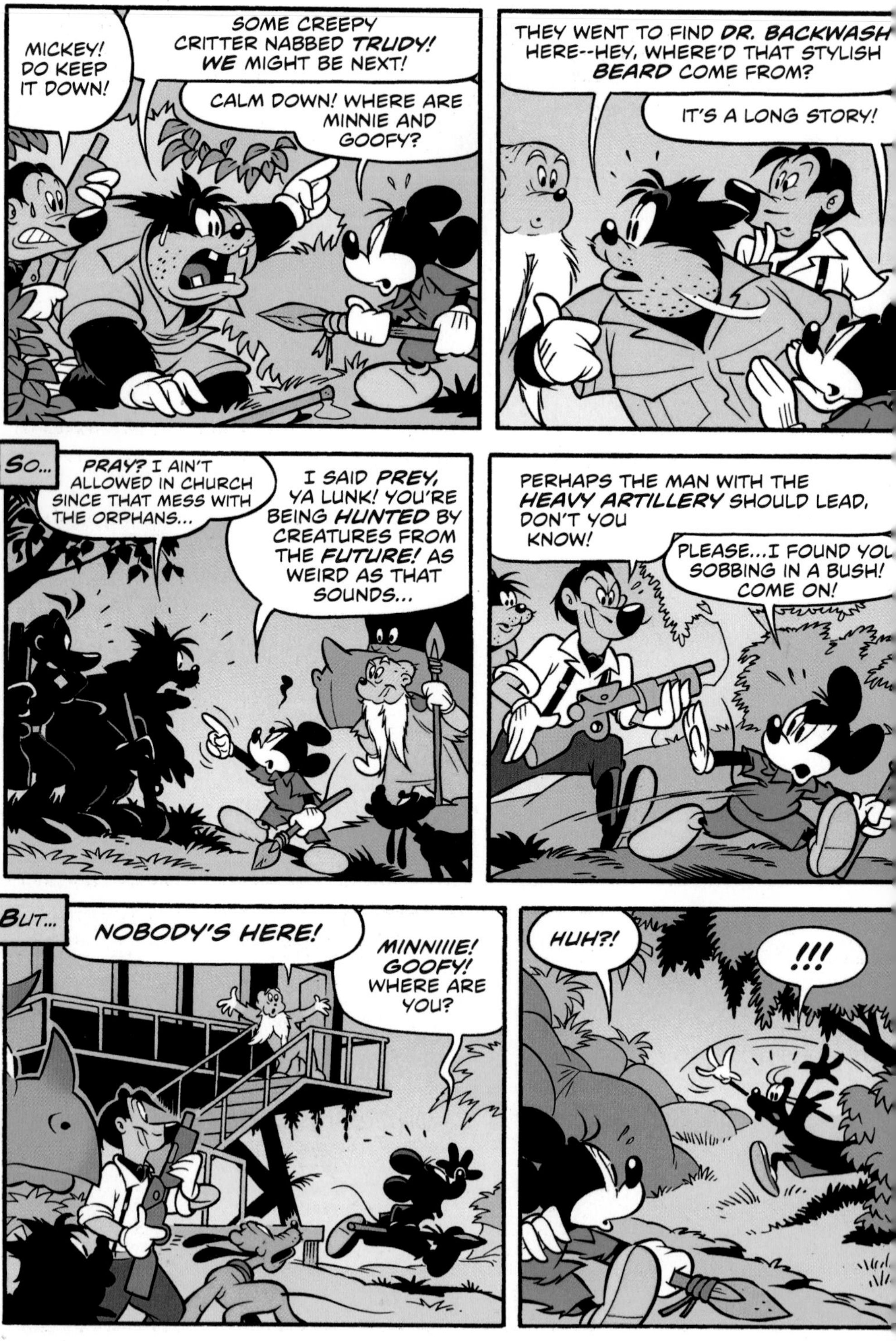

MICKEY! DO KEEP IT DOWN!
SOME CREEPY CRITTER NABBED TRUDY! WE MIGHT BE NEXT!
CALM DOWN! WHERE ARE MINNIE AND GOOFY?
THEY WENT TO FIND DR. BACKWASH HERE--HEY, WHERE'D THAT STYLISH BEARD COME FROM?
IT'S A LONG STORY!
SO...
PRAY? I AIN'T ALLOWED IN CHURCH SINCE THAT MESS WITH THE ORPHANS...
I SAID PREY, YA LUNK! YOU'RE BEING HUNTED BY CREATURES FROM THE FUTURE! AS WEIRD AS THAT SOUNDS...
PERHAPS THE MAN WITH THE HEAVY ARTILLERY SHOULD LEAD, DON'T YOU KNOW!
PLEASE...I FOUND YOU SOBBING IN A BUSH! COME ON!
BUT...
NOBODY'S HERE!
MINNIIIE! GOOFY! WHERE ARE YOU?
HUH?!
!!!

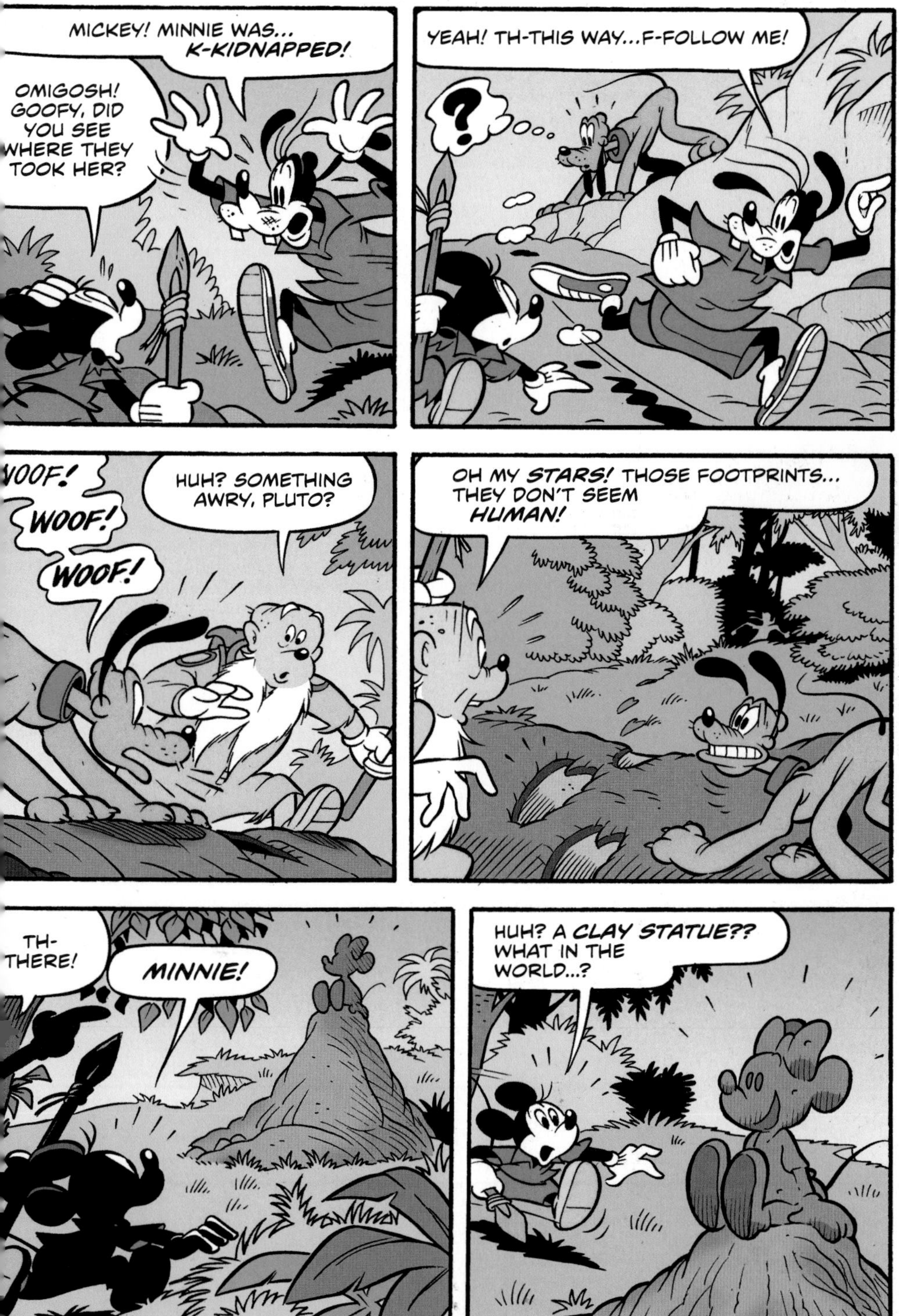
MICKEY! MINNIE WAS... K-KIDNAPPED!
OMIGOSH! GOOFY, DID YOU SEE WHERE THEY TOOK HER?
YEAH! TH-THIS WAY...F-FOLLOW ME!
?
WOOF! WOOF! WOOF!
HUH? SOMETHING AWRY, PLUTO?
OH MY STARS! THOSE FOOTPRINTS... THEY DON'T SEEM HUMAN!
TH-THERE!
MINNIE!
HUH? A CLAY STATUE?? WHAT IN THE WORLD...?

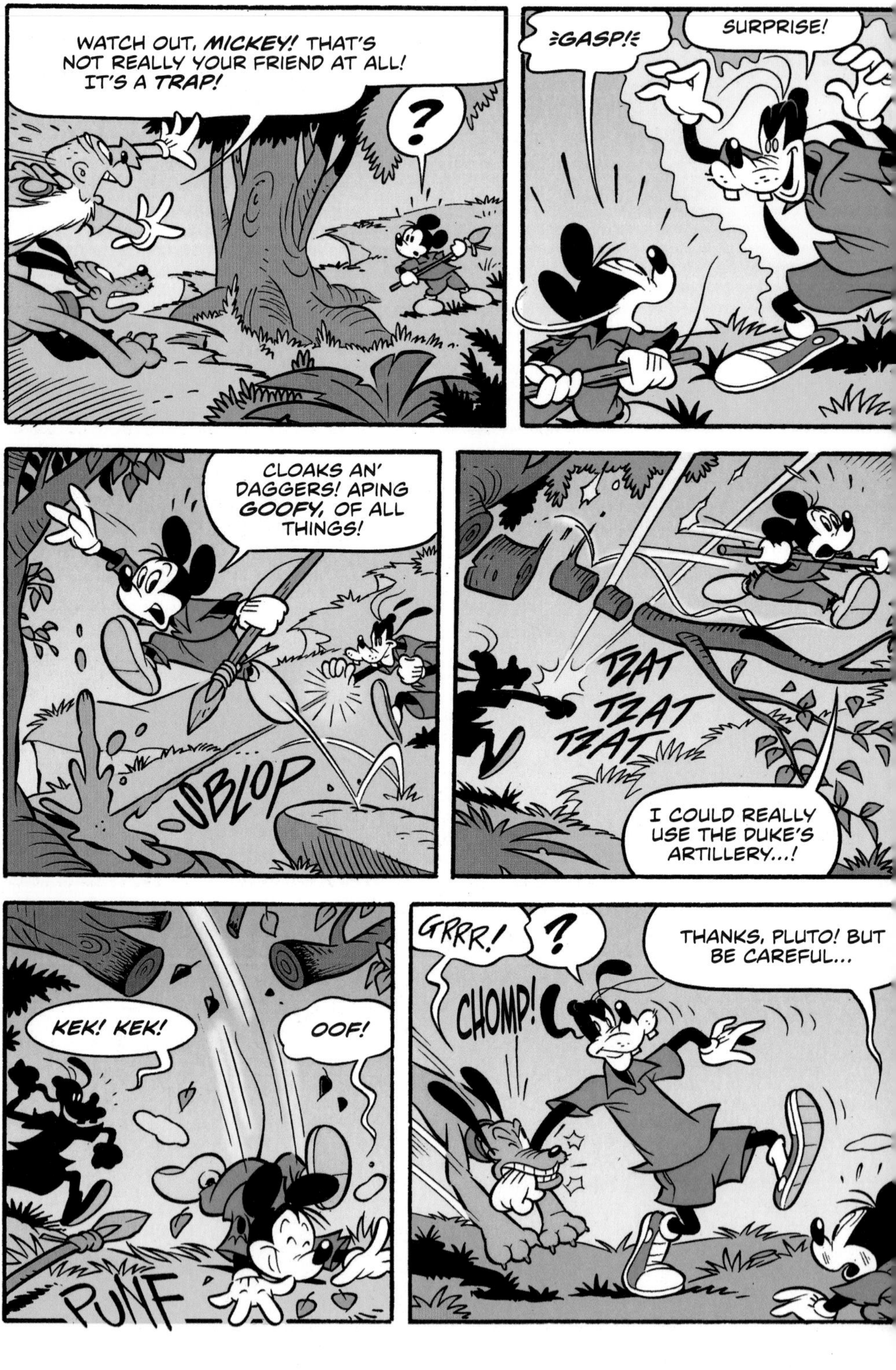
WATCH OUT, MICKEY! THAT'S NOT REALLY YOUR FRIEND AT ALL! IT'S A TRAP!
?
GASP!
SURPRISE!
CLOAKS AN' DAGGERS! APING GOOFY, OF ALL THINGS!
SBLOP
TZAT TZAT TZAT
I COULD REALLY USE THE DUKE'S ARTILLERY...!
KEK! KEK!
OOF!
PUNF
GRRR!
?
THANKS, PLUTO! BUT BE CAREFUL...
CHOMP!

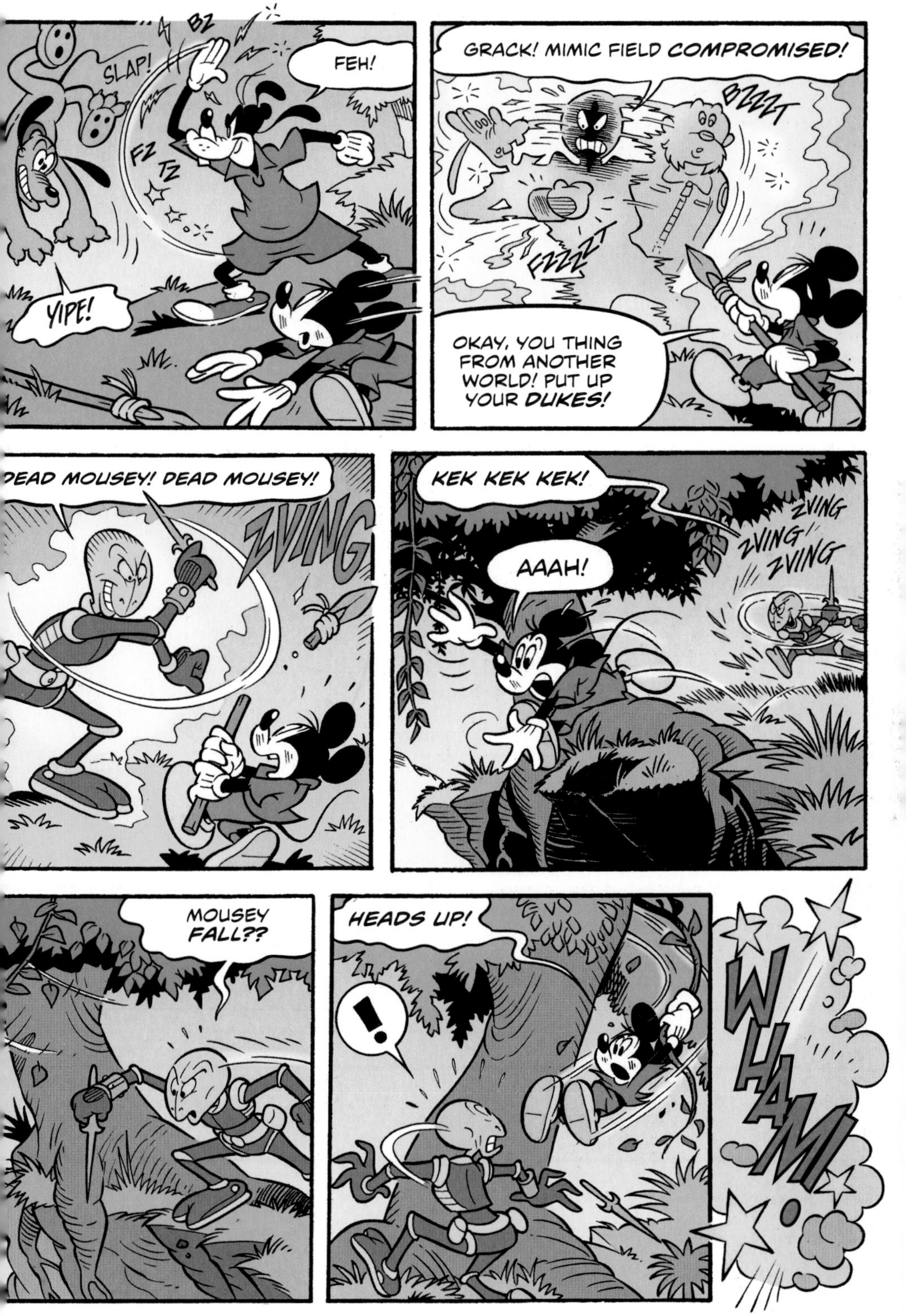
SLAP!
BZ
FEH!
FZ
ZZ
YIPE!
GRACK! MIMIC FIELD COMPROMISED!
BZZZT
FZZZZT
OKAY, YOU THING FROM ANOTHER WORLD! PUT UP YOUR DUKES!
DEAD MOUSEY! DEAD MOUSEY!
ZVING
KEK KEK KEK!
AAAH!
ZVING
ZVING
ZVING
MOUSEY FALL??
HEADS UP!
!
WHAM!

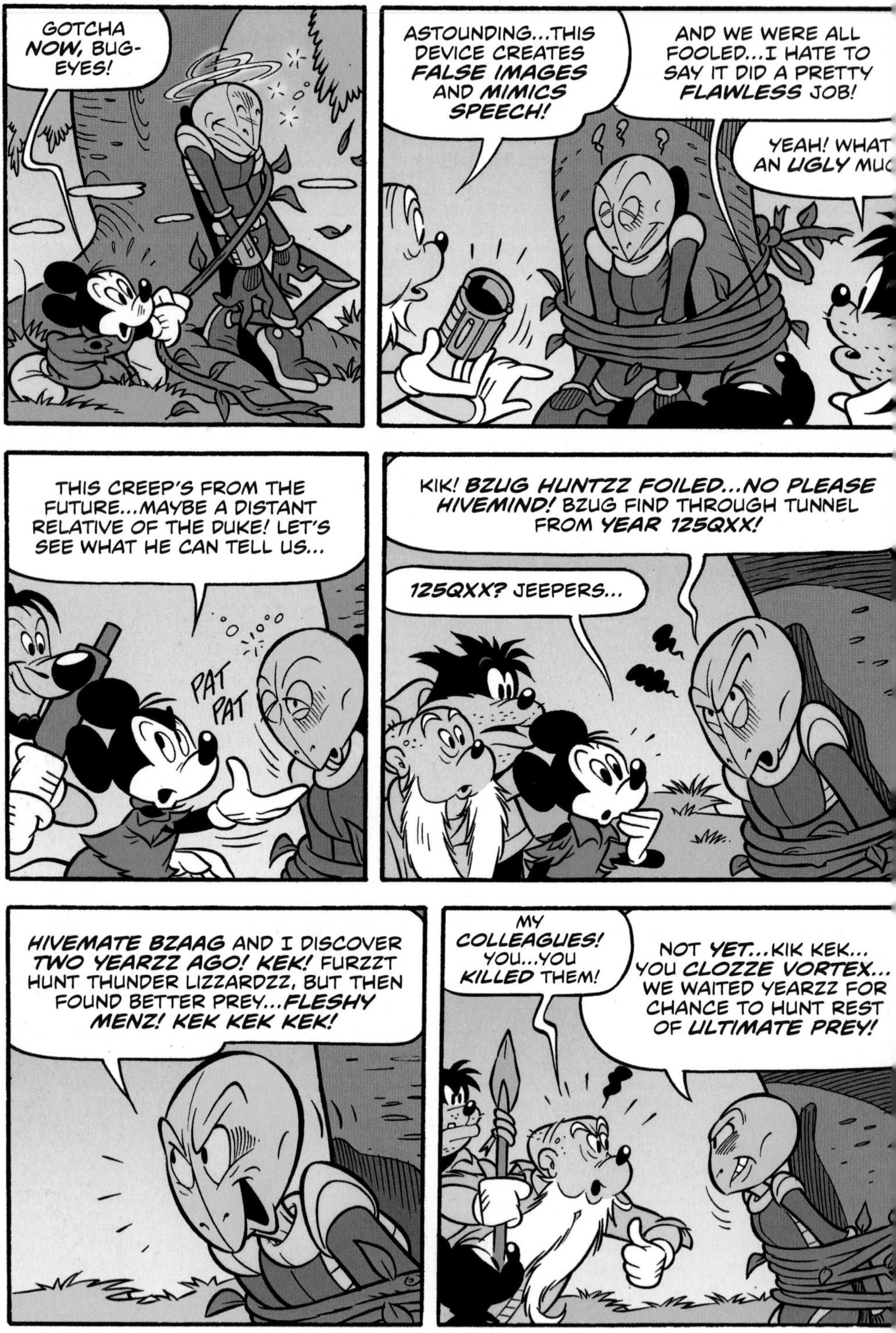
GOTCHA NOW, BUG-EYES!
ASTOUNDING...THIS DEVICE CREATES FALSE IMAGES AND MIMICS SPEECH!
AND WE WERE ALL FOOLED...I HATE TO SAY IT DID A PRETTY FLAWLESS JOB!
YEAH! WHAT AN UGLY MU
THIS CREEP'S FROM THE FUTURE...MAYBE A DISTANT RELATIVE OF THE DUKE! LET'S SEE WHAT HE CAN TELL US...
PAT PAT
KIK! BZUG HUNTZZ FOILED...NO PLEASE HIVEMIND! BZUG FIND THROUGH TUNNEL FROM YEAR 125QXX!
125QXX? JEEPERS...
HIVEMATE BZAAG AND I DISCOVER TWO YEARZZ AGO! KEK! FURZZT HUNT THUNDER LIZZARDZZ, BUT THEN FOUND BETTER PREY...FLESHY MENZ! KEK KEK KEK!
MY COLLEAGUES! YOU...YOU KILLED THEM!
NOT YET...KIK KEK... YOU CLOZZE VORTEX... WE WAITED YEARZZ FOR CHANCE TO HUNT REST OF ULTIMATE PREY!

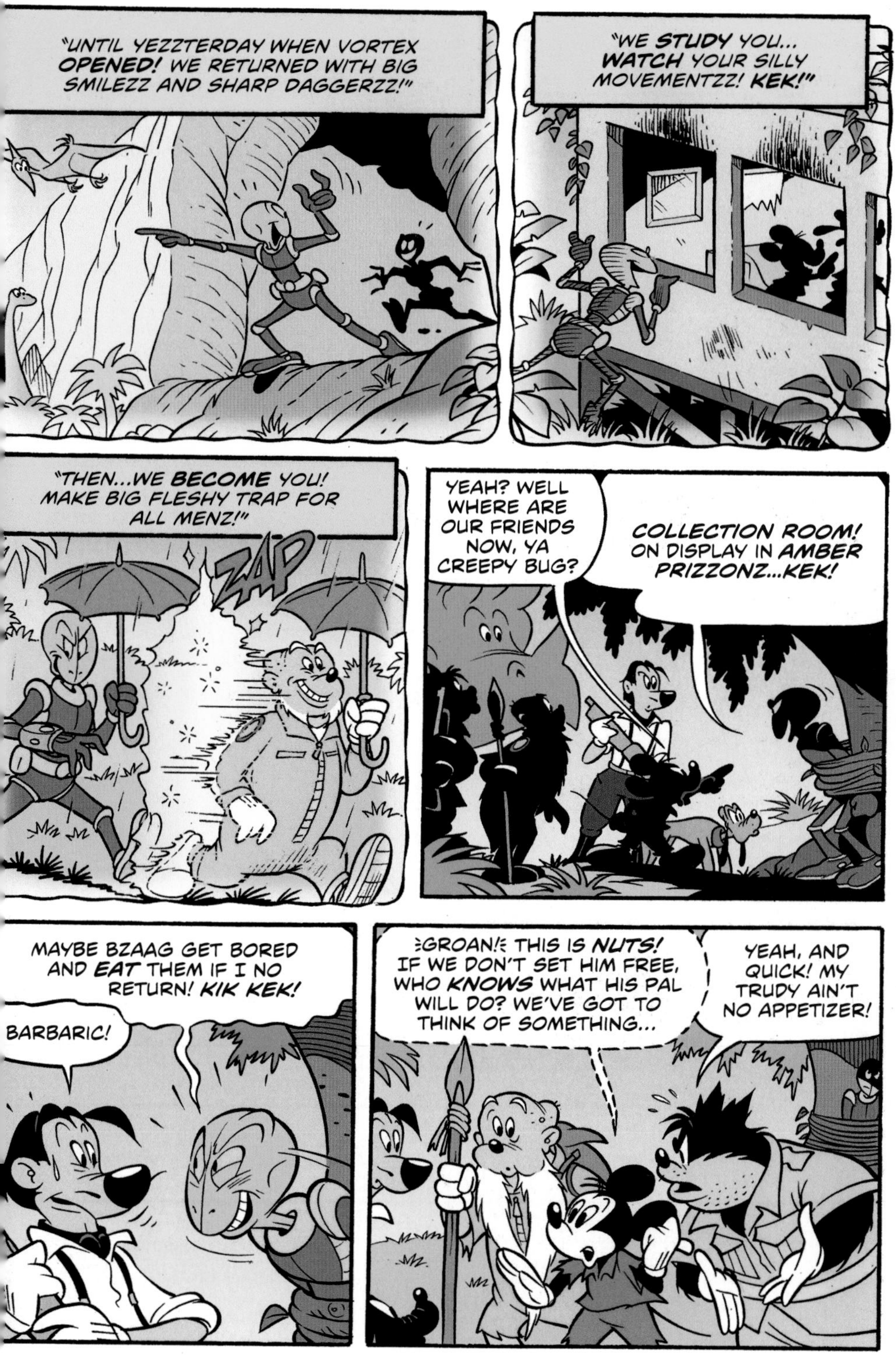
"UNTIL YEZZTERDAY WHEN VORTEX OPENED! WE RETURNED WITH BIG SMILEZZ AND SHARP DAGGERZZ!"
"WE STUDY YOU... WATCH YOUR SILLY MOVEMENTZZ! KEK!"
"THEN...WE BECOME YOU! MAKE BIG FLESHY TRAP FOR ALL MENZ!"
ZAP
YEAH? WELL WHERE ARE OUR FRIENDS NOW, YA CREEPY BUG?
COLLECTION ROOM! ON DISPLAY IN AMBER PRIZZONZ...KEK!
MAYBE BZAAG GET BORED AND EAT THEM IF I NO RETURN! KIK KEK!
BARBARIC!
GROAN! THIS IS NUTS! IF WE DON'T SET HIM FREE, WHO KNOWS WHAT HIS PAL WILL DO? WE'VE GOT TO THINK OF SOMETHING...
YEAH, AND QUICK! MY TRUDY AIN'T NO APPETIZER!

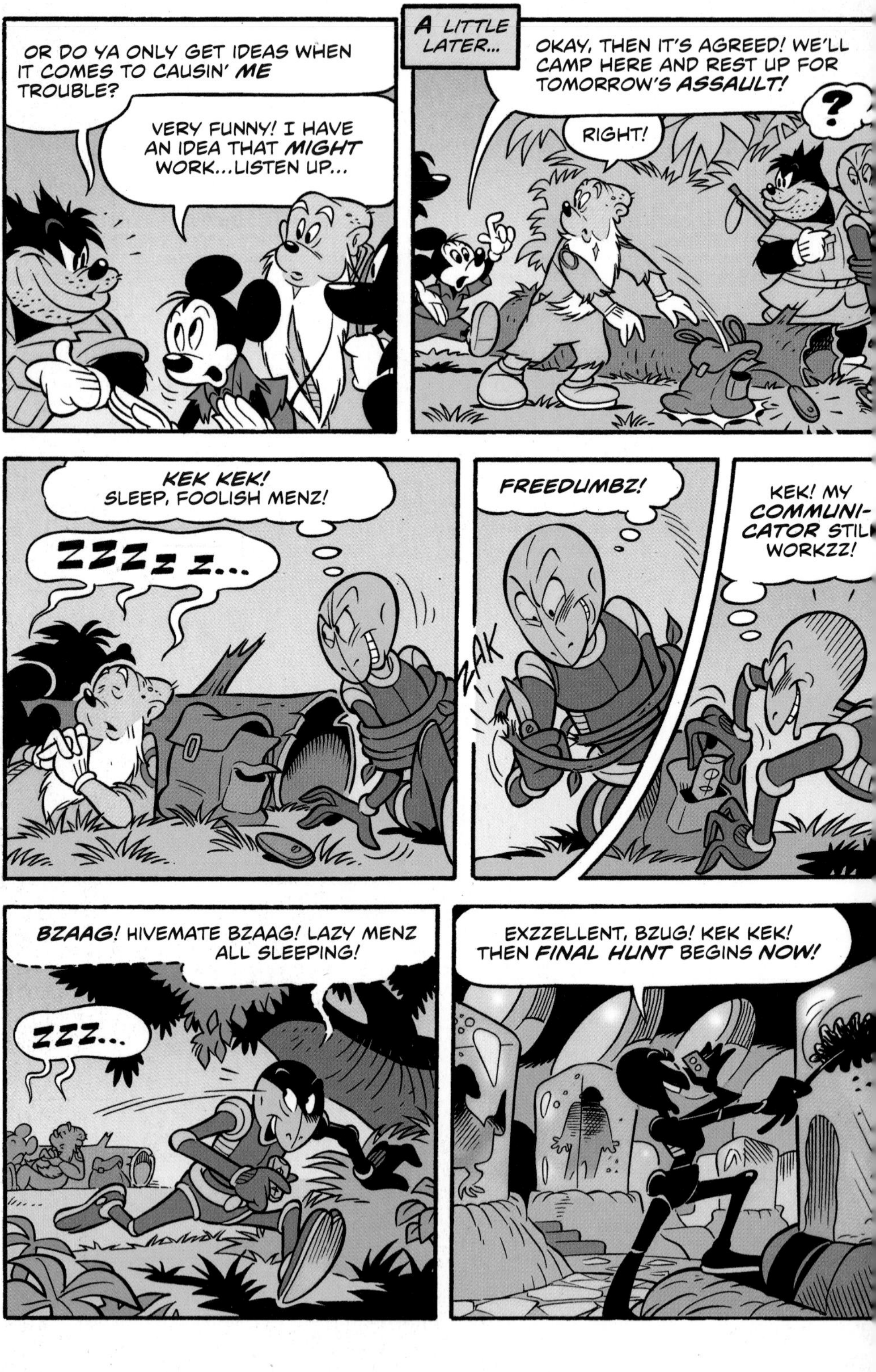
OR DO YA ONLY GET IDEAS WHEN IT COMES TO CAUSIN' *ME* TROUBLE?
VERY FUNNY! I HAVE AN IDEA THAT *MIGHT* WORK...LISTEN UP...
A LITTLE LATER...
OKAY, THEN IT'S AGREED! WE'LL CAMP HERE AND REST UP FOR TOMORROW'S *ASSAULT!*
RIGHT!
?
KEK KEK! SLEEP, FOOLISH MENZ!
ZZZz z...
FREEDUMBZ!
KEK! MY *COMMUNI-CATOR* STIL
WORKZZ!
BZAAG! HIVEMATE BZAAG! LAZY MENZ ALL SLEEPING!
ZZZ...
EXZZELLENT, BZUG! KEK KEK! THEN *FINAL HUNT* BEGINS *NOW!*

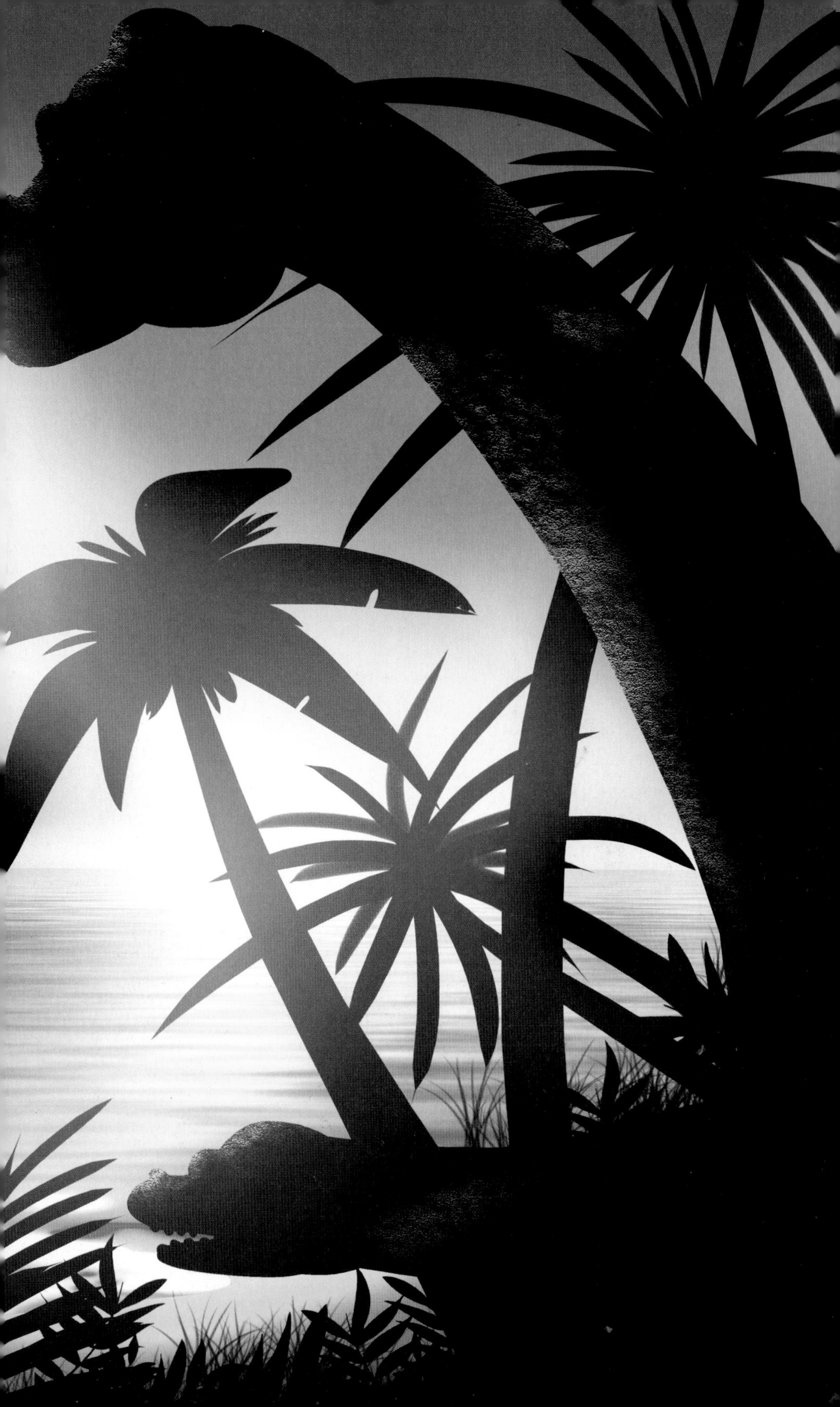

CHAPTER FOUR

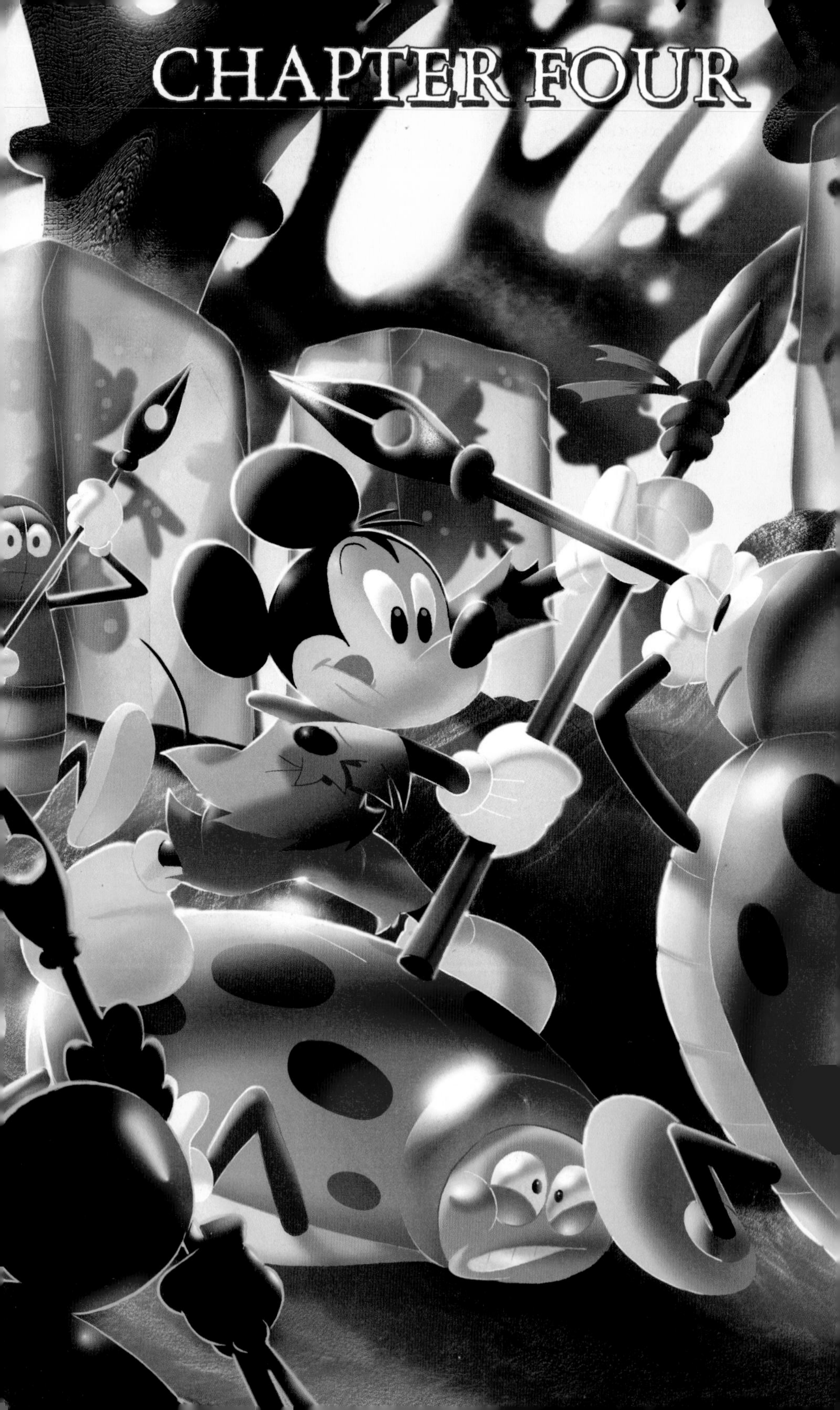

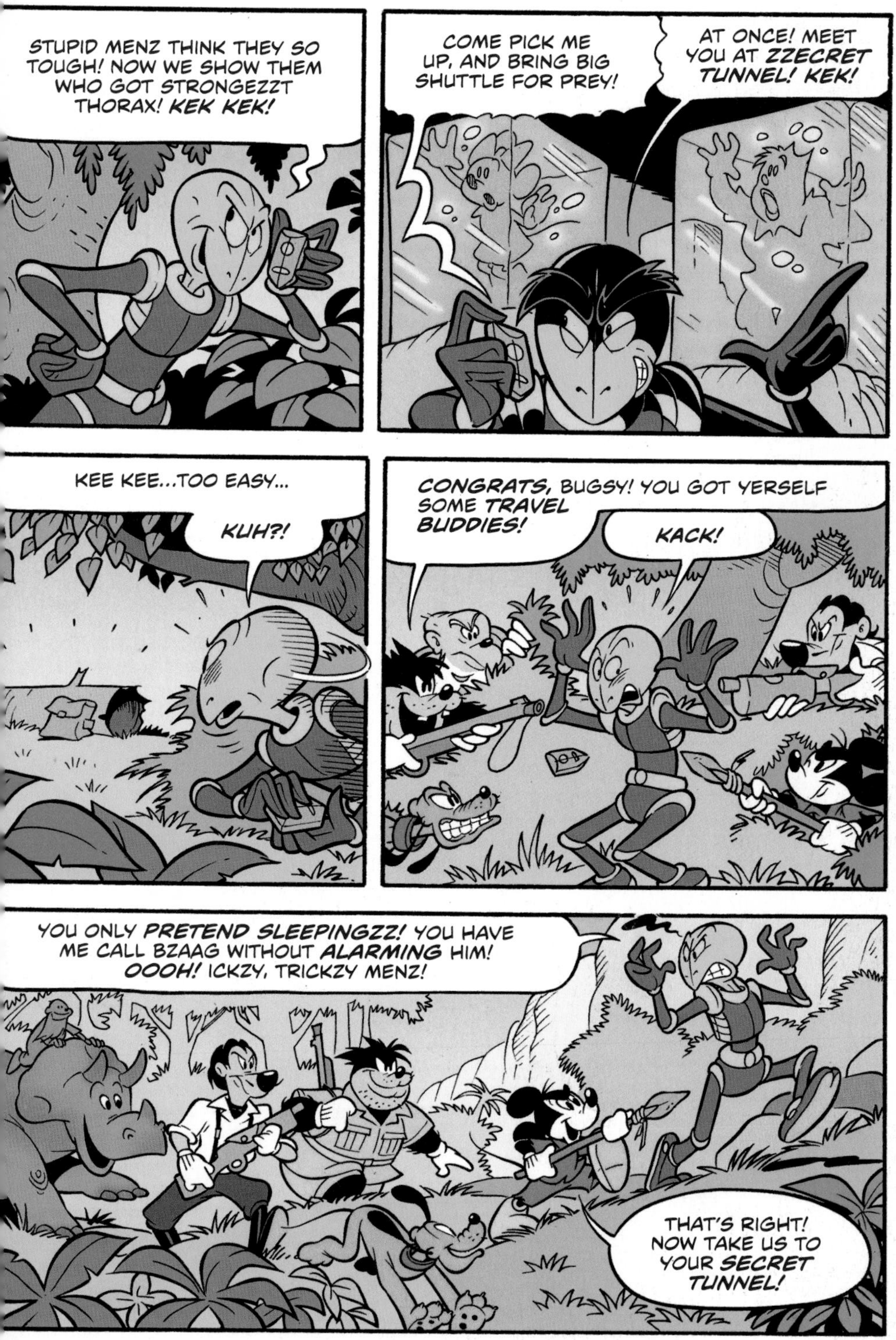
STUPID MENZ THINK THEY SO TOUGH! NOW WE SHOW THEM WHO GOT STRONGEZZT THORAX! KEK KEK!
COME PICK ME UP, AND BRING BIG SHUTTLE FOR PREY!
AT ONCE! MEET YOU AT ZZECRET TUNNEL! KEK!
KEE KEE...TOO EASY...
KUH?!
CONGRATS, BUGSY! YOU GOT YERSELF SOME TRAVEL BUDDIES!
KACK!
YOU ONLY PRETEND SLEEPINGZZ! YOU HAVE ME CALL BZAAG WITHOUT ALARMING HIM! OOOH! ICKZY, TRICKZY MENZ!
THAT'S RIGHT! NOW TAKE US TO YOUR SECRET TUNNEL!

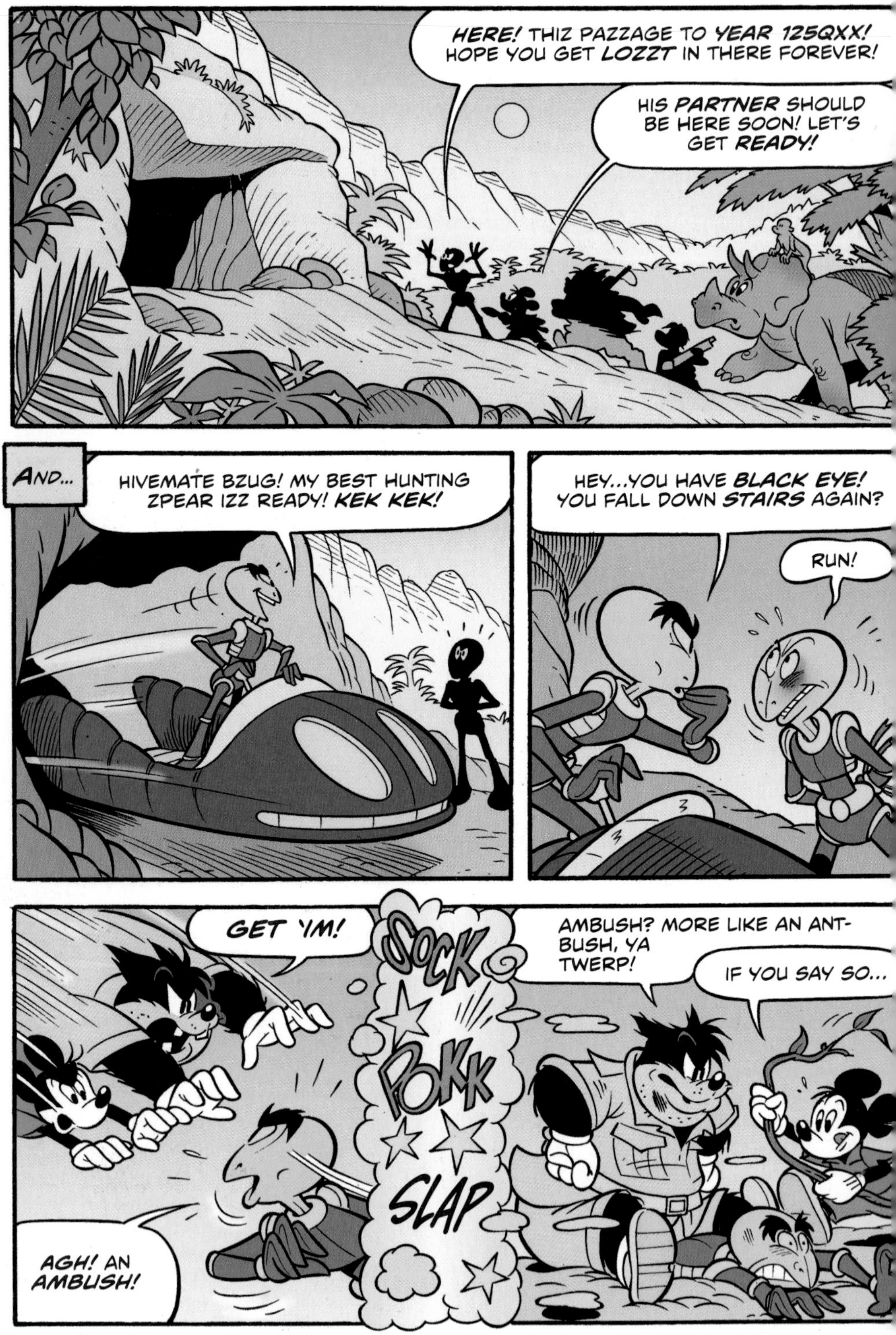
HERE! THIZ PAZZAGE TO YEAR 125QXX! HOPE YOU GET LOZZT IN THERE FOREVER!
HIS PARTNER SHOULD BE HERE SOON! LET'S GET READY!
AND...
HIVEMATE BZUG! MY BEST HUNTING ZPEAR IZZ READY! KEK KEK!
HEY...YOU HAVE BLACK EYE! YOU FALL DOWN STAIRS AGAIN?
RUN!
GET 'IM!
SOCK
POKK
SLAP
AMBUSH? MORE LIKE AN ANT-BUSH, YA TWERP!
IF YOU SAY SO...
AGH! AN AMBUSH!

GET ON, DUKEY! THAT *LIGHT GUN* OF YOURS MIGHT FINALLY DO SOME *GOOD!*

NOW JUST A *MINUTE--*

WHAT ABOUT *ME,* RAT?

SORRY, PETE, THERE'S NOT ENOUGH SPACE ON THE HOVERCAR! I MAY NOT BE ABLE TO COME BACK FOR THE REST OF YOU!

BUT...BUT I GOTTA SAVE *TRUDY...*

WE MAY NOT EXACTLY BE *FRIENDS,* PETE -- BUT I'LL BRING *EVERYONE* BACK SAFE AN' SOUND! *PROMISE!*

WOOF!

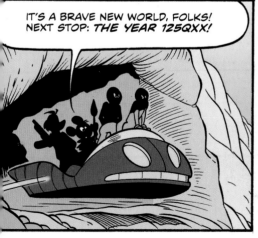

IT'S A BRAVE NEW WORLD, FOLKS! NEXT STOP: *THE YEAR 125QXX!*

ZOUNDS AND GADZOOKS! IT'S...

NO...

VZZZZ

VZZZZzz

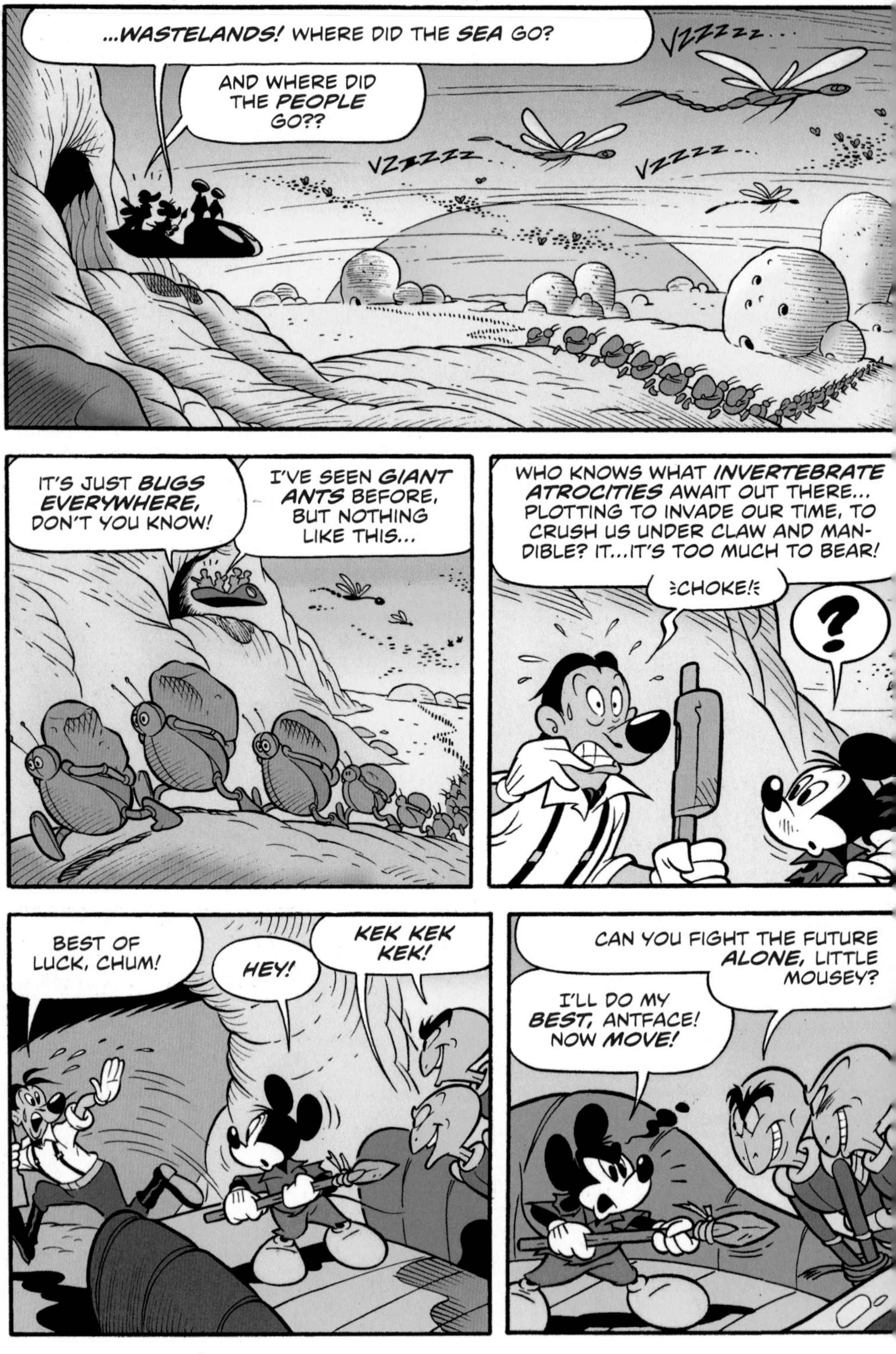
...WASTELANDS! WHERE DID THE SEA GO?
AND WHERE DID THE PEOPLE GO??
VZZZZZ...
VZZZZZ
VZZZZZ...
IT'S JUST BUGS EVERYWHERE, DON'T YOU KNOW!
I'VE SEEN GIANT ANTS BEFORE, BUT NOTHING LIKE THIS...
WHO KNOWS WHAT INVERTEBRATE ATROCITIES AWAIT OUT THERE... PLOTTING TO INVADE OUR TIME, TO CRUSH US UNDER CLAW AND MAN-DIBLE? IT...IT'S TOO MUCH TO BEAR!
CHOKE!
?
BEST OF LUCK, CHUM!
HEY!
KEK KEK KEK!
CAN YOU FIGHT THE FUTURE ALONE, LITTLE MOUSEY?
I'LL DO MY BEST, ANTFACE! NOW MOVE!

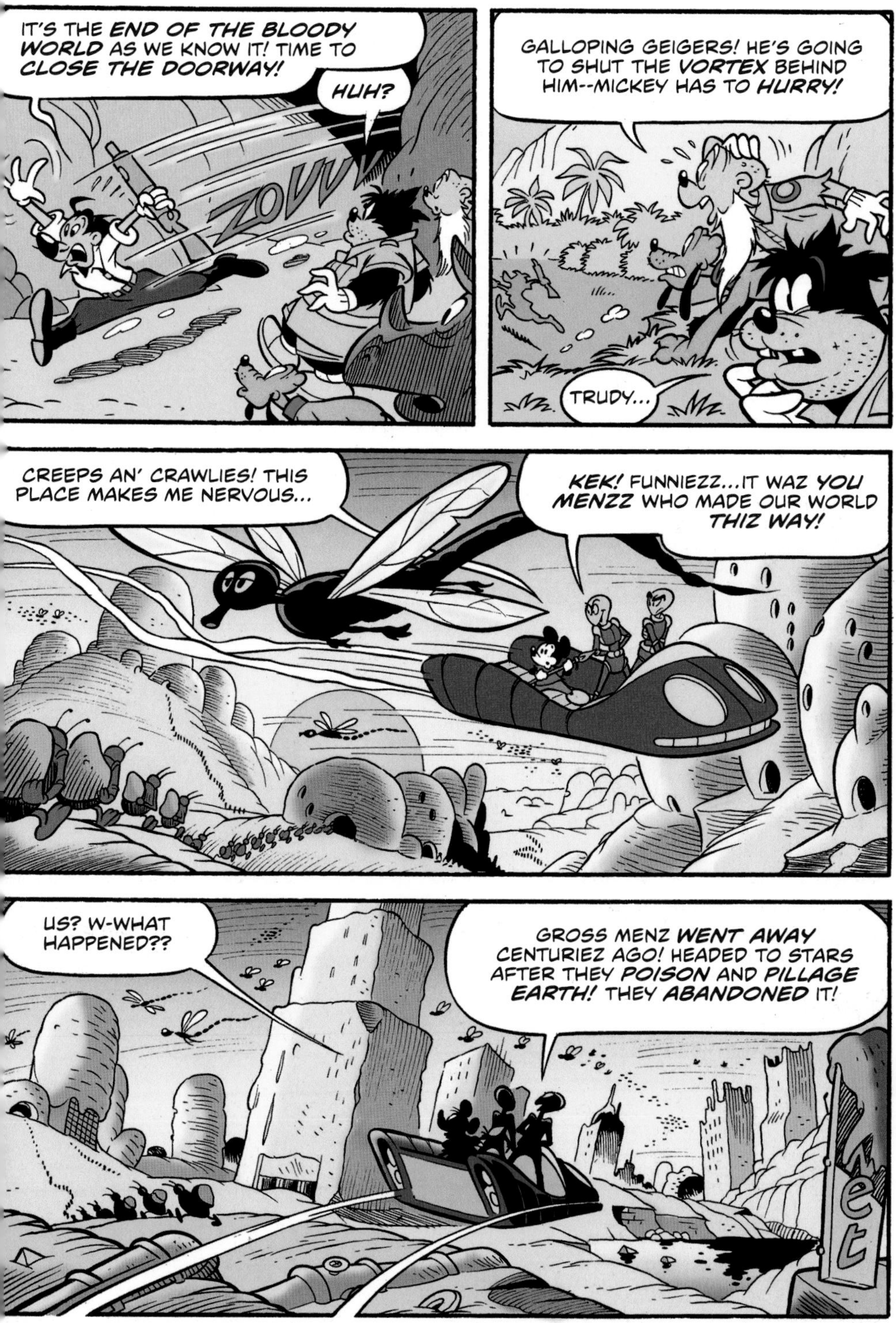
IT'S THE END OF THE BLOODY WORLD AS WE KNOW IT! TIME TO CLOSE THE DOORWAY!
HUH?
ZOVVV
GALLOPING GEIGERS! HE'S GOING TO SHUT THE VORTEX BEHIND HIM--MICKEY HAS TO HURRY!
TRUDY...
CREEPS AN' CRAWLIES! THIS PLACE MAKES ME NERVOUS...
KEK! FUNNIEZZ...IT WAZ YOU MENZZ WHO MADE OUR WORLD THIZ WAY!
US? W-WHAT HAPPENED??
GROSS MENZ WENT AWAY CENTURIEZ AGO! HEADED TO STARS AFTER THEY POISON AND PILLAGE EARTH! THEY ABANDONED IT!

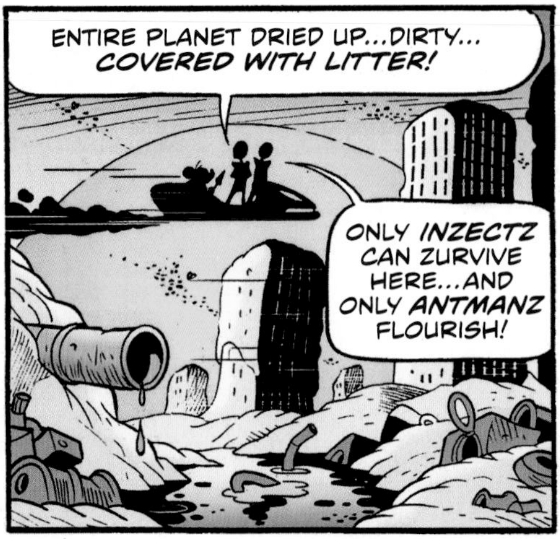
ENTIRE PLANET DRIED UP...DIRTY... COVERED WITH LITTER!
ONLY INZECTZ CAN ZURVIVE HERE...AND ONLY ANTMANZ FLOURISH!

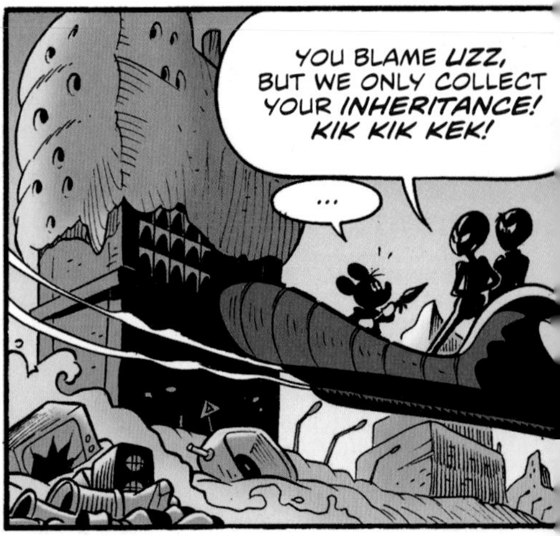
YOU BLAME UZZ, BUT WE ONLY COLLECT YOUR INHERITANCE! KIK KIK KEK!
...

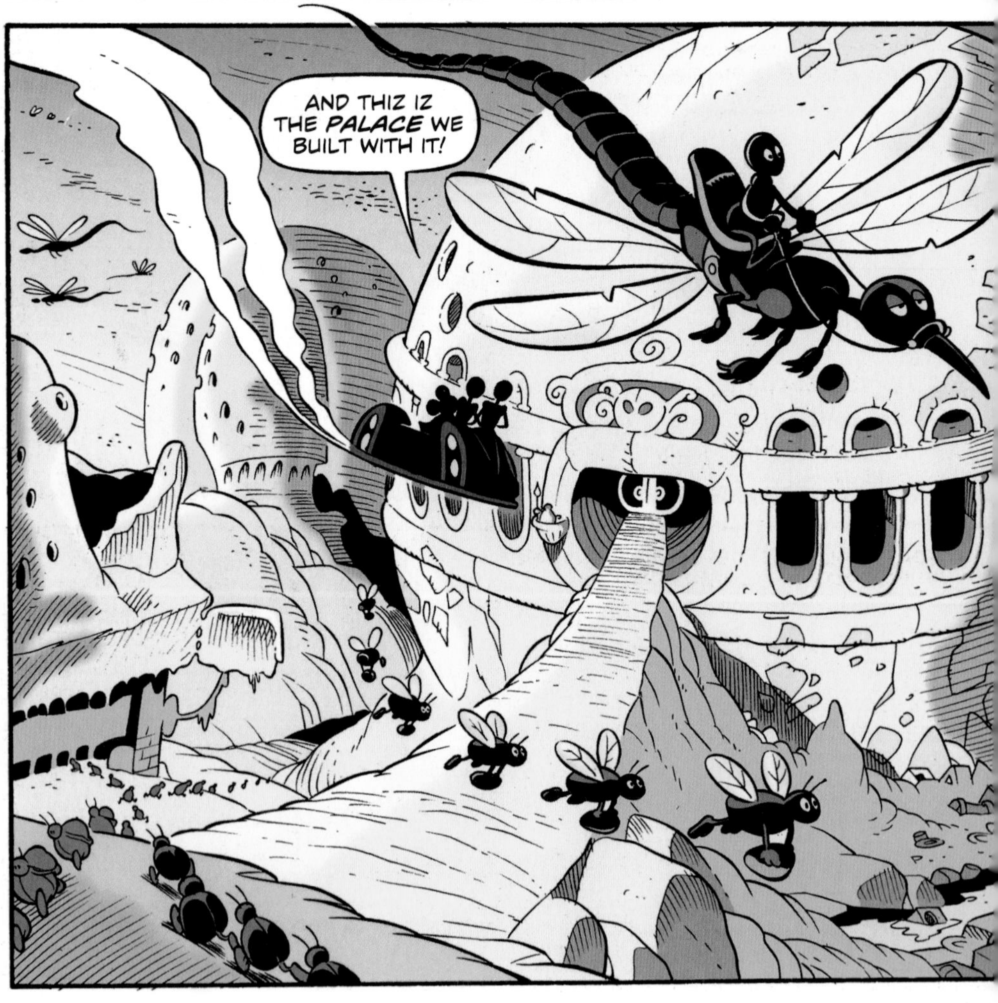
AND THIZ IZ THE PALACE WE BUILT WITH IT!

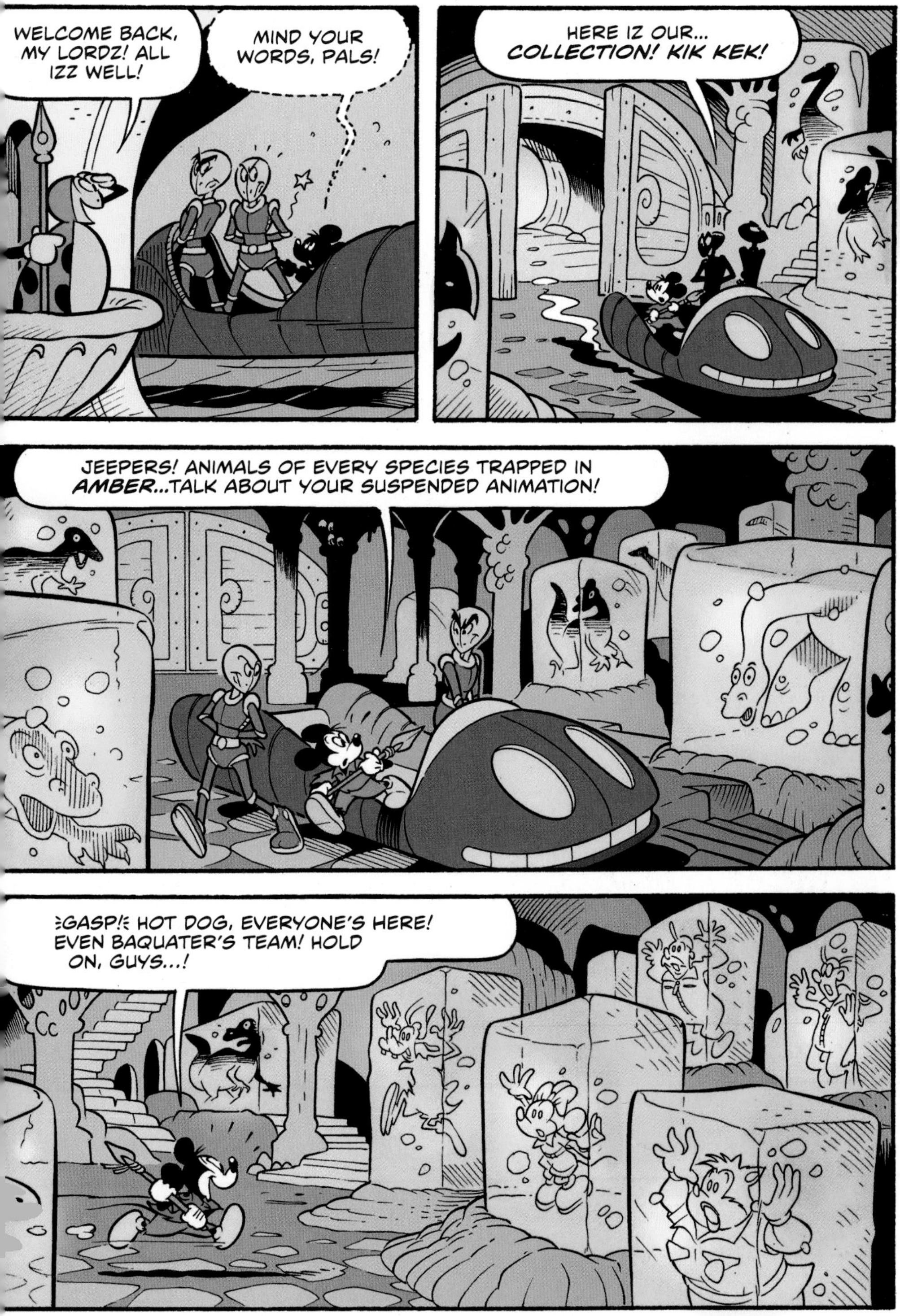
WELCOME BACK, MY LORDZ! ALL IZZ WELL!
MIND YOUR WORDS, PALS!
HERE IZ OUR... COLLECTION! KIK KEK!
JEEPERS! ANIMALS OF EVERY SPECIES TRAPPED IN AMBER...TALK ABOUT YOUR SUSPENDED ANIMATION!
GASP! HOT DOG, EVERYONE'S HERE! EVEN BAQUATER'S TEAM! HOLD ON, GUYS...!

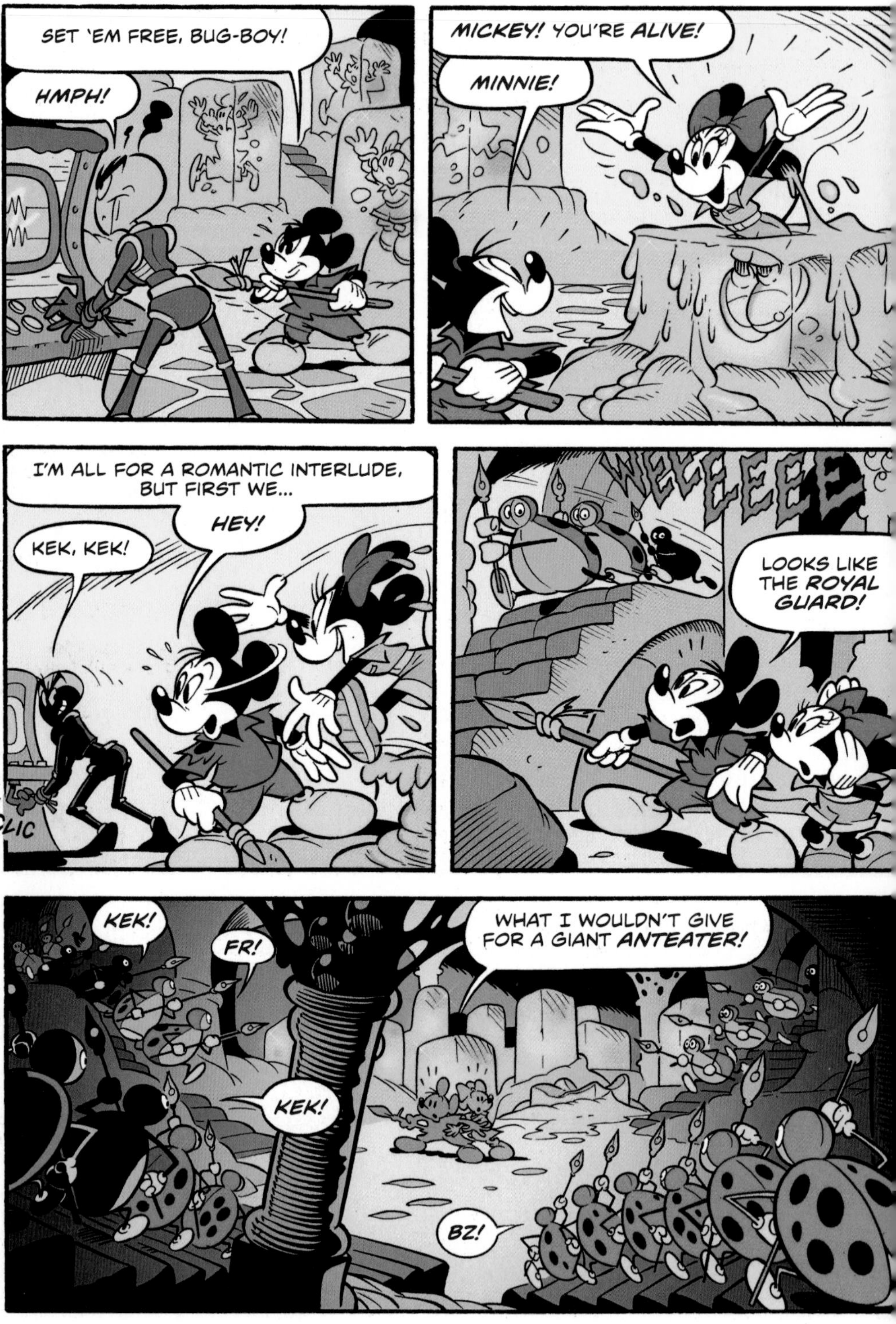
SET 'EM FREE, BUG-BOY!
HMPH!
MICKEY! YOU'RE ALIVE!
MINNIE!
I'M ALL FOR A ROMANTIC INTERLUDE, BUT FIRST WE...
HEY!
KEK, KEK!
CLIC
WEEEEE
LOOKS LIKE THE ROYAL GUARD!
KEK!
FR!
WHAT I WOULDN'T GIVE FOR A GIANT ANTEATER!
KEK!
BZ!

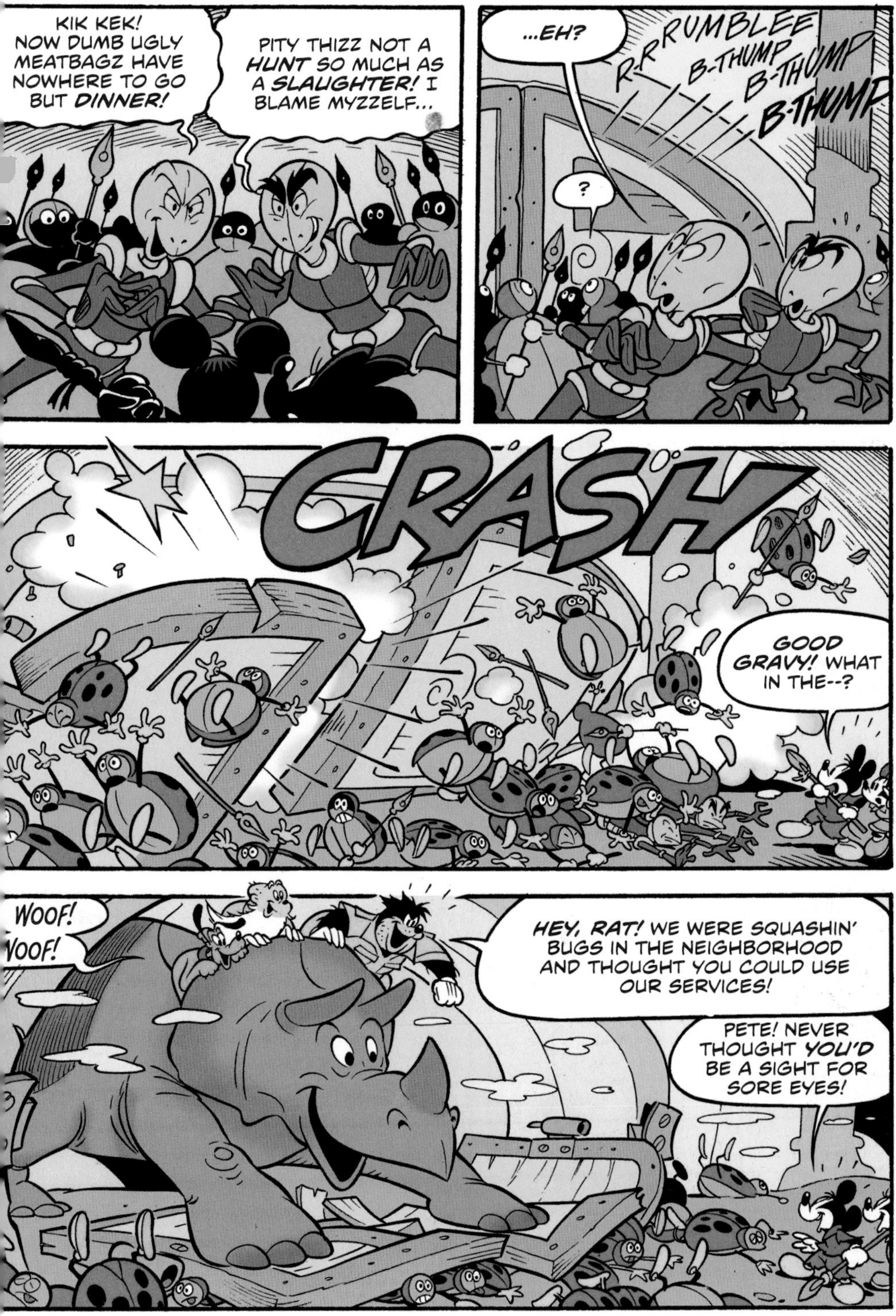
KIK KEK! NOW DUMB UGLY MEATBAGZ HAVE NOWHERE TO GO BUT DINNER!
PITY THIZZ NOT A HUNT SO MUCH AS A SLAUGHTER! I BLAME MYZZELF...
...EH?
R-R-RUMBLEE
B-THUMP
B-THUMP
B-THUMP
?
CRASH
GOOD GRAVY! WHAT IN THE--?
WOOF! WOOF!
HEY, RAT! WE WERE SQUASHIN' BUGS IN THE NEIGHBORHOOD AND THOUGHT YOU COULD USE OUR SERVICES!
PETE! NEVER THOUGHT YOU'D BE A SIGHT FOR SORE EYES!

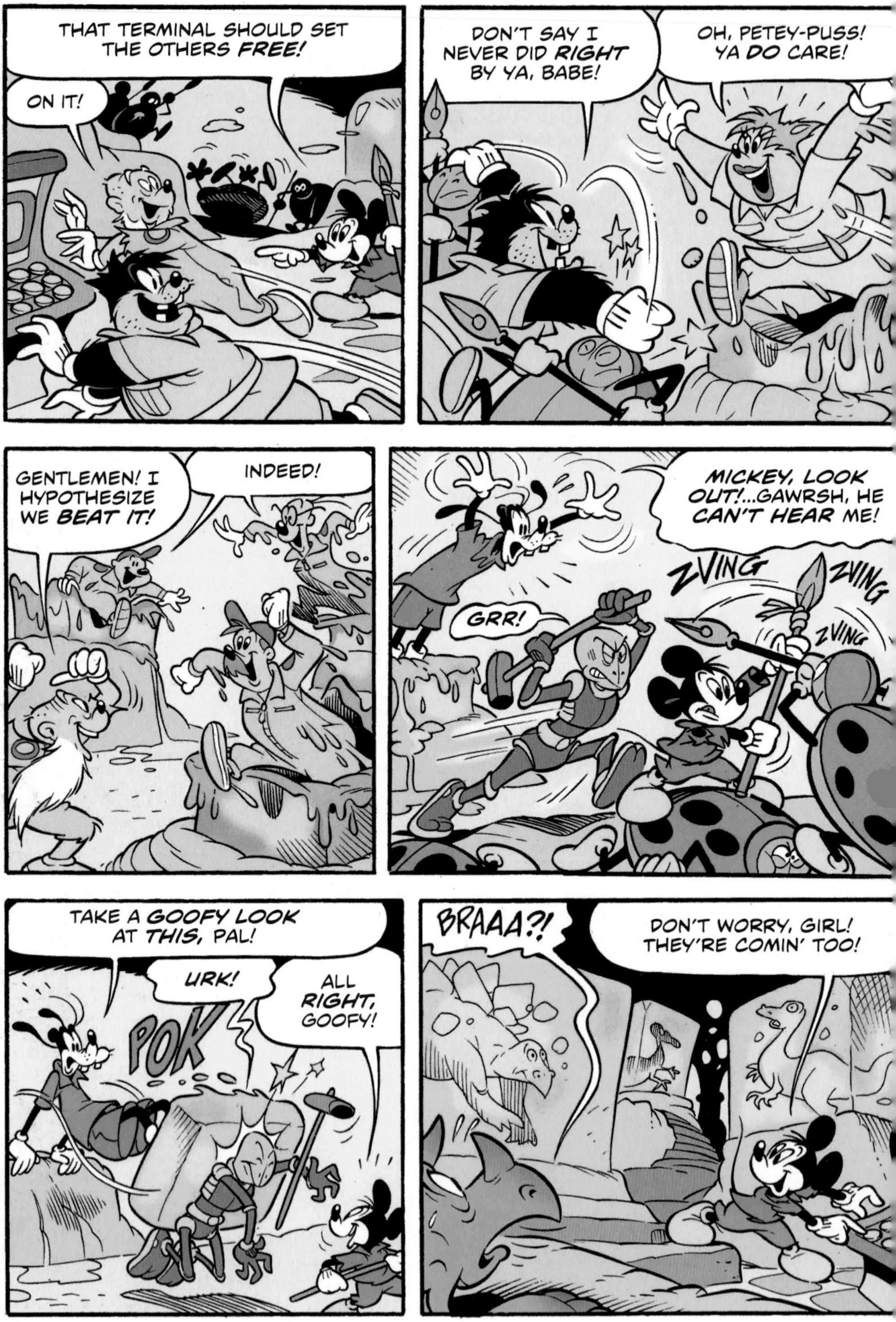
THAT TERMINAL SHOULD SET THE OTHERS FREE!
ON IT!
DON'T SAY I NEVER DID RIGHT BY YA, BABE!
OH, PETEY-PUSS! YA DO CARE!
GENTLEMEN! I HYPOTHESIZE WE BEAT IT!
INDEED!
MICKEY, LOOK OUT!...GAWRSH, HE CAN'T HEAR ME!
ZVING
ZVING
GRR!
ZVING
TAKE A GOOFY LOOK AT THIS, PAL!
URK!
ALL RIGHT, GOOFY!
POK
BRAAA?!
DON'T WORRY, GIRL! THEY'RE COMIN' TOO!

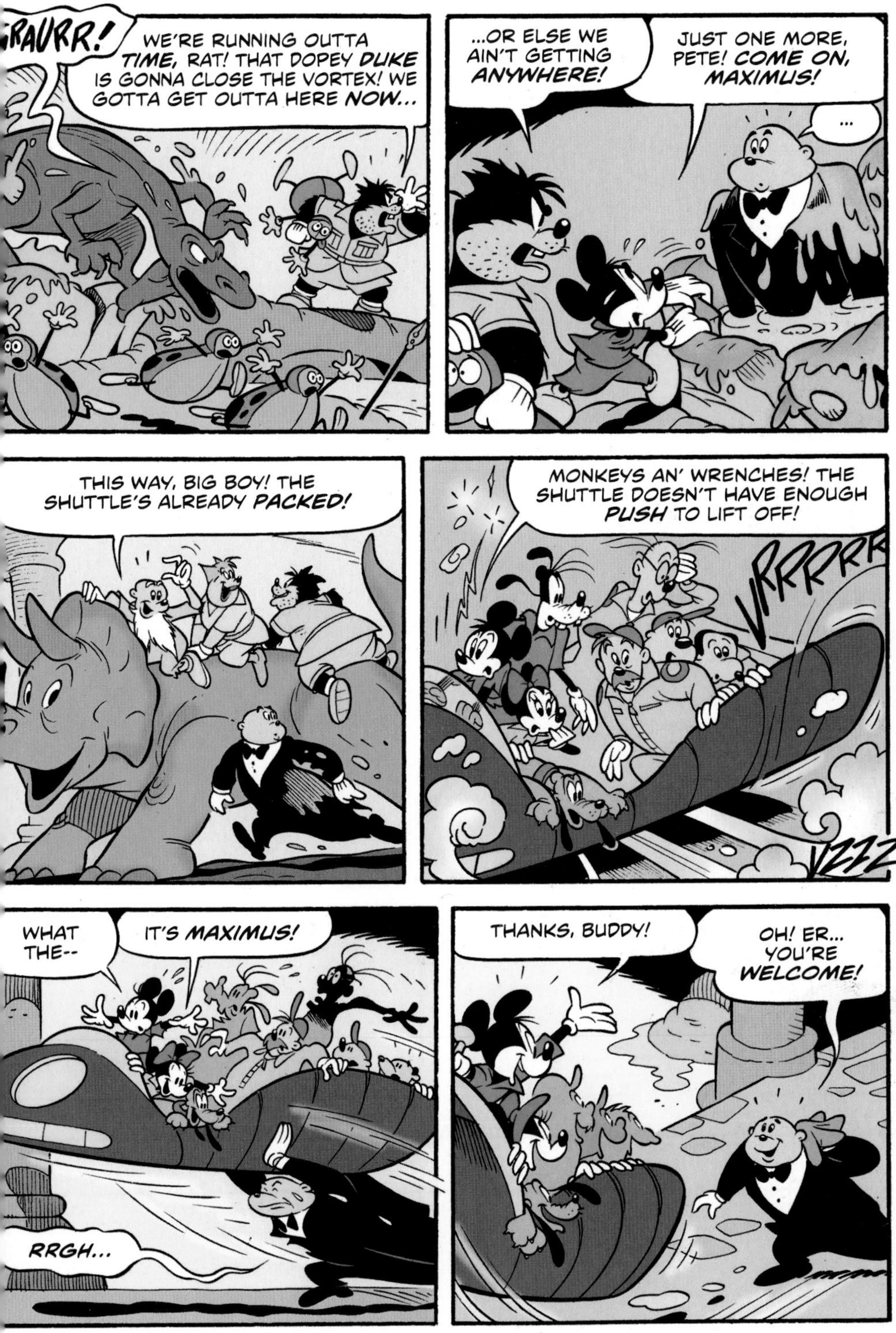
GRAURR!
WE'RE RUNNING OUTTA TIME, RAT! THAT DOPEY DUKE IS GONNA CLOSE THE VORTEX! WE GOTTA GET OUTTA HERE NOW...
...OR ELSE WE AIN'T GETTING ANYWHERE!
JUST ONE MORE, PETE! COME ON, MAXIMUS!
...
THIS WAY, BIG BOY! THE SHUTTLE'S ALREADY PACKED!
MONKEYS AN' WRENCHES! THE SHUTTLE DOESN'T HAVE ENOUGH PUSH TO LIFT OFF!
VRRRRR
VZZZ
WHAT THE--
IT'S MAXIMUS!
RRGH...
THANKS, BUDDY!
OH! ER... YOU'RE WELCOME!

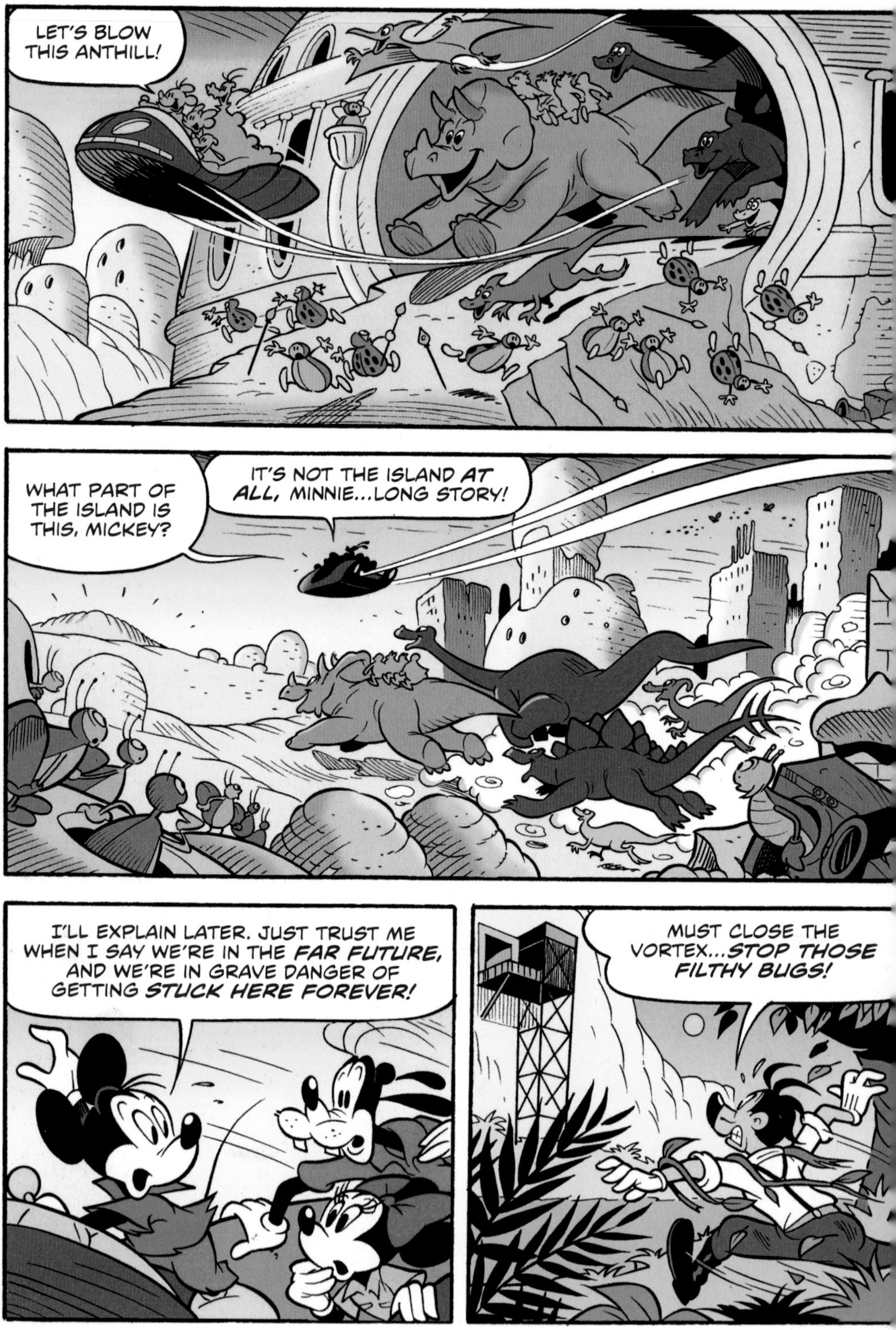
LET'S BLOW THIS ANTHILL!
WHAT PART OF THE ISLAND IS THIS, MICKEY?
IT'S NOT THE ISLAND AT ALL, MINNIE...LONG STORY!
I'LL EXPLAIN LATER. JUST TRUST ME WHEN I SAY WE'RE IN THE FAR FUTURE, AND WE'RE IN GRAVE DANGER OF GETTING STUCK HERE FOREVER!
MUST CLOSE THE VORTEX...STOP THOSE FILTHY BUGS!

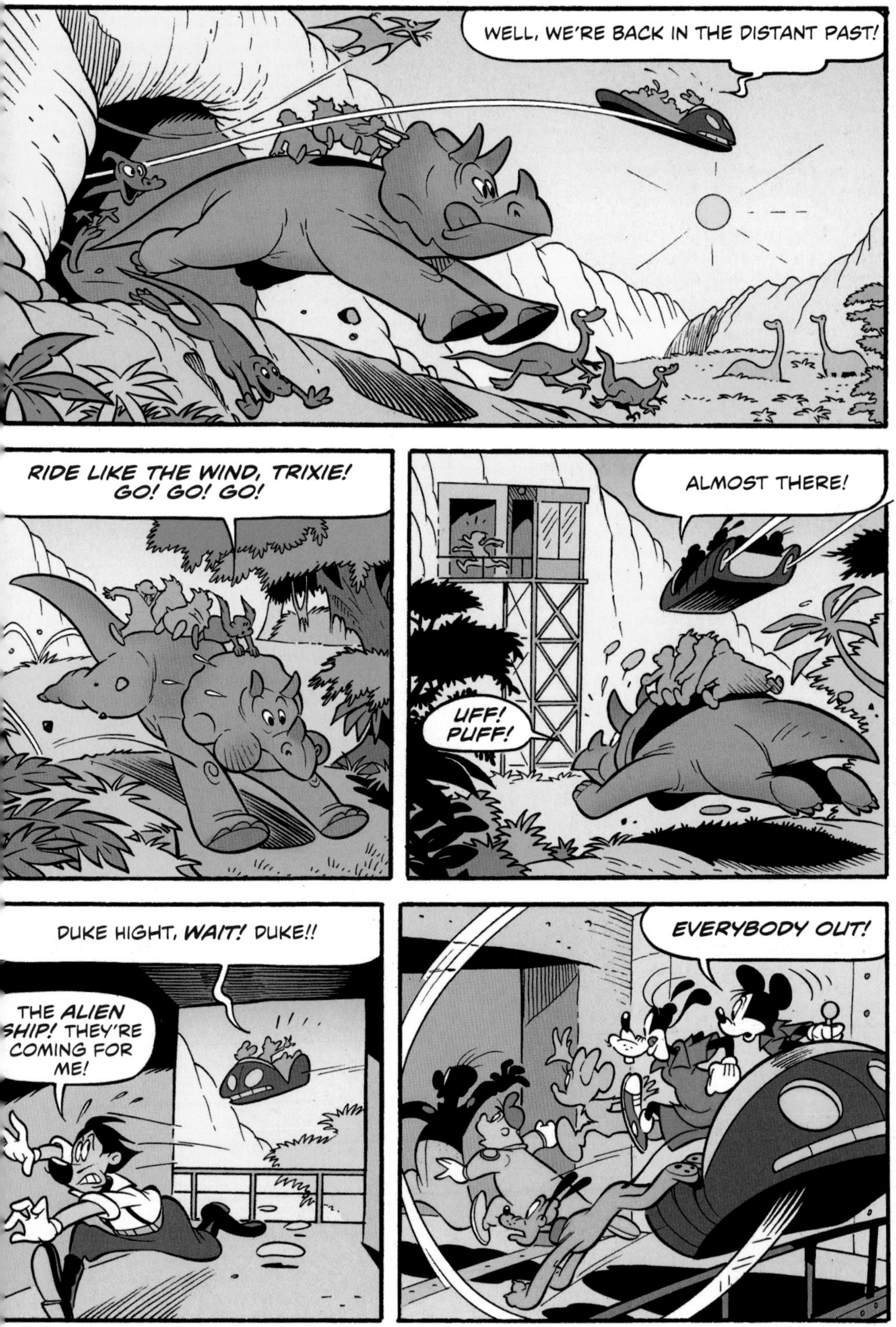
WELL, WE'RE BACK IN THE DISTANT PAST!
RIDE LIKE THE WIND, TRIXIE! GO! GO! GO!
ALMOST THERE!
UFF! PUFF!
DUKE HIGHT, WAIT! DUKE!!
THE ALIEN SHIP! THEY'RE COMING FOR ME!
EVERYBODY OUT!

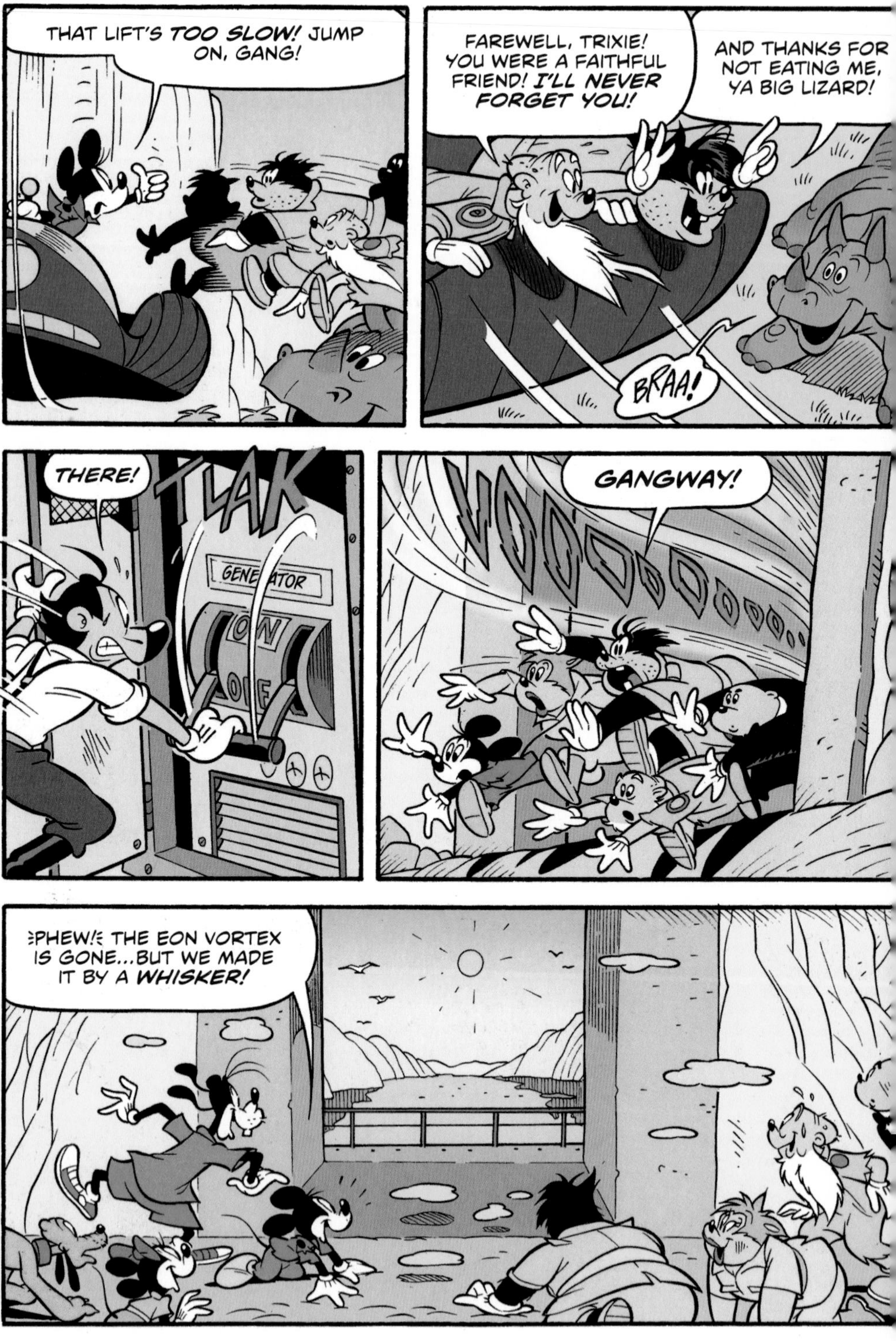

THAT LIFT'S *TOO SLOW!* JUMP ON, GANG!
FAREWELL, TRIXIE! YOU WERE A FAITHFUL FRIEND! *I'LL NEVER FORGET YOU!*
AND THANKS FOR NOT EATING ME, YA BIG LIZARD!
BRAA!
THERE!
TLAK
GENERATOR
ON
OFF
GANGWAY!
VOOOOOOOOOOOV
PHEW! THE EON VORTEX IS GONE...BUT WE MADE IT BY A *WHISKER!*

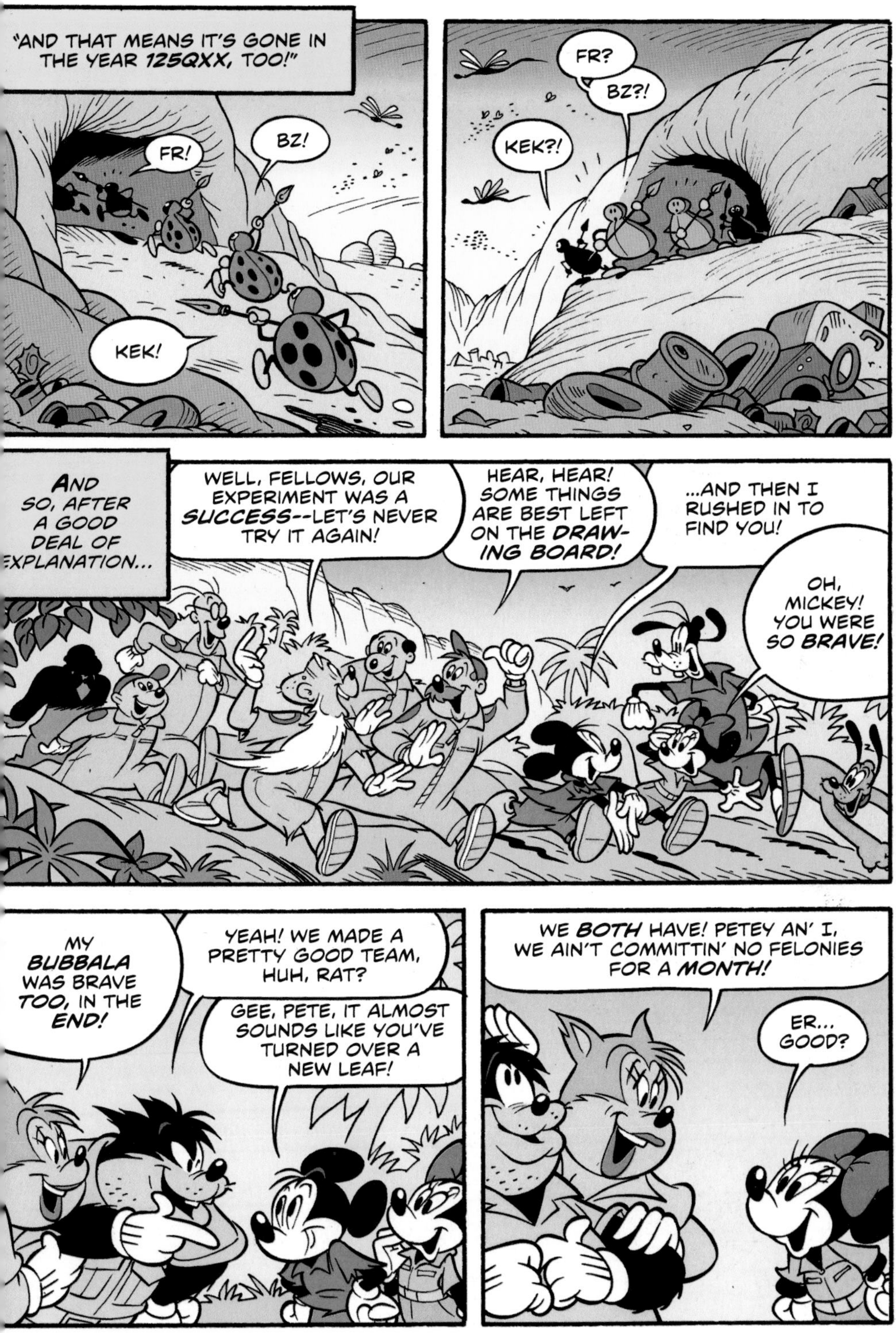

"AND THAT MEANS IT'S GONE IN THE YEAR 125QXX, TOO!"
FR!
BZ!
KEK!
FR?
BZ?!
KEK?!
AND SO, AFTER A GOOD DEAL OF EXPLANATION...
WELL, FELLOWS, OUR EXPERIMENT WAS A SUCCESS--LET'S NEVER TRY IT AGAIN!
HEAR, HEAR! SOME THINGS ARE BEST LEFT ON THE DRAWING BOARD!
...AND THEN I RUSHED IN TO FIND YOU!
OH, MICKEY! YOU WERE SO BRAVE!
MY BUBBALA WAS BRAVE TOO, IN THE END!
YEAH! WE MADE A PRETTY GOOD TEAM, HUH, RAT?
GEE, PETE, IT ALMOST SOUNDS LIKE YOU'VE TURNED OVER A NEW LEAF!
WE BOTH HAVE! PETEY AN' I, WE AIN'T COMMITTIN' NO FELONIES FOR A MONTH!
ER... GOOD?

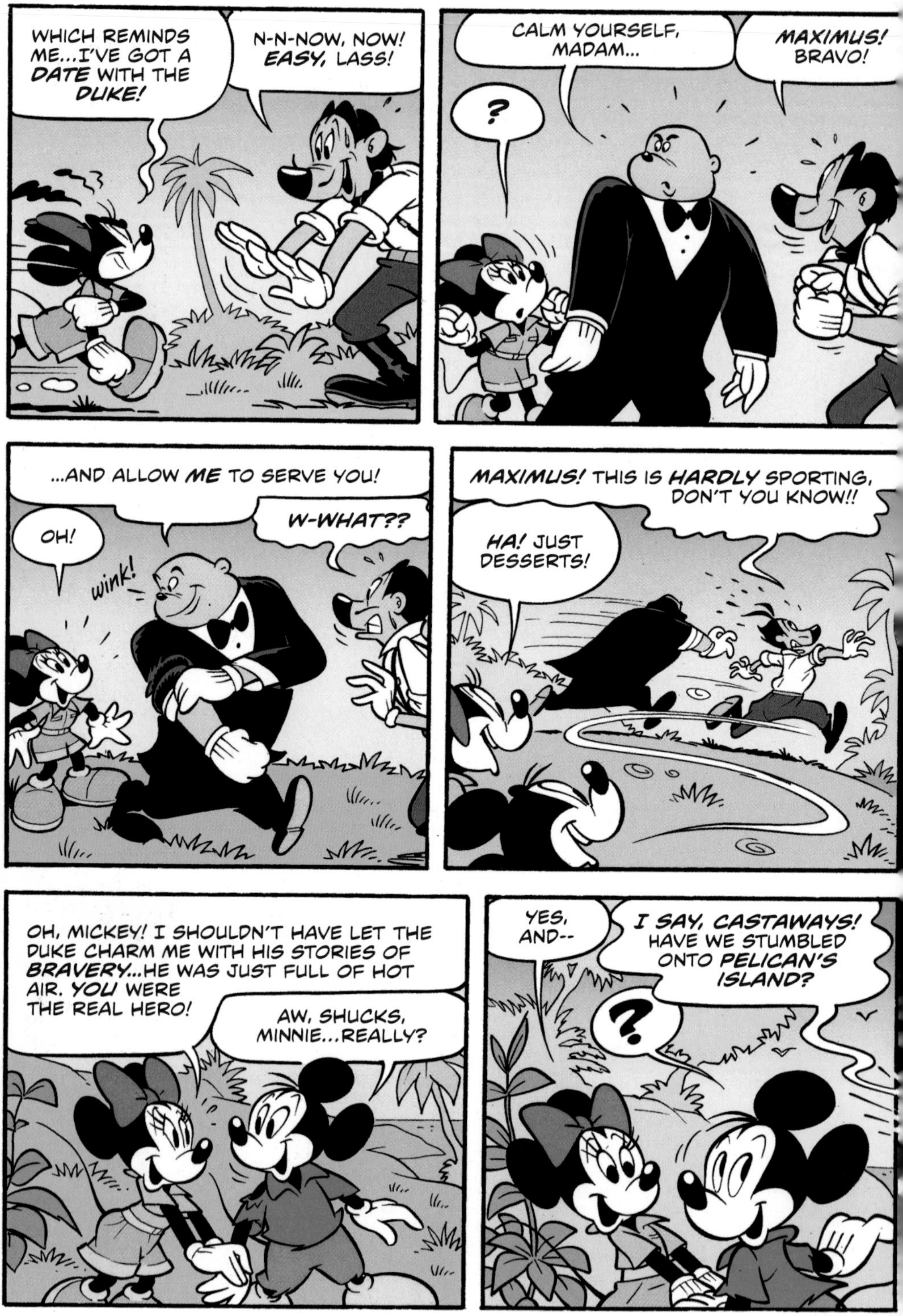
WHICH REMINDS ME...I'VE GOT A *DATE* WITH THE *DUKE!*
N-N-NOW, NOW! *EASY,* LASS!
CALM YOURSELF, MADAM...
MAXIMUS! BRAVO!
?
...AND ALLOW *ME* TO SERVE YOU!
OH!
W-WHAT??
wink!
MAXIMUS! THIS IS *HARDLY* SPORTING, DON'T YOU KNOW!!
HA! JUST DESSERTS!
OH, MICKEY! I SHOULDN'T HAVE LET THE DUKE CHARM ME WITH HIS STORIES OF *BRAVERY*...HE WAS JUST FULL OF HOT AIR. *YOU* WERE THE REAL HERO!
AW, SHUCKS, MINNIE...REALLY?
YES, AND--
I SAY, CASTAWAYS! HAVE WE STUMBLED ONTO *PELICAN'S ISLAND?*
?

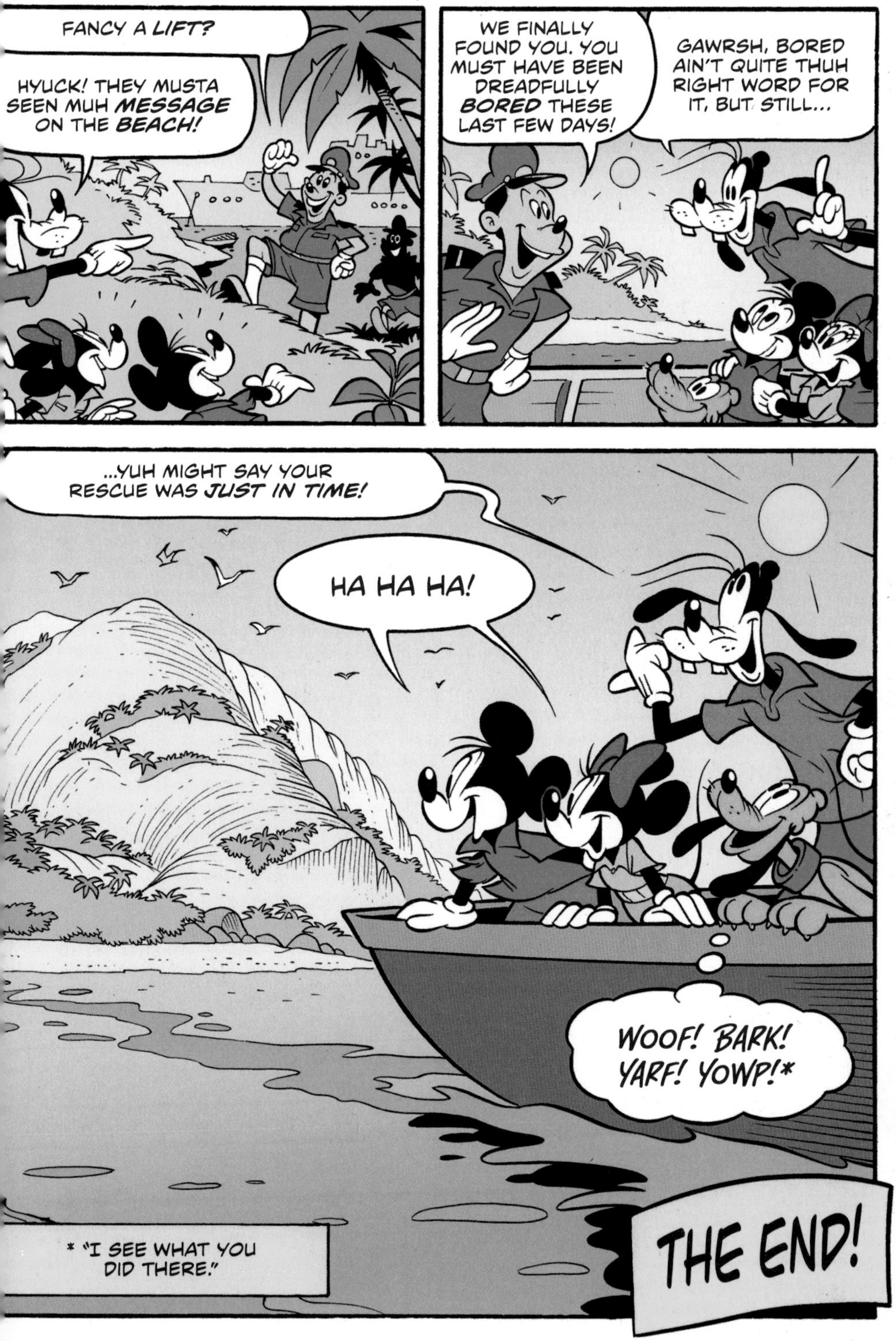
FANCY A LIFT?
HYUCK! THEY MUSTA SEEN MUH MESSAGE ON THE BEACH!
WE FINALLY FOUND YOU. YOU MUST HAVE BEEN DREADFULLY BORED THESE LAST FEW DAYS!
GAWRSH, BORED AIN'T QUITE THUH RIGHT WORD FOR IT, BUT STILL...
...YUH MIGHT SAY YOUR RESCUE WAS JUST IN TIME!
HA HA HA!
WOOF! BARK! YARF! YOWP!*
* "I SEE WHAT YOU DID THERE."
THE END!

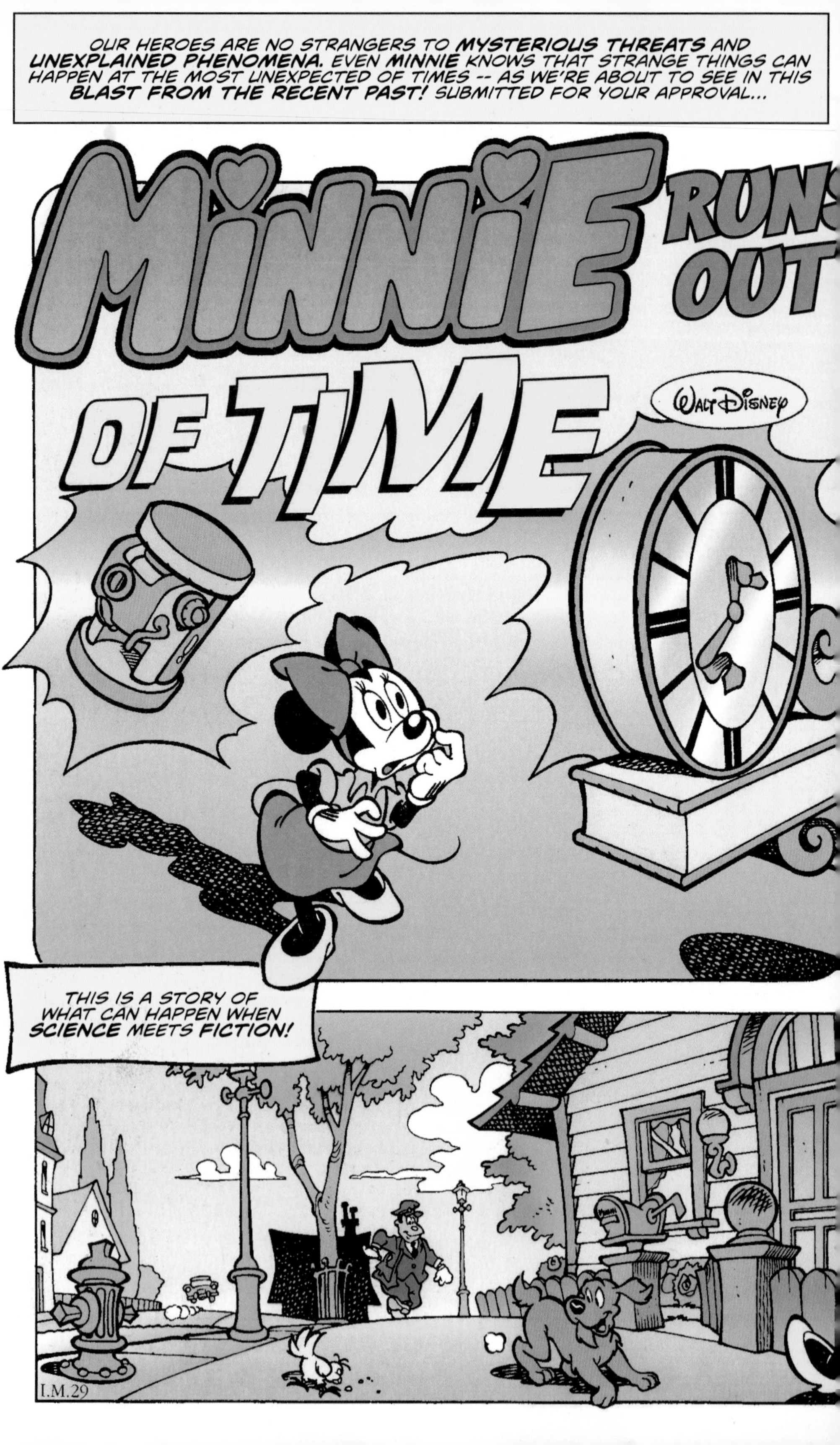
OUR HEROES ARE NO STRANGERS TO **MYSTERIOUS THREATS** AND **UNEXPLAINED PHENOMENA.** EVEN **MINNIE** KNOWS THAT STRANGE THINGS CAN HAPPEN AT THE MOST UNEXPECTED OF TIMES -- AS WE'RE ABOUT TO SEE IN THIS **BLAST FROM THE RECENT PAST!** SUBMITTED FOR YOUR APPROVAL...
MINNIE RUNS OUT OF TIME
WALT DISNEY
THIS IS A STORY OF WHAT CAN HAPPEN WHEN **SCIENCE** MEETS **FICTION!**
I.M.29

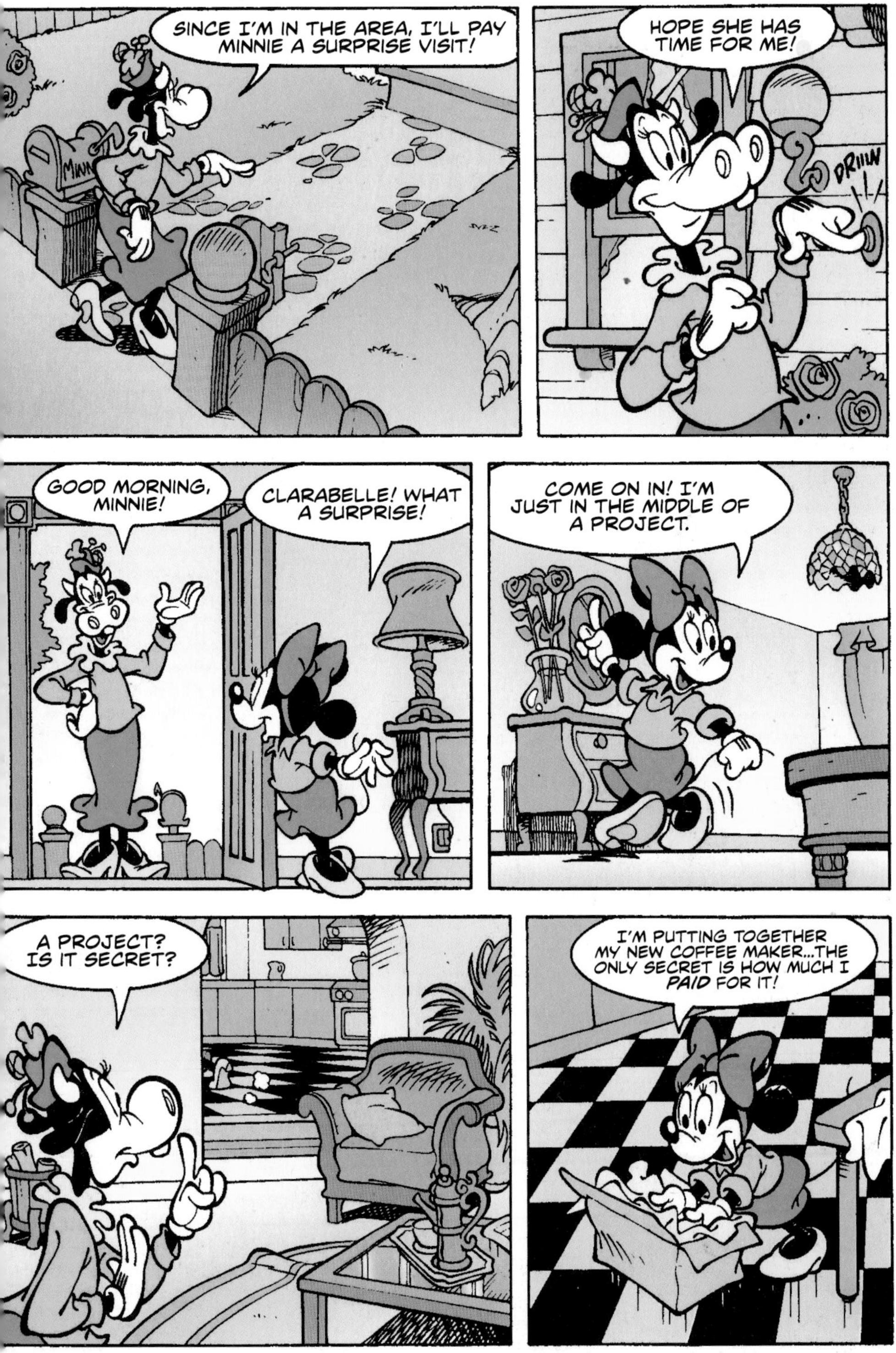

SINCE I'M IN THE AREA, I'LL PAY MINNIE A SURPRISE VISIT!
MINN
HOPE SHE HAS TIME FOR ME!
DRIIIN
GOOD MORNING, MINNIE!
CLARABELLE! WHAT A SURPRISE!
COME ON IN! I'M JUST IN THE MIDDLE OF A PROJECT.
A PROJECT? IS IT SECRET?
I'M PUTTING TOGETHER MY NEW COFFEE MAKER...THE ONLY SECRET IS HOW MUCH I *PAID* FOR IT!

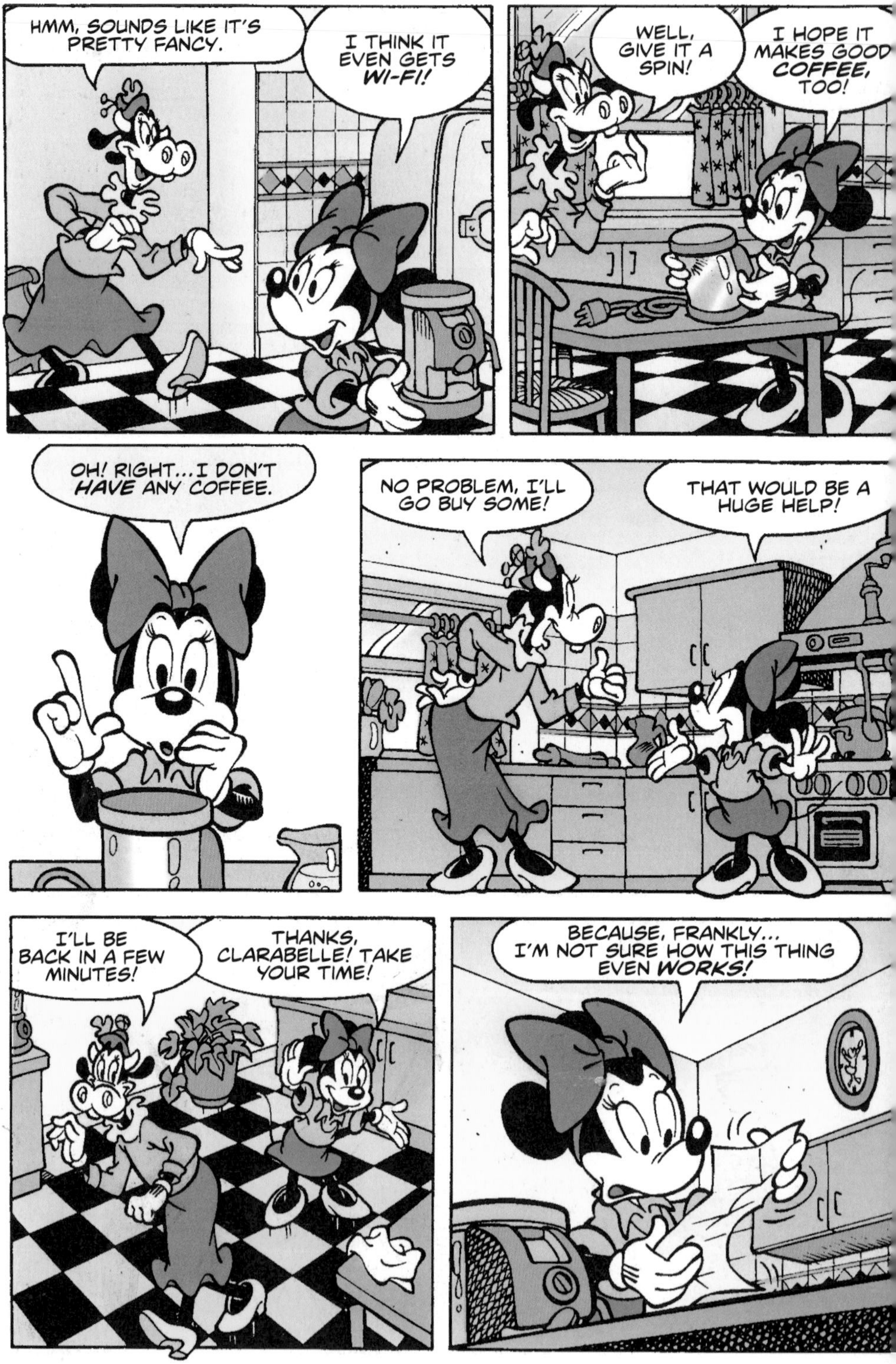
HMM, SOUNDS LIKE IT'S PRETTY FANCY.
I THINK IT EVEN GETS WI-FI!
WELL, GIVE IT A SPIN!
I HOPE IT MAKES GOOD COFFEE, TOO!
OH! RIGHT...I DON'T HAVE ANY COFFEE.
NO PROBLEM, I'LL GO BUY SOME!
THAT WOULD BE A HUGE HELP!
I'LL BE BACK IN A FEW MINUTES!
THANKS, CLARABELLE! TAKE YOUR TIME!
BECAUSE, FRANKLY... I'M NOT SURE HOW THIS THING EVEN WORKS!

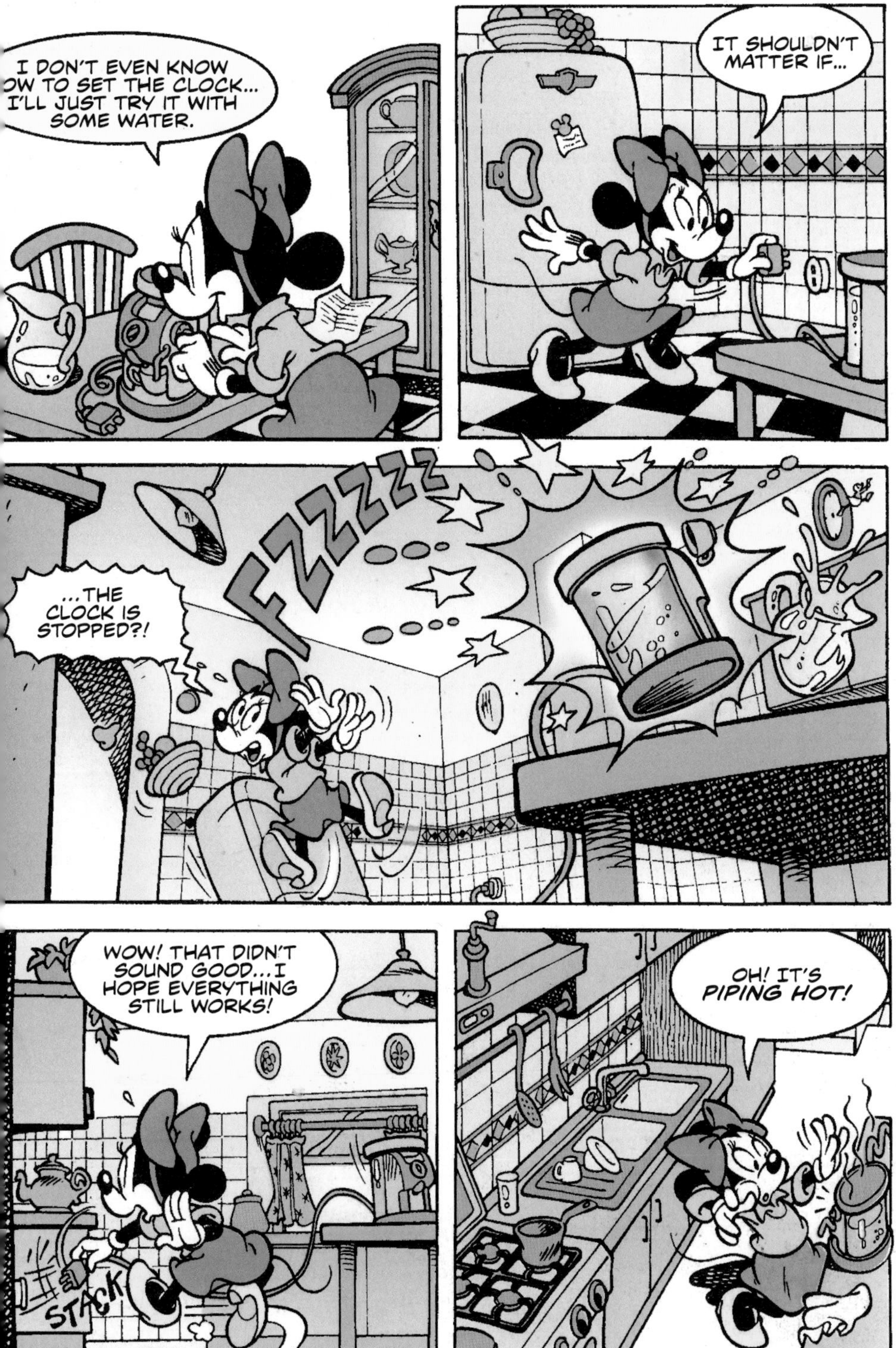
I DON'T EVEN KNOW
OW TO SET THE CLOCK...
I'LL JUST TRY IT WITH
SOME WATER.
IT SHOULDN'T
MATTER IF...
...THE
CLOCK IS
STOPPED?!
FZZZZZZ
WOW! THAT DIDN'T
SOUND GOOD...I
HOPE EVERYTHING
STILL WORKS!
STACK
OH! IT'S
PIPING HOT!

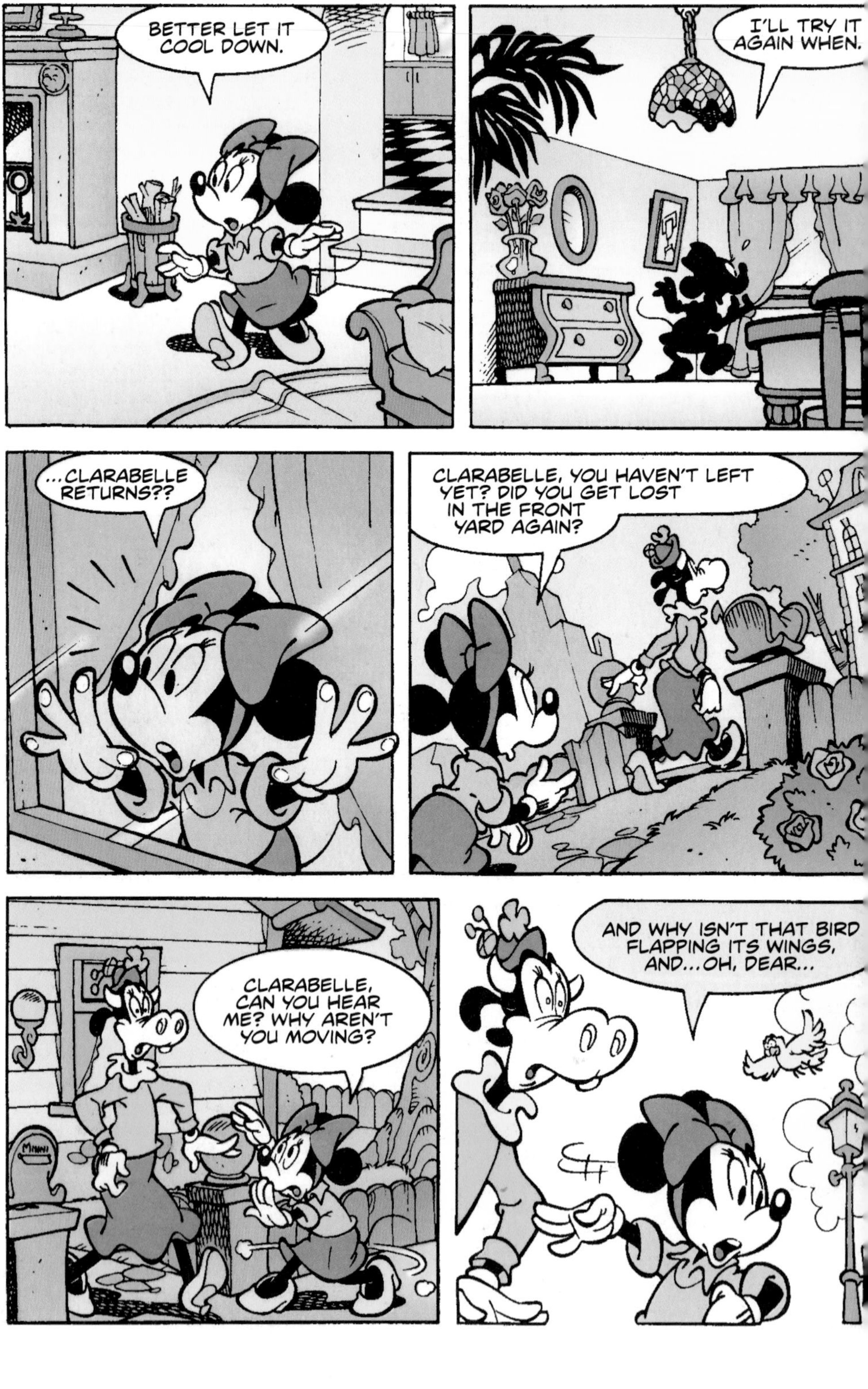
BETTER LET IT COOL DOWN.
I'LL TRY IT AGAIN WHEN.
...CLARABELLE RETURNS??
CLARABELLE, YOU HAVEN'T LEFT YET? DID YOU GET LOST IN THE FRONT YARD AGAIN?
CLARABELLE, CAN YOU HEAR ME? WHY AREN'T YOU MOVING?
AND WHY ISN'T THAT BIRD FLAPPING ITS WINGS, AND...OH, DEAR...

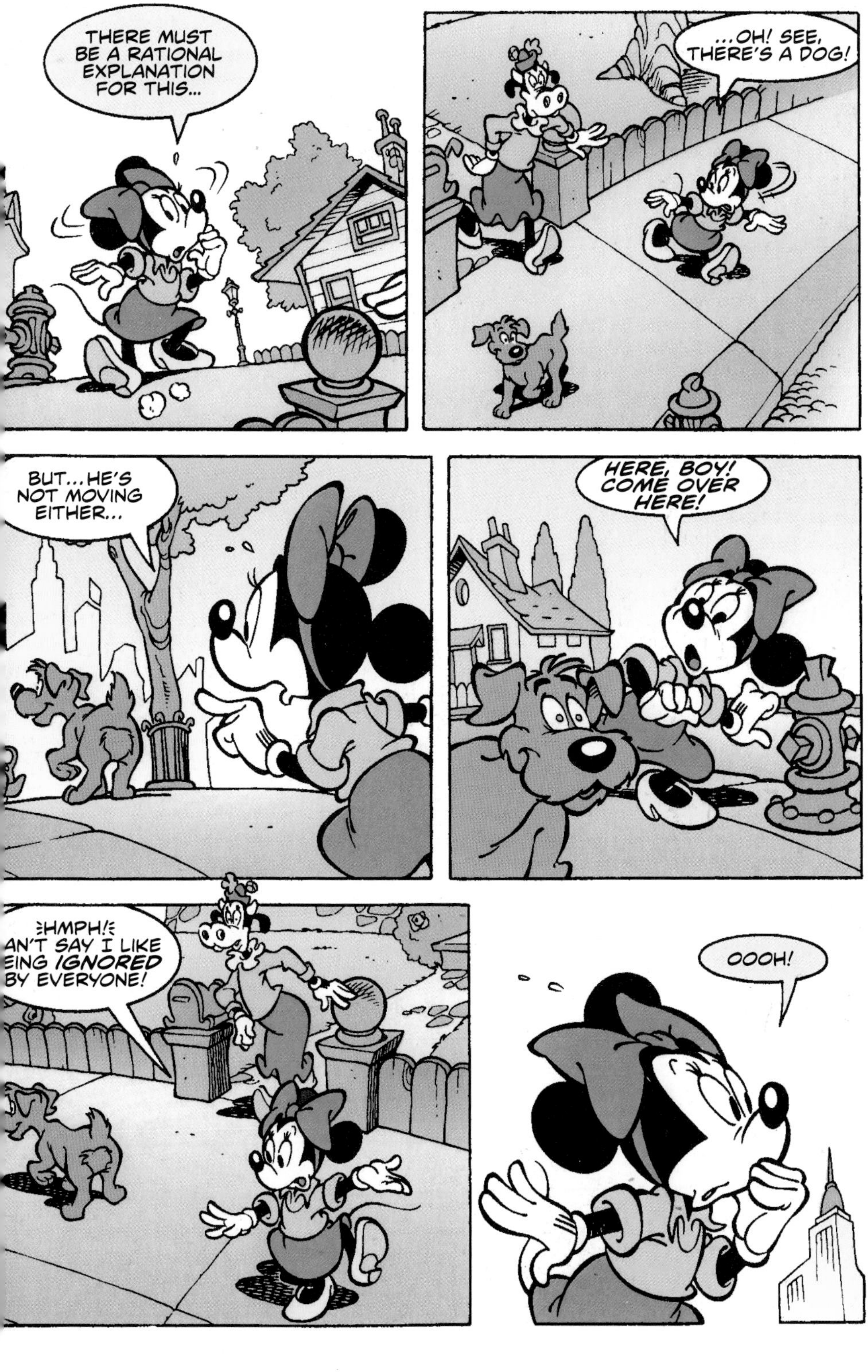
THERE MUST BE A RATIONAL EXPLANATION FOR THIS...
...OH! SEE, THERE'S A DOG!
BUT... HE'S NOT MOVING EITHER...
HERE, BOY! COME OVER HERE!
HMPH! AN'T SAY I LIKE EING IGNORED BY EVERYONE!
OOOH!

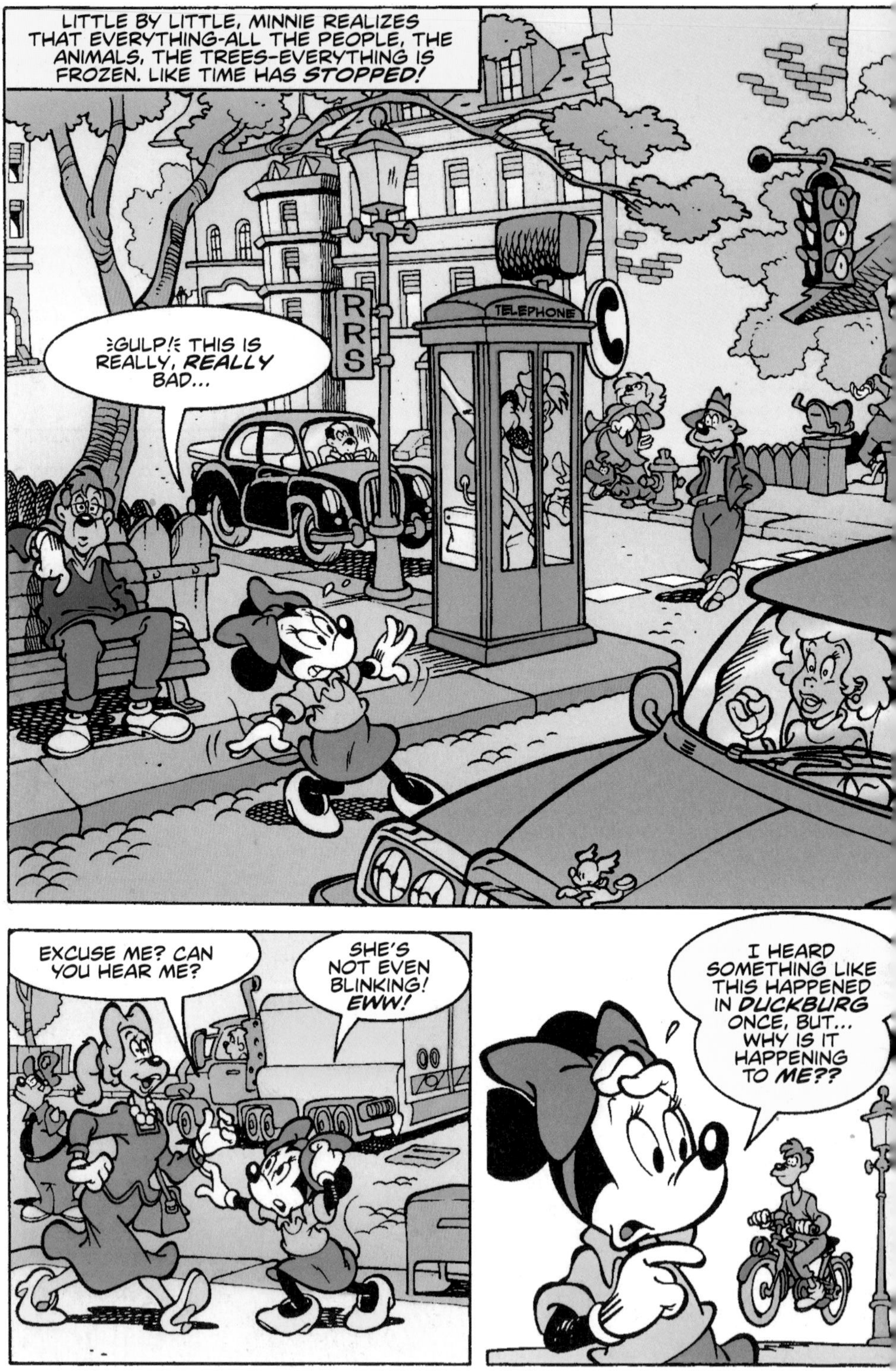

LITTLE BY LITTLE, MINNIE REALIZES THAT EVERYTHING-ALL THE PEOPLE, THE ANIMALS, THE TREES-EVERYTHING IS FROZEN. LIKE TIME HAS STOPPED!
GULP! THIS IS REALLY, REALLY BAD...
RRS
TELEPHONE
EXCUSE ME? CAN YOU HEAR ME?
SHE'S NOT EVEN BLINKING! EWW!
I HEARD SOMETHING LIKE THIS HAPPENED IN DUCKBURG ONCE, BUT... WHY IS IT HAPPENING TO ME??

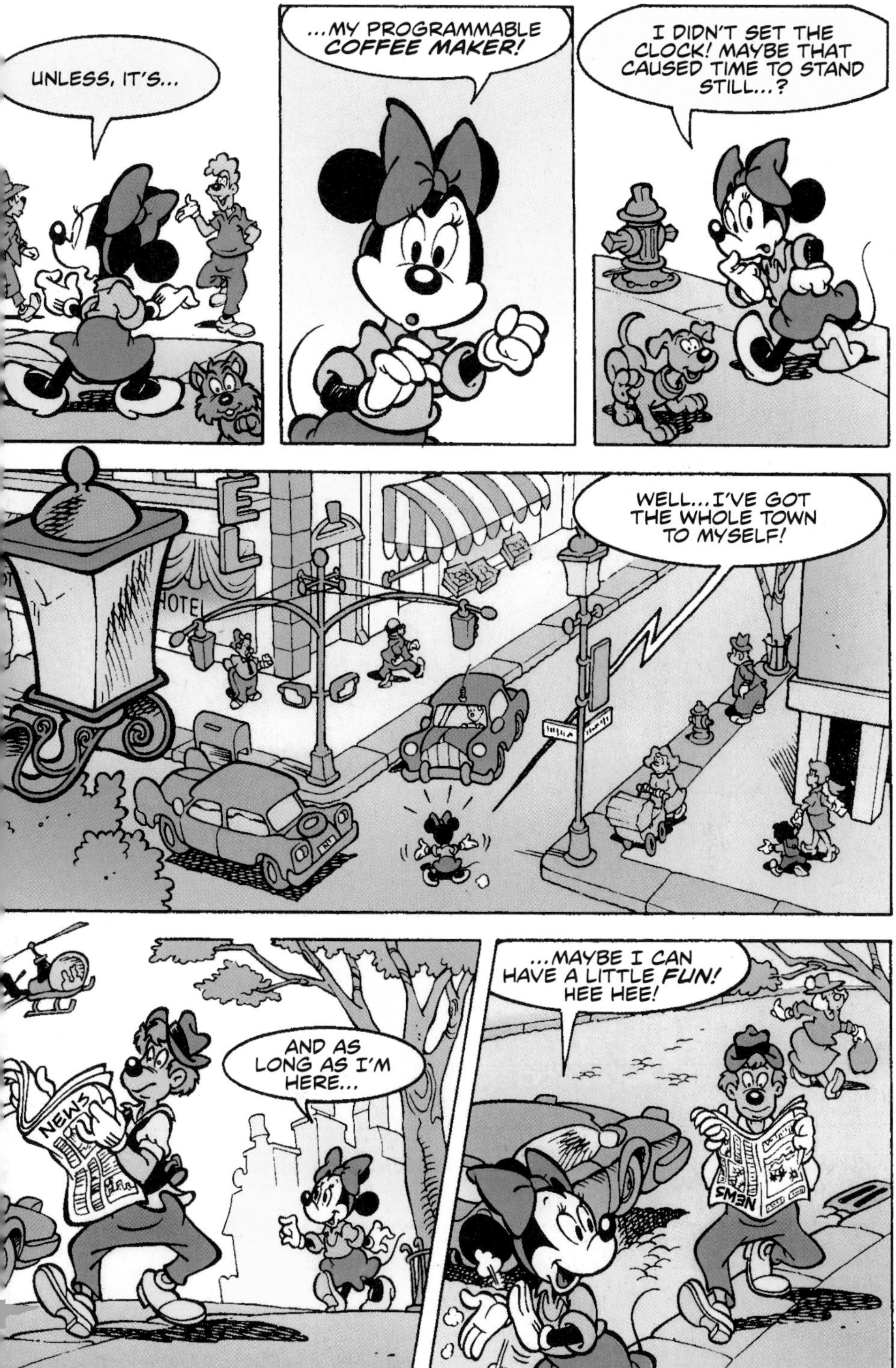

UNLESS, IT'S...
...MY PROGRAMMABLE COFFEE MAKER!
I DIDN'T SET THE CLOCK! MAYBE THAT CAUSED TIME TO STAND STILL...?
HOTEL
WELL...I'VE GOT THE WHOLE TOWN TO MYSELF!
NEWS
AND AS LONG AS I'M HERE...
...MAYBE I CAN HAVE A LITTLE FUN! HEE HEE!
NEWS

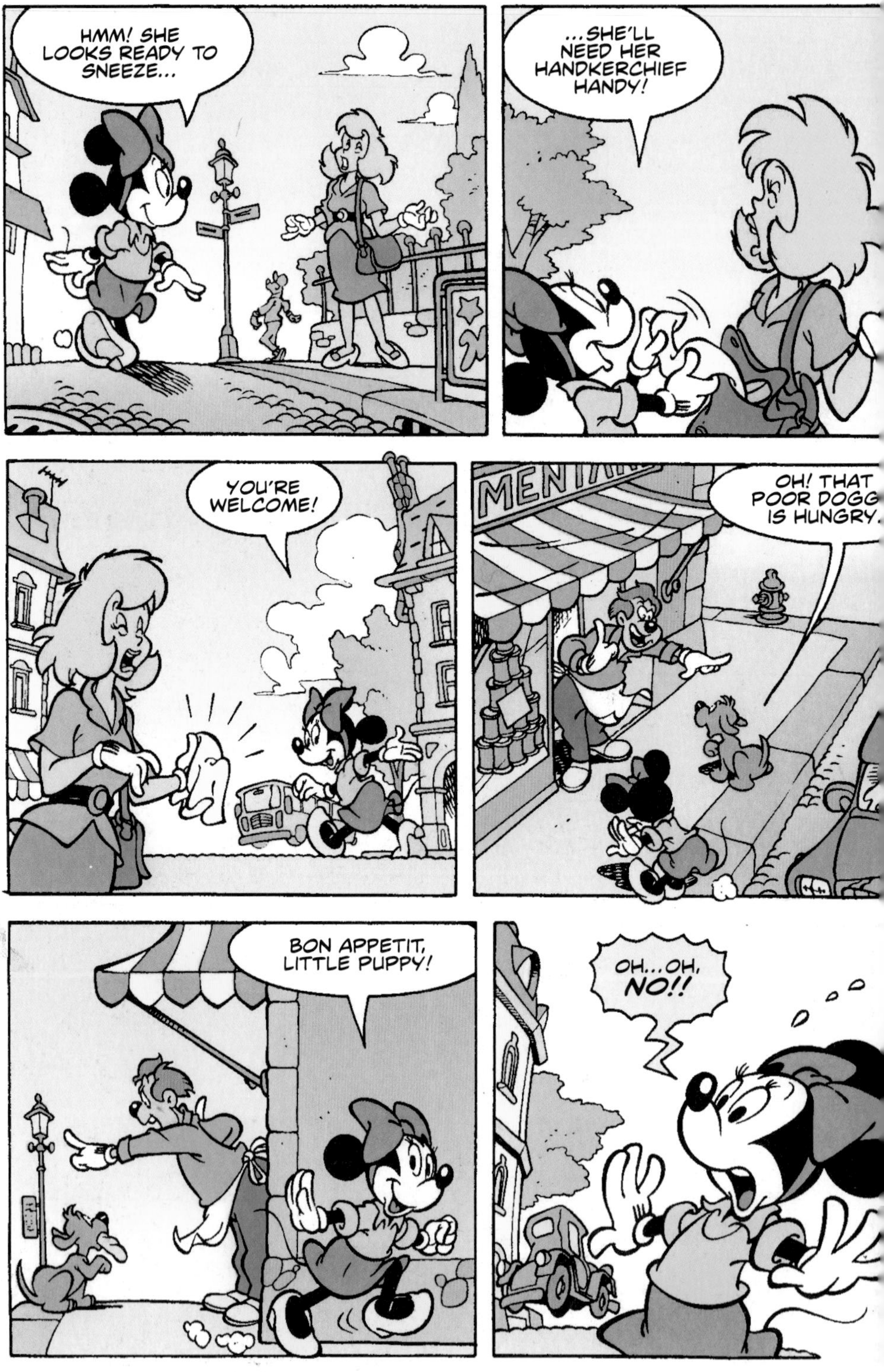
HMM! SHE LOOKS READY TO SNEEZE...
...SHE'LL NEED HER HANDKERCHIEF HANDY!
YOU'RE WELCOME!
MENTA
OH! THAT POOR DOGG IS HUNGRY.
BON APPETIT, LITTLE PUPPY!
OH...OH, NO!!

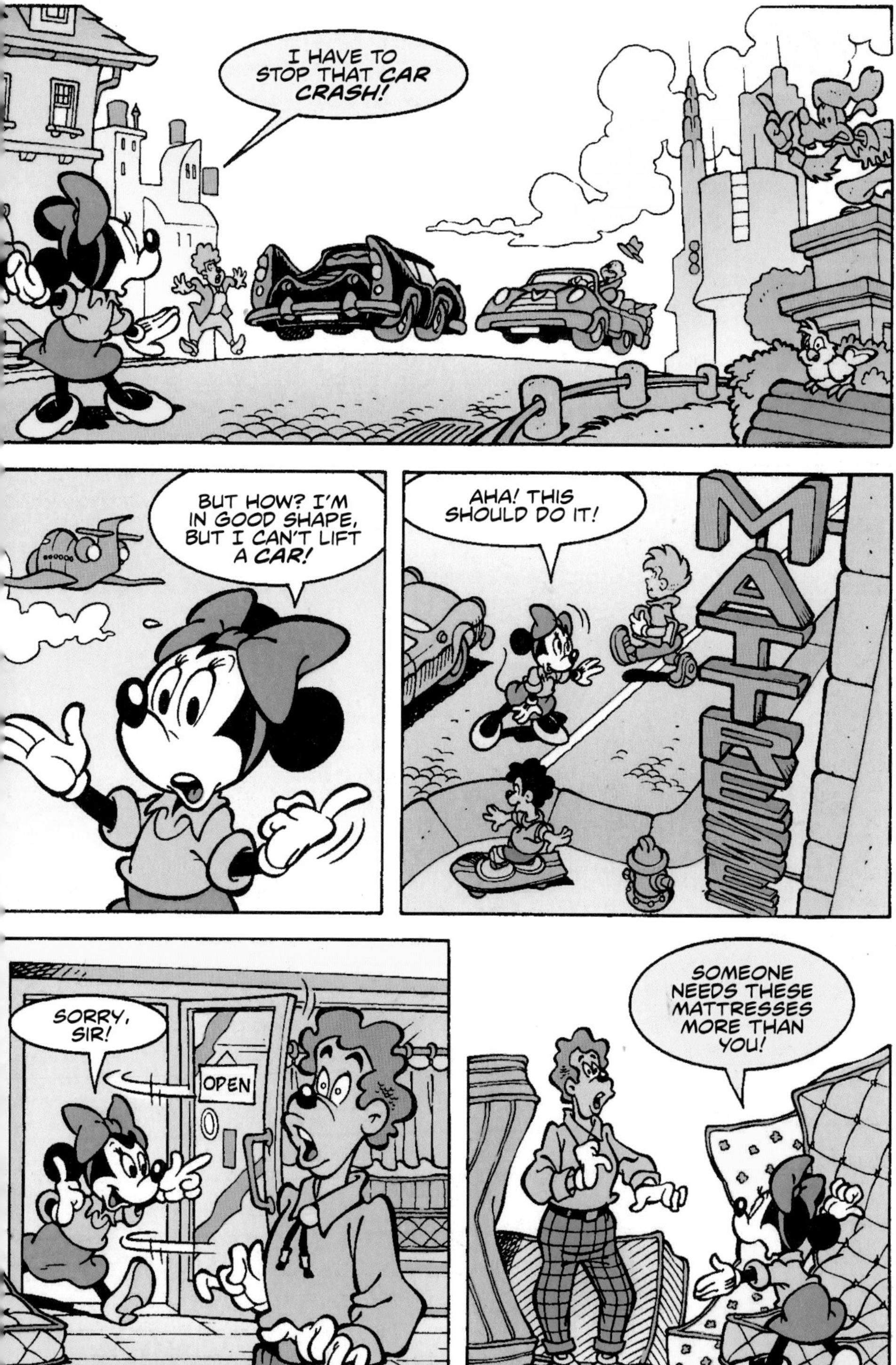
I HAVE TO STOP THAT CAR CRASH!
BUT HOW? I'M IN GOOD SHAPE, BUT I CAN'T LIFT A CAR!
AHA! THIS SHOULD DO IT!
MATTRE
SORRY, SIR!
OPEN
SOMEONE NEEDS THESE MATTRESSES MORE THAN YOU!

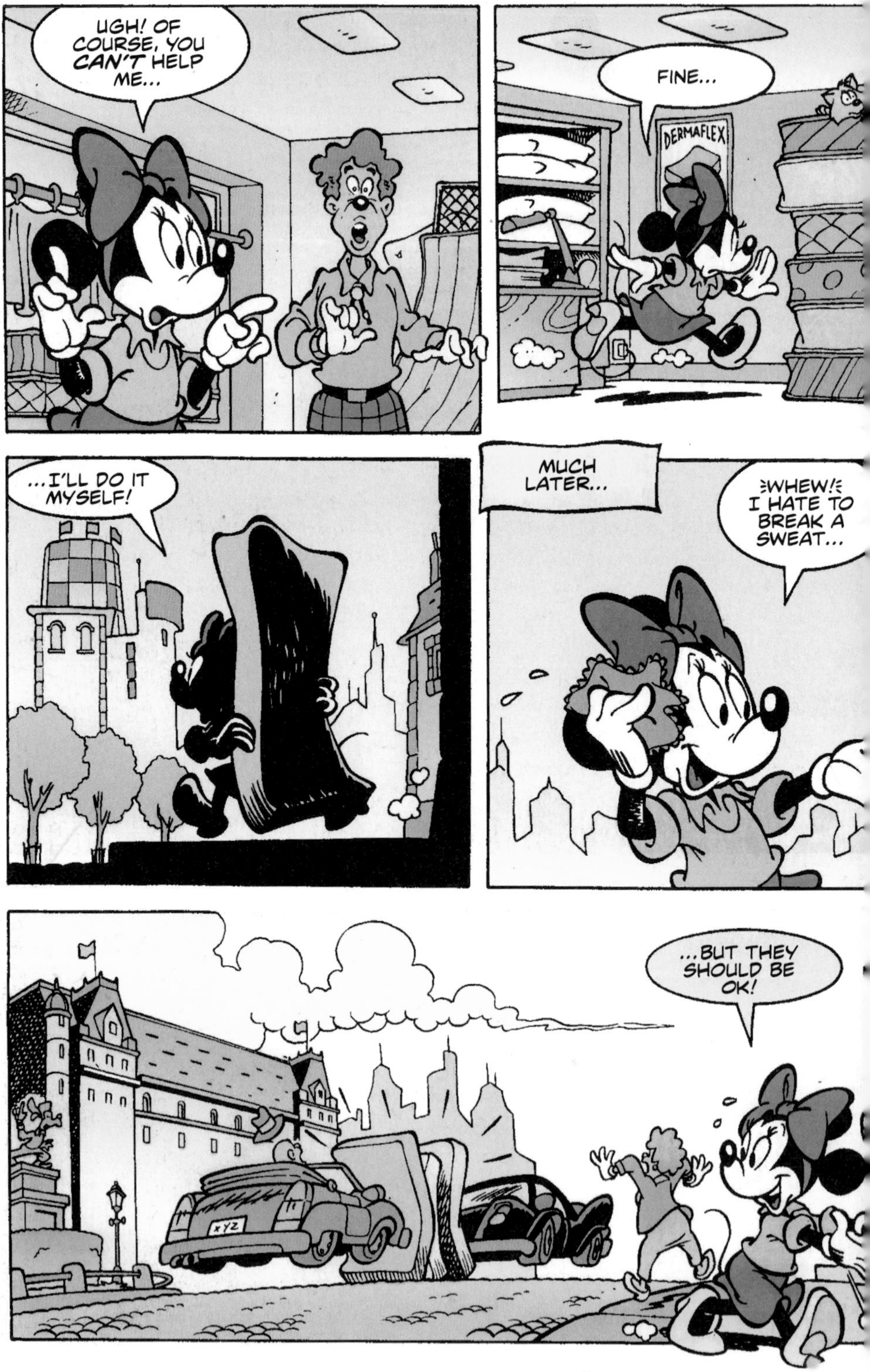
UGH! OF COURSE, YOU CAN'T HELP ME...
FINE...
DERMAFLEX
...I'LL DO IT MYSELF!
MUCH LATER...
WHEW! I HATE TO BREAK A SWEAT...
...BUT THEY SHOULD BE OK!
XYZ

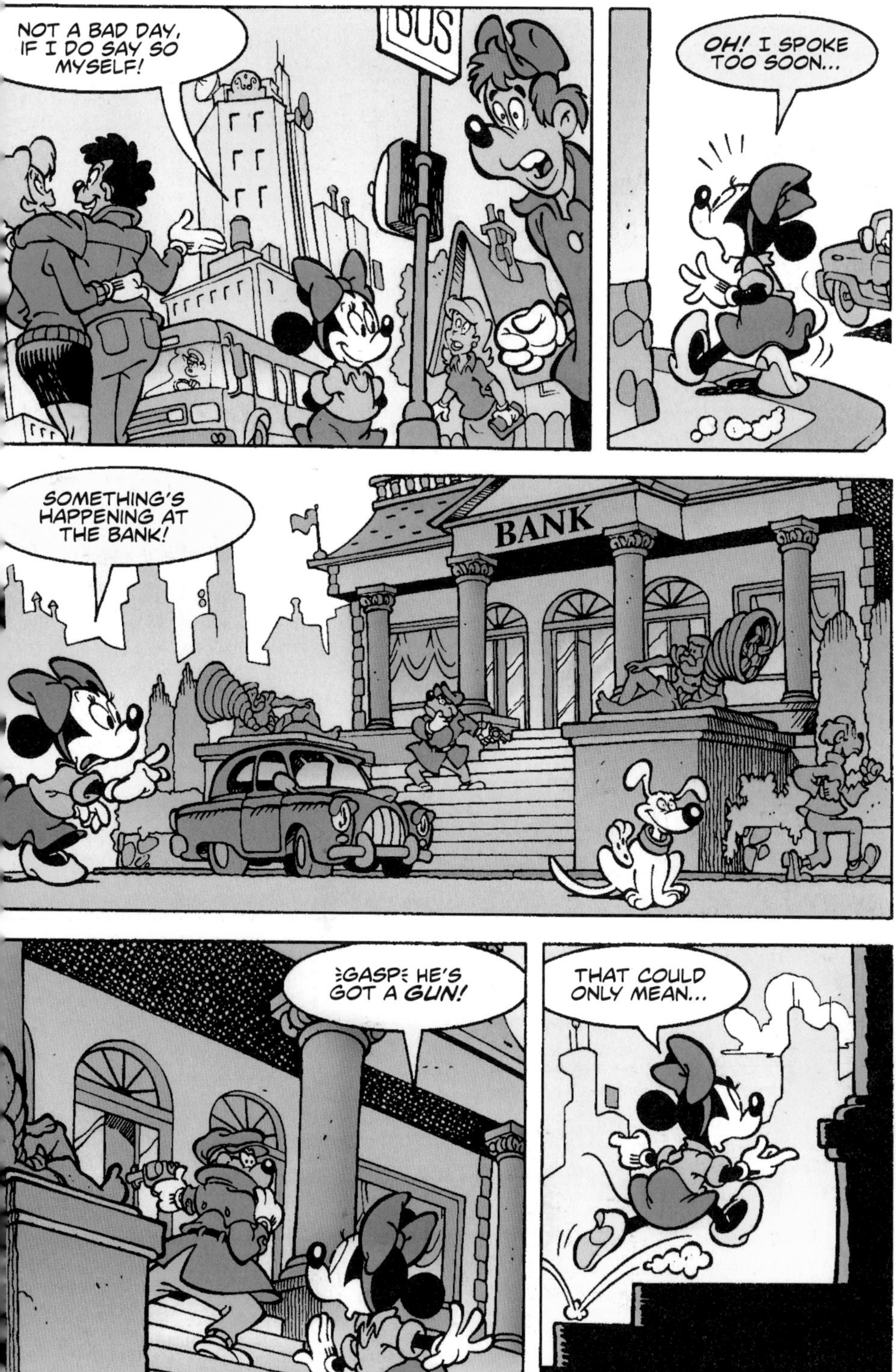
NOT A BAD DAY, IF I DO SAY SO MYSELF!
BUS
OH! I SPOKE TOO SOON...
SOMETHING'S HAPPENING AT THE BANK!
BANK
GASP HE'S GOT A GUN!
THAT COULD ONLY MEAN...

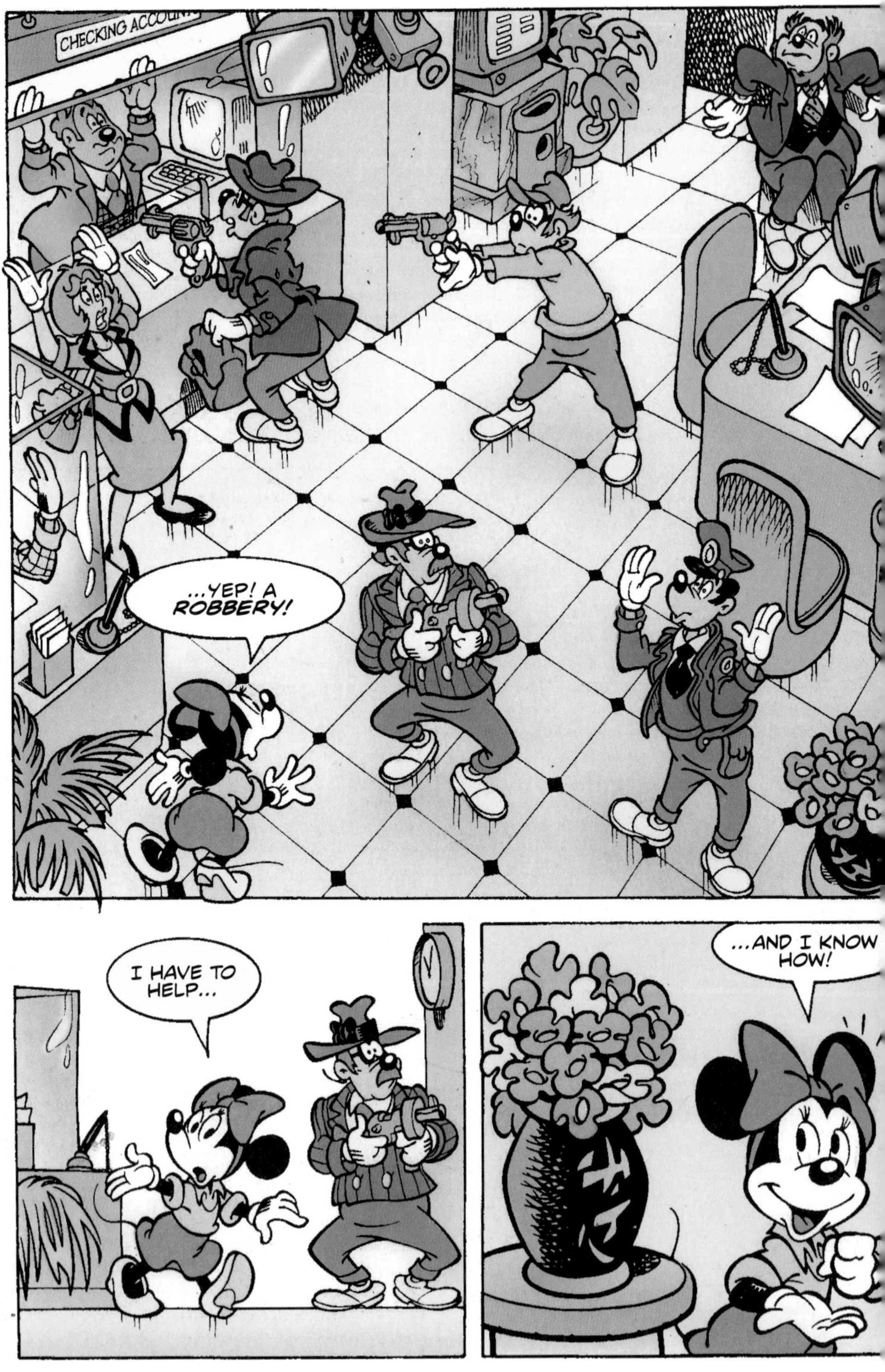
CHECKING
...YEP! A ROBBERY!
I HAVE TO HELP...
...AND I KNOW HOW!

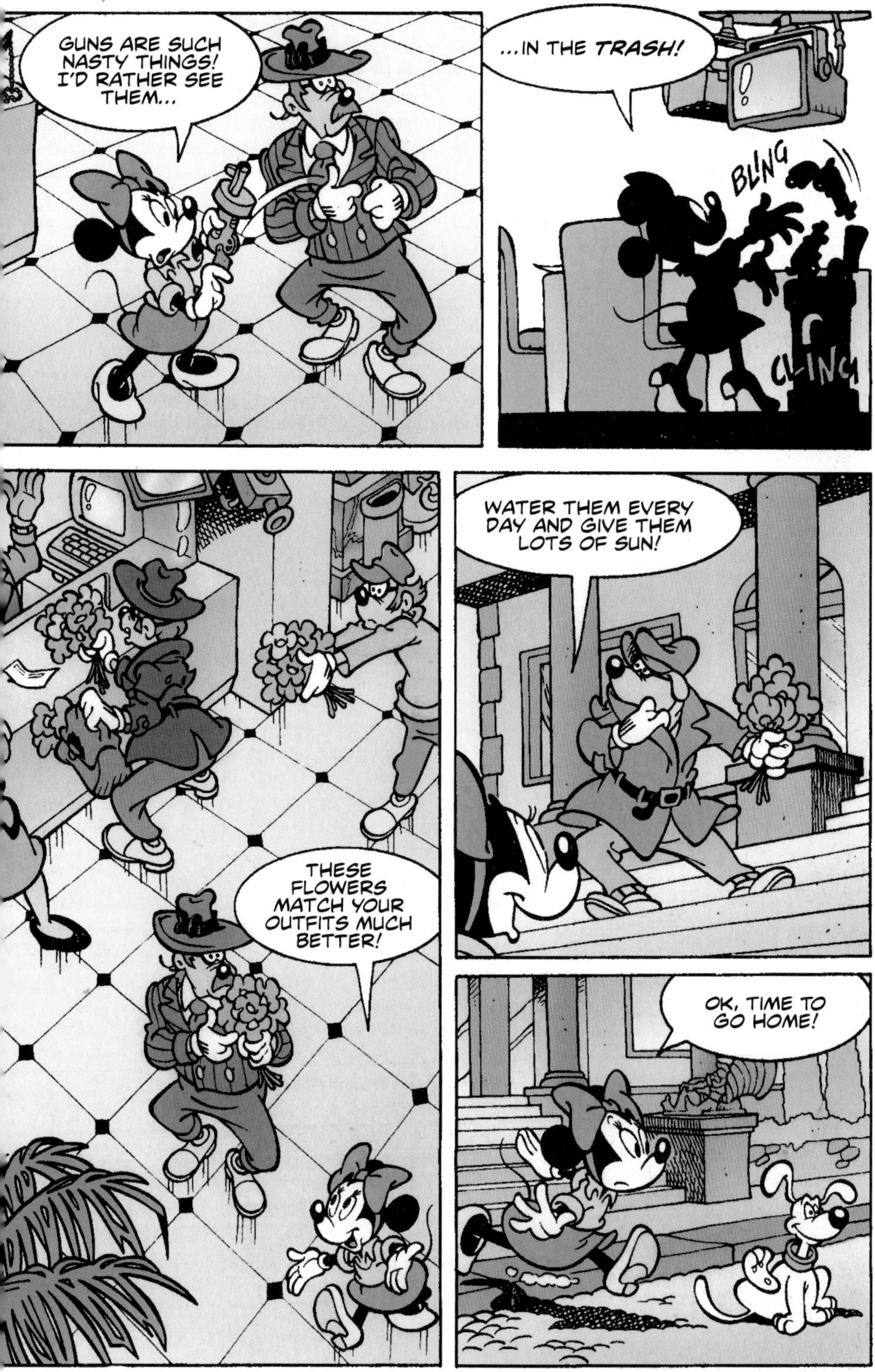
GUNS ARE SUCH NASTY THINGS! I'D RATHER SEE THEM...
...IN THE TRASH!
BLING
CLING
THESE FLOWERS MATCH YOUR OUTFITS MUCH BETTER!
WATER THEM EVERY DAY AND GIVE THEM LOTS OF SUN!
OK, TIME TO GO HOME!

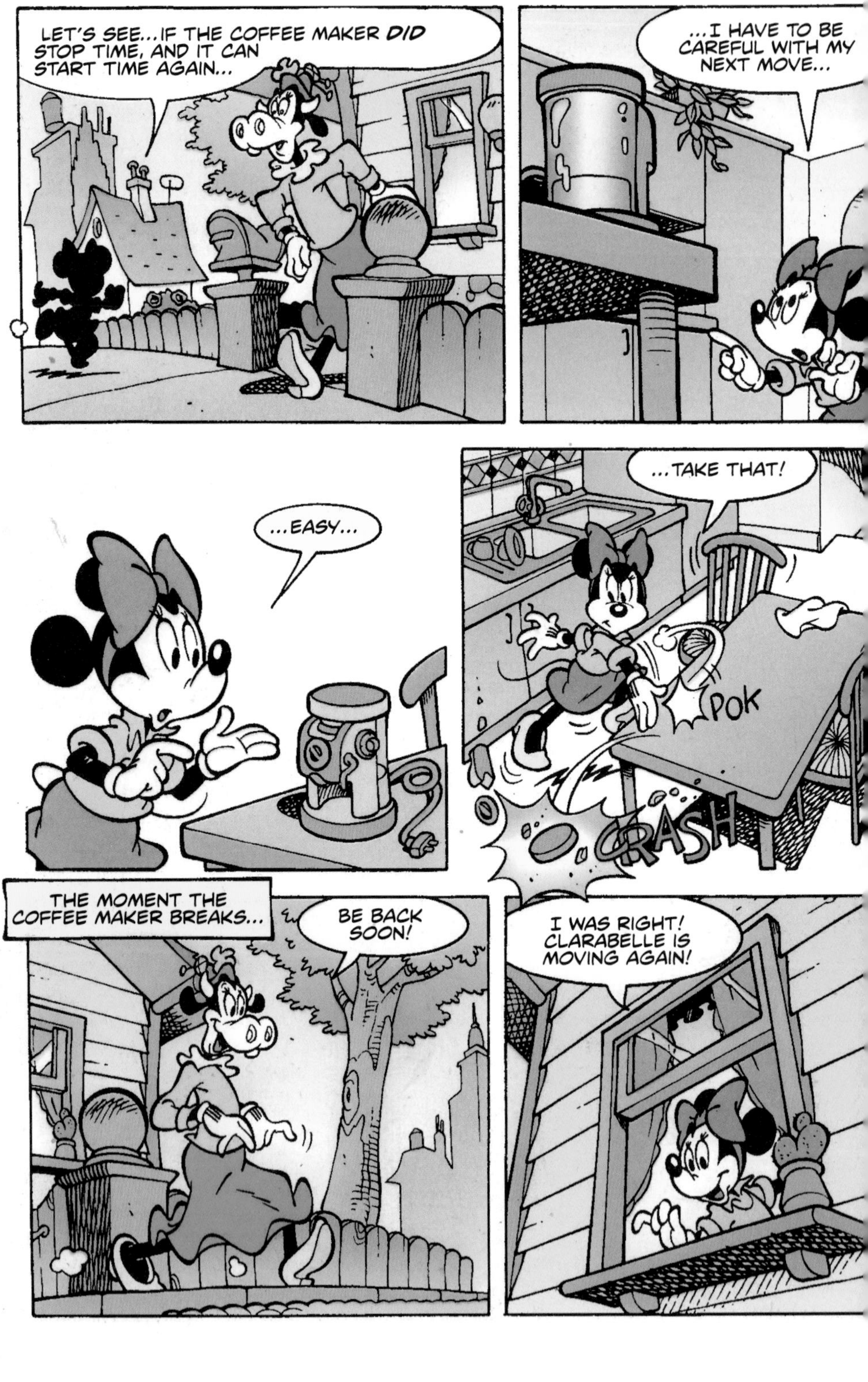
LET'S SEE... IF THE COFFEE MAKER DID STOP TIME, AND IT CAN START TIME AGAIN...
...I HAVE TO BE CAREFUL WITH MY NEXT MOVE...
...EASY...
...TAKE THAT!
POK
CRASH
THE MOMENT THE COFFEE MAKER BREAKS...
BE BACK SOON!
I WAS RIGHT! CLARABELLE IS MOVING AGAIN!

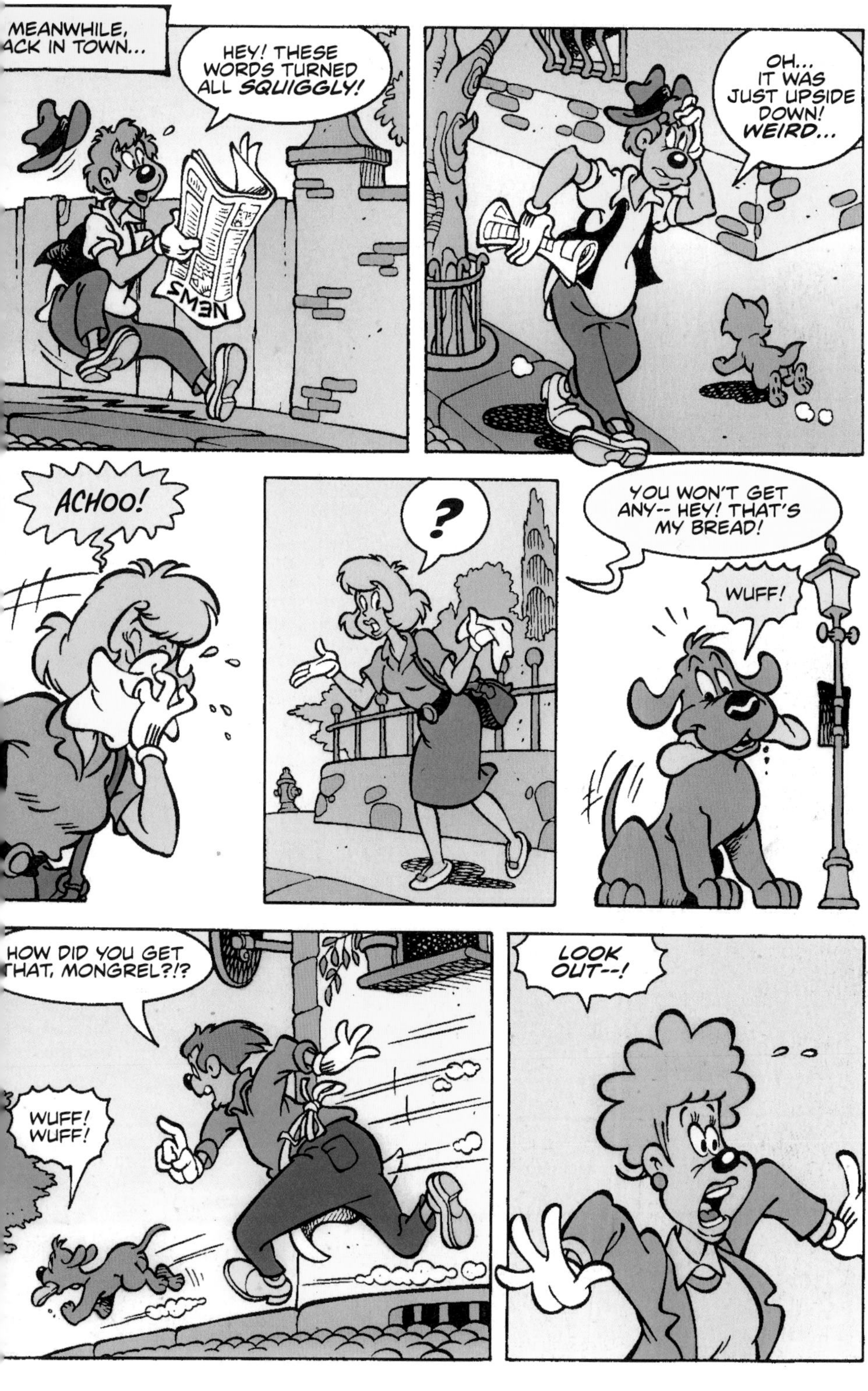
MEANWHILE, ACK IN TOWN...
HEY! THESE WORDS TURNED ALL SQUIGGLY!
NEWS
OH... IT WAS JUST UPSIDE DOWN! WEIRD...
ACHOO!
?
YOU WON'T GET ANY-- HEY! THAT'S MY BREAD!
WUFF!
HOW DID YOU GET THAT, MONGREL?!?
WUFF! WUFF!
LOOK OUT--!

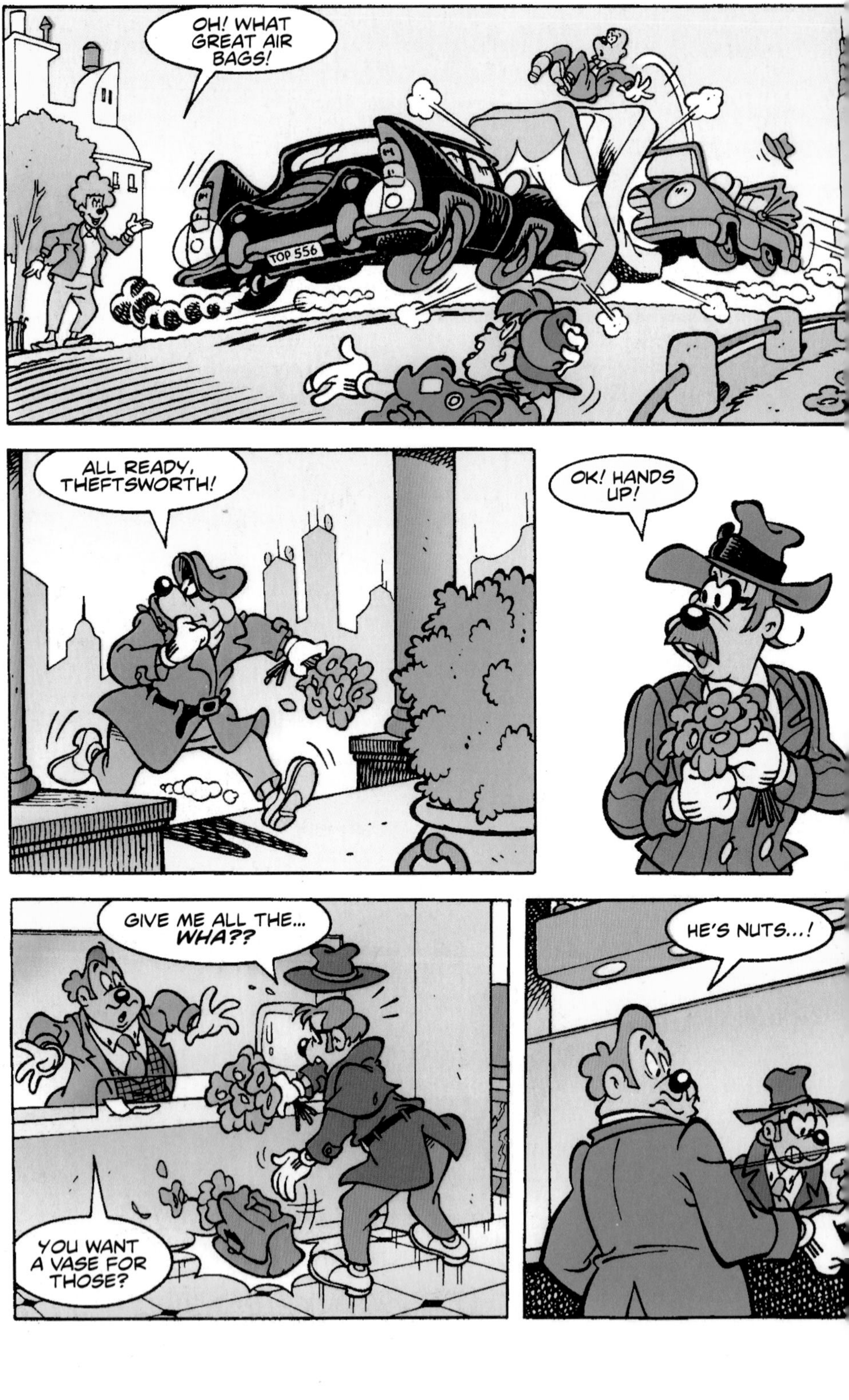
OH! WHAT GREAT AIR BAGS!
TOP 556
ALL READY, THEFTSWORTH!
OK! HANDS UP!
GIVE ME ALL THE... WHA??
YOU WANT A VASE FOR THOSE?
HE'S NUTS...!

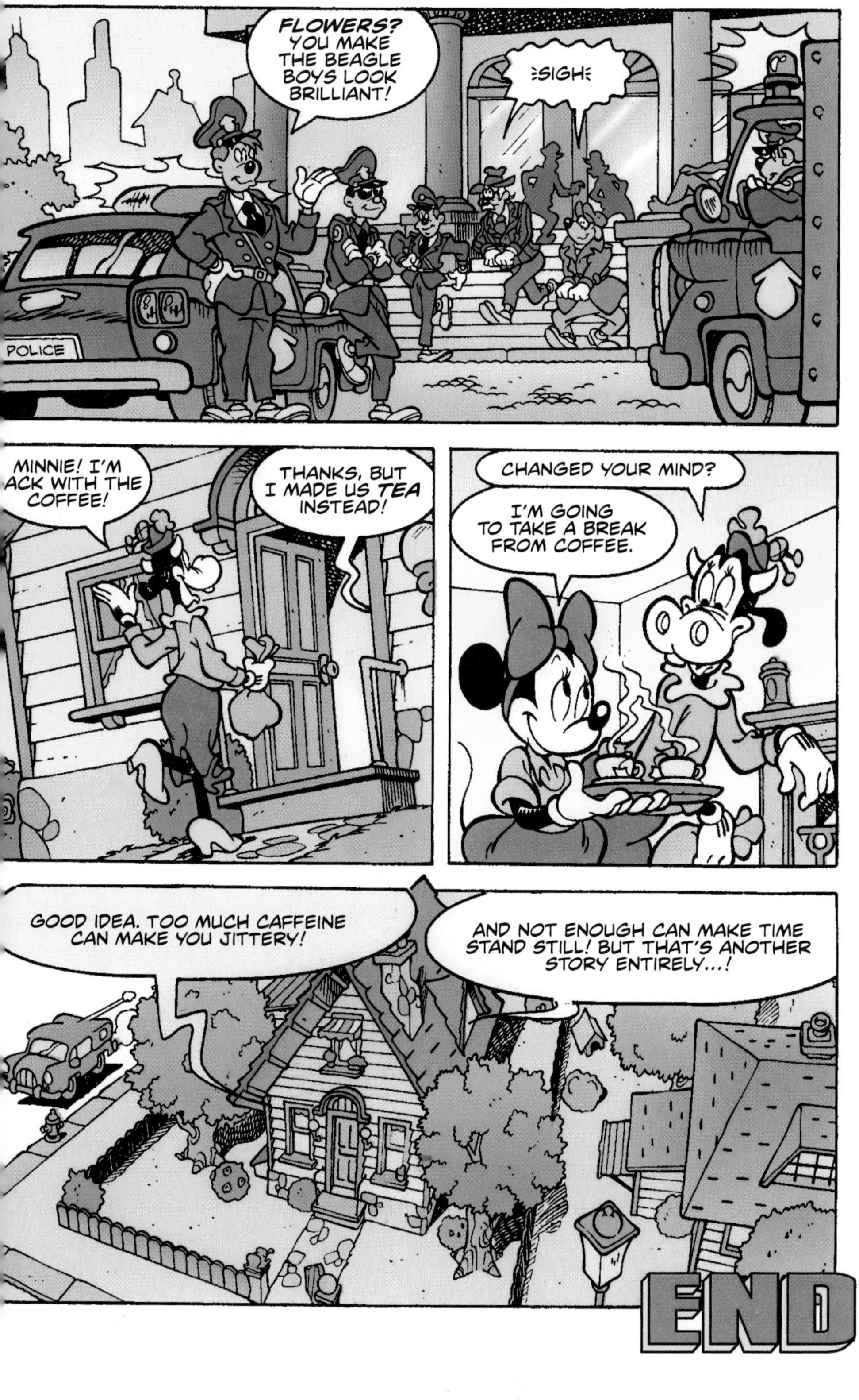
FLOWERS? YOU MAKE THE BEAGLE BOYS LOOK BRILLIANT!
SIGH
POLICE
MINNIE! I'M ACK WITH THE COFFEE!
THANKS, BUT I MADE US TEA INSTEAD!
CHANGED YOUR MIND?
I'M GOING TO TAKE A BREAK FROM COFFEE.
GOOD IDEA. TOO MUCH CAFFEINE CAN MAKE YOU JITTERY!
AND NOT ENOUGH CAN MAKE TIME STAND STILL! BUT THAT'S ANOTHER STORY ENTIRELY...!
END

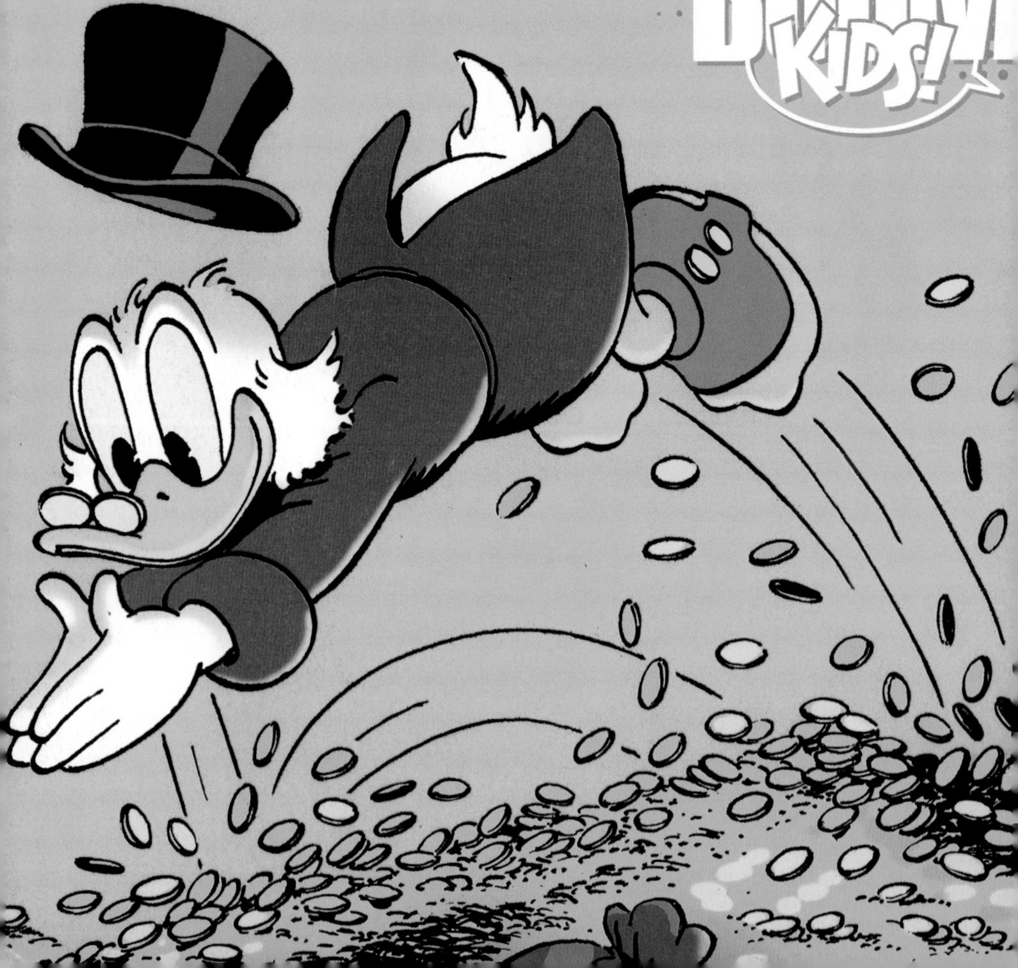

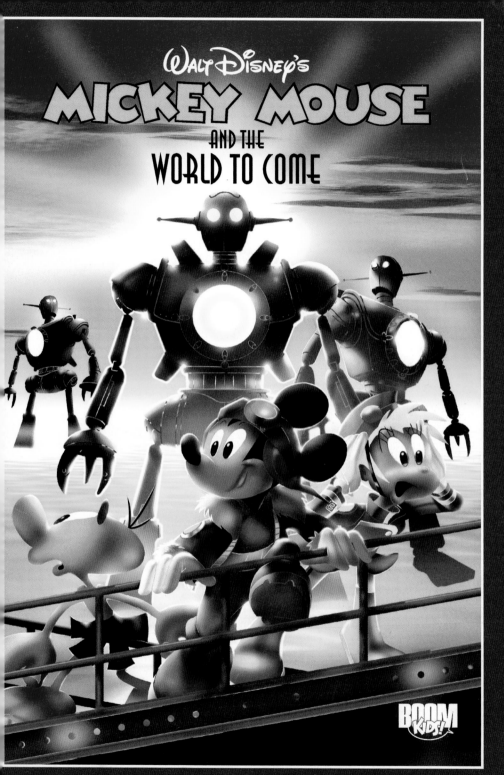

Join Mickey Mouse, Minnie and Eega Beeva on a
high-flying adventure to stop a terrifying possible
future from coming true!

MICKEY MOUSE AND THE
WORLD TO COME
DIAMOND CODE: MAR100814
SC $9.99 ISBN 9781608865628

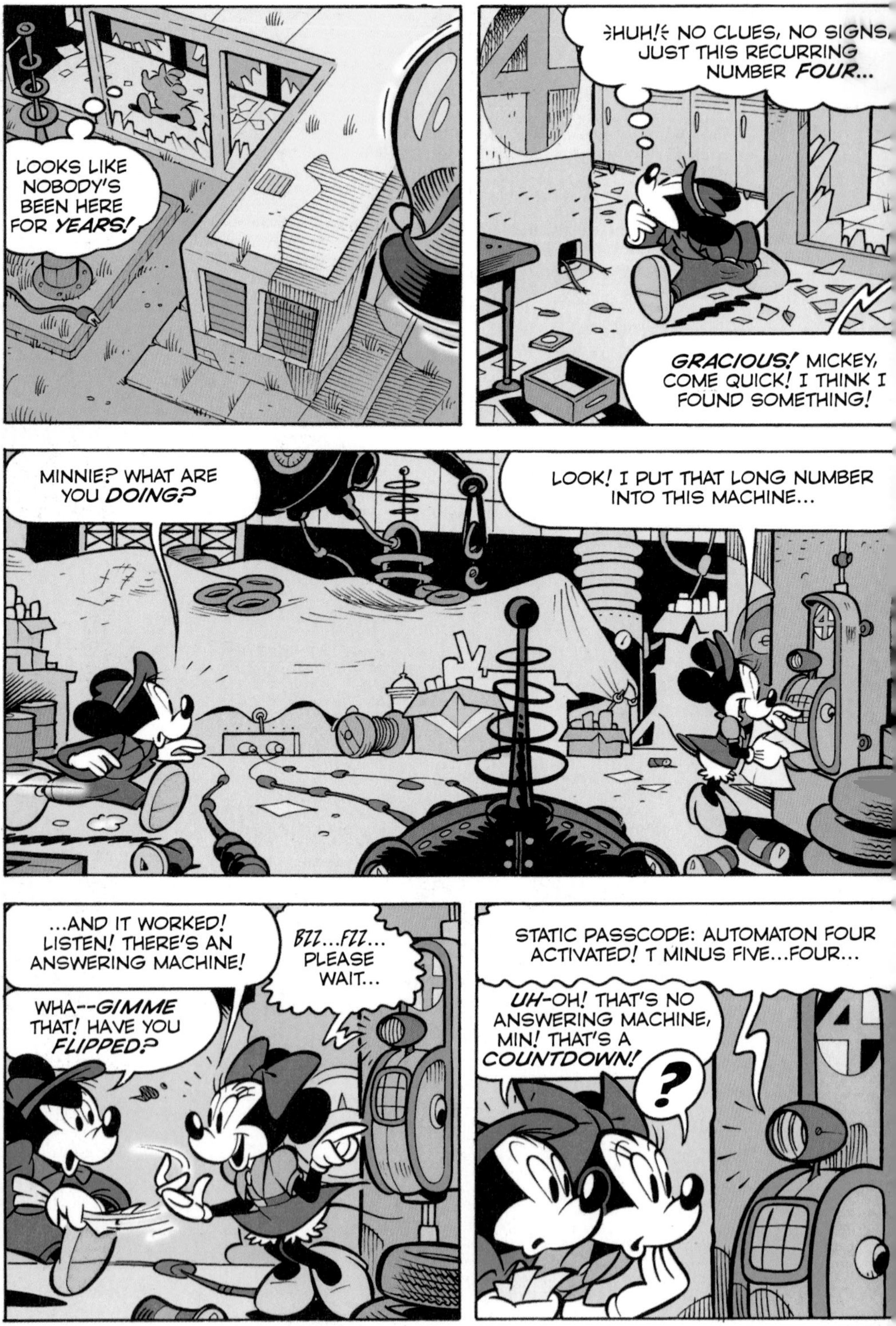
LOOKS LIKE NOBODY'S BEEN HERE FOR *YEARS!*
HUH! NO CLUES, NO SIGNS, JUST THIS RECURRING NUMBER *FOUR*...
GRACIOUS! MICKEY, COME QUICK! I THINK I FOUND SOMETHING!
MINNIE? WHAT ARE YOU *DOING?*
LOOK! I PUT THAT LONG NUMBER INTO THIS MACHINE...
...AND IT WORKED! LISTEN! THERE'S AN ANSWERING MACHINE!
BZZ...FZZ... PLEASE WAIT...
WHA--*GIMME* THAT! HAVE YOU *FLIPPED?*
STATIC PASSCODE: AUTOMATON FOUR ACTIVATED! T MINUS FIVE...FOUR...
UH-OH! THAT'S NO ANSWERING MACHINE, MIN! THAT'S A *COUNTDOWN!*
?

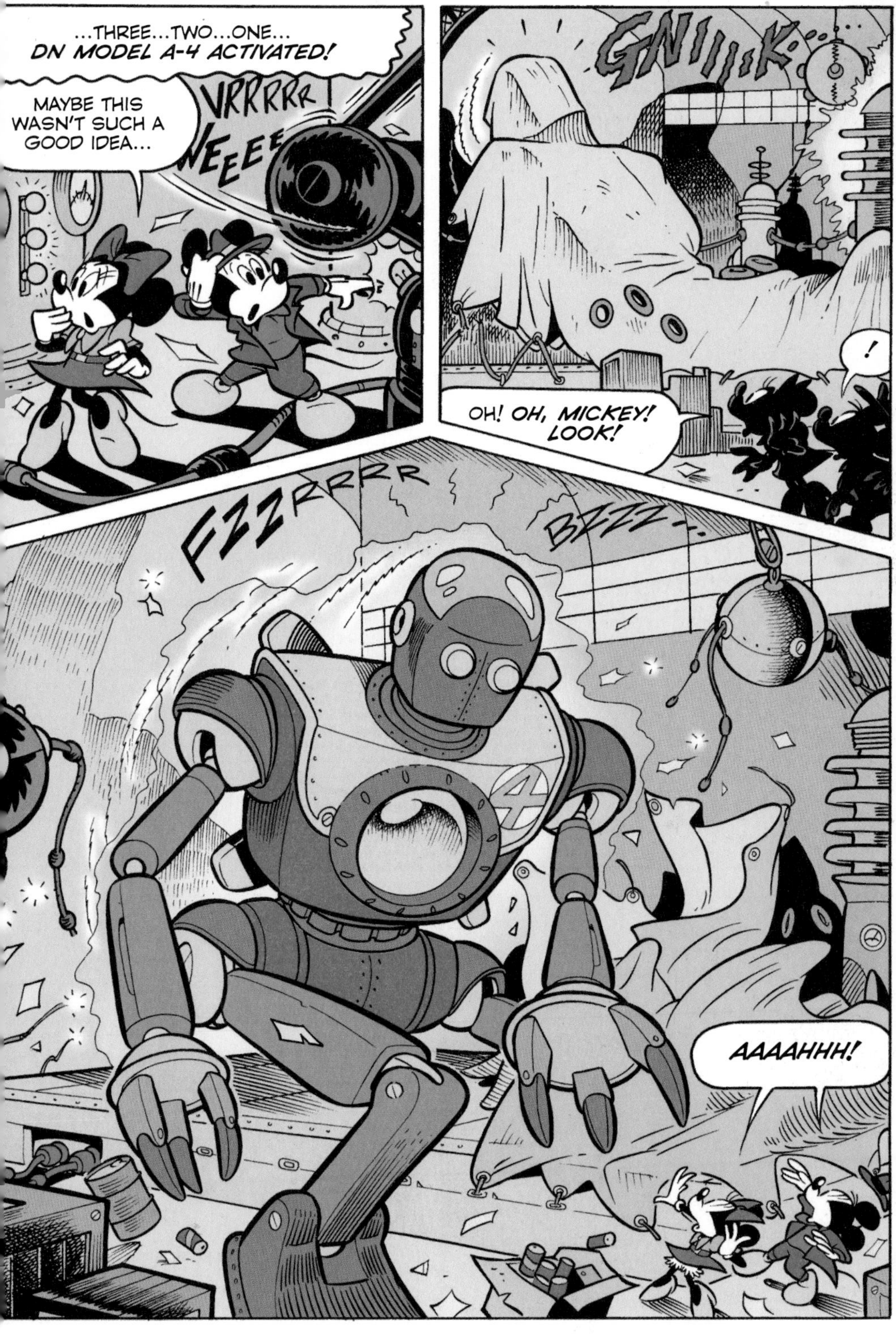
...THREE...TWO...ONE...
DN MODEL A-4 ACTIVATED!
MAYBE THIS WASN'T SUCH A GOOD IDEA...
VRRRRR
WEEEE
GNIIIIK...
!
OH! OH, MICKEY! LOOK!
FZZRRRRR
BZZZ...
AAAAHHH!

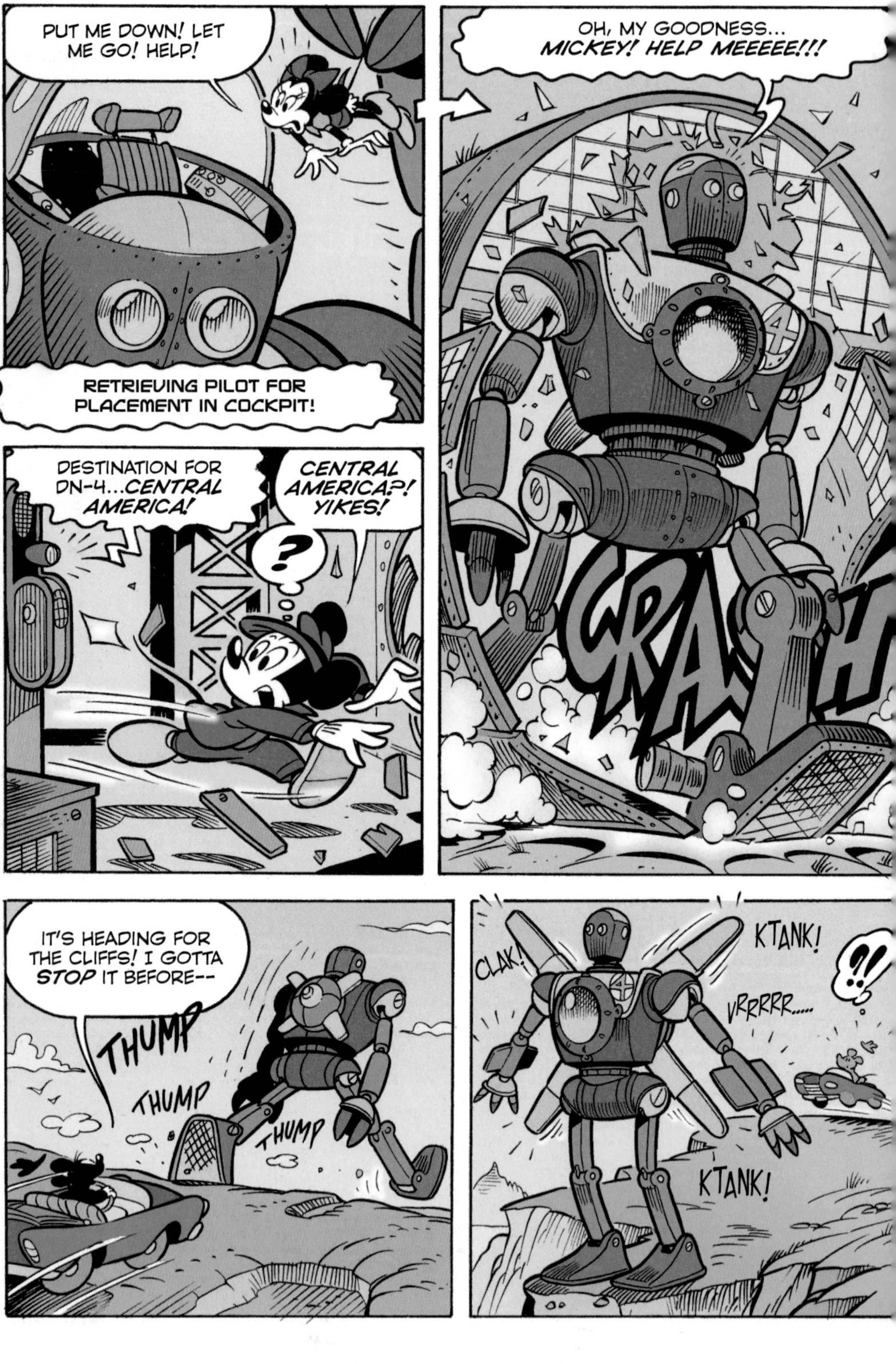
PUT ME DOWN! LET ME GO! HELP!
RETRIEVING PILOT FOR PLACEMENT IN COCKPIT!
OH, MY GOODNESS... MICKEY! HELP MEEEEE!!!
DESTINATION FOR DN-4...CENTRAL AMERICA!
CENTRAL AMERICA?! YIKES!
?
CRASH
IT'S HEADING FOR THE CLIFFS! I GOTTA STOP IT BEFORE--
THUMP
THUMP
THUMP
CLAK!
KTANK!
VRRRRR.....
!!
KTANK!

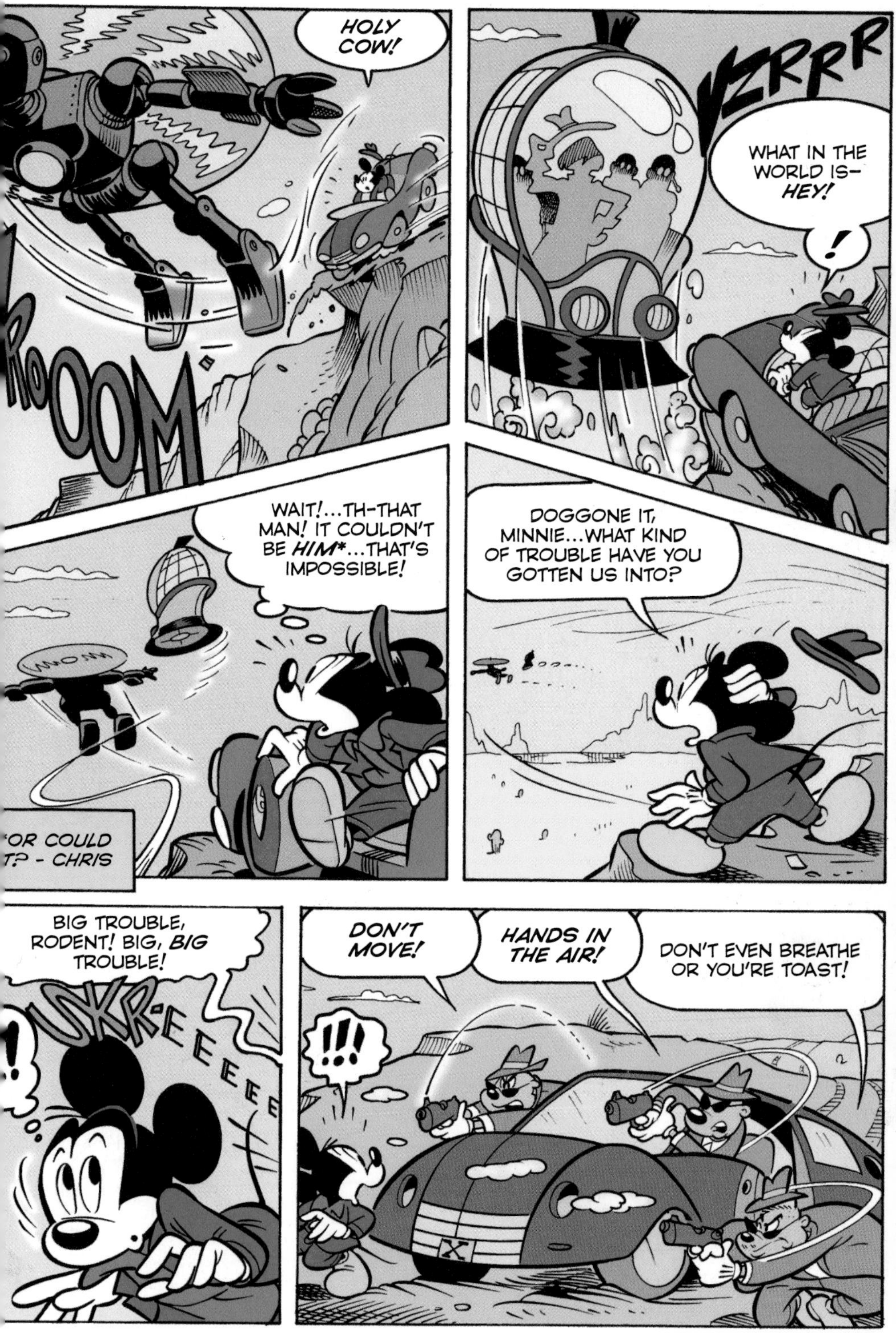
HOLY COW!
ROOOM
VZRRR
WHAT IN THE WORLD IS— HEY!
!
WAIT!...TH-THAT MAN! IT COULDN'T BE HIM*...THAT'S IMPOSSIBLE!
DOGGONE IT, MINNIE...WHAT KIND OF TROUBLE HAVE YOU GOTTEN US INTO?
*OR COULD IT? - CHRIS
BIG TROUBLE, RODENT! BIG, BIG TROUBLE!
SKR-EEEEEE
!
DON'T MOVE!
HANDS IN THE AIR!
DON'T EVEN BREATHE OR YOU'RE TOAST!
!!!

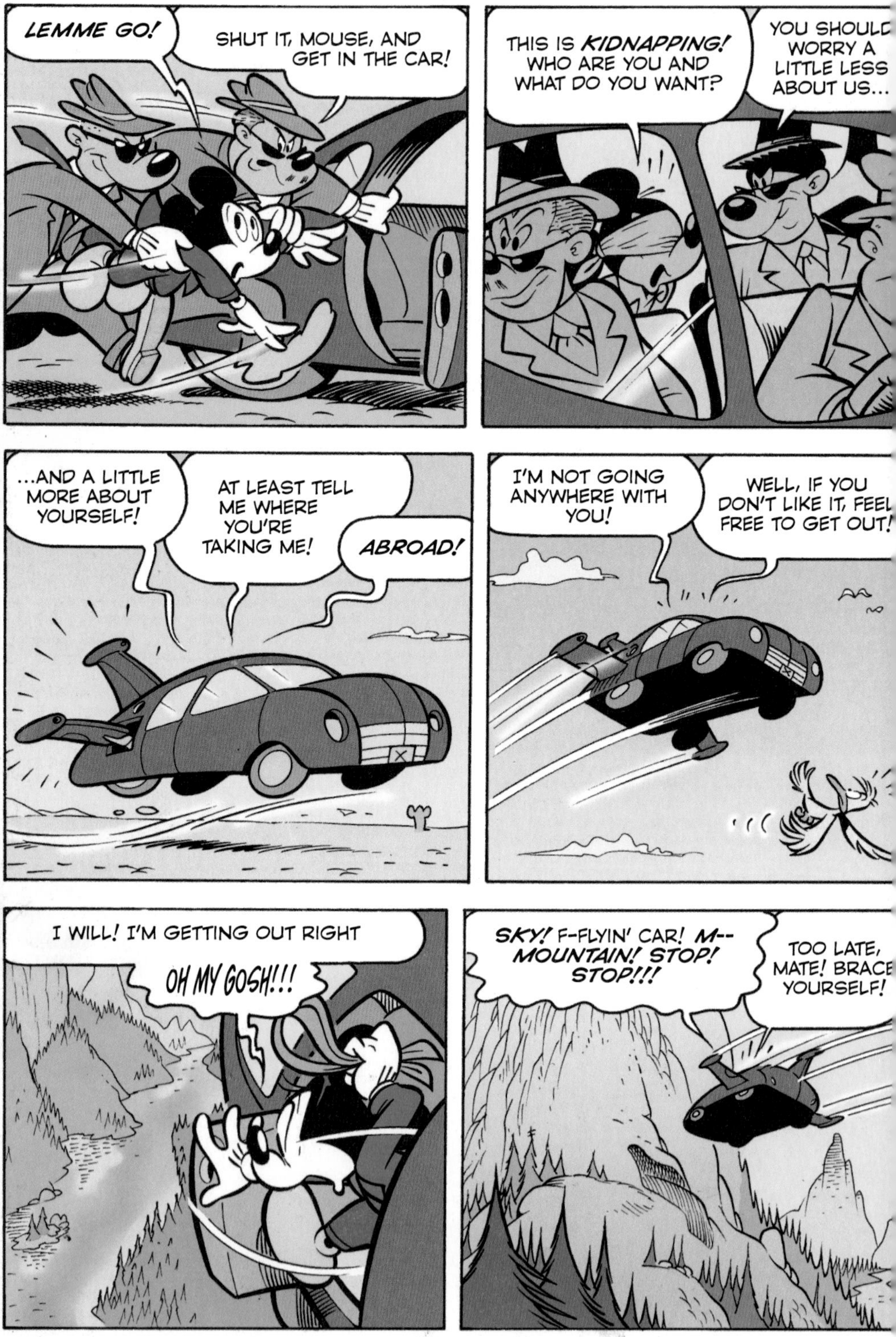
LEMME GO!
SHUT IT, MOUSE, AND GET IN THE CAR!
THIS IS KIDNAPPING! WHO ARE YOU AND WHAT DO YOU WANT?
YOU SHOULD WORRY A LITTLE LESS ABOUT US...
...AND A LITTLE MORE ABOUT YOURSELF!
AT LEAST TELL ME WHERE YOU'RE TAKING ME!
ABROAD!
I'M NOT GOING ANYWHERE WITH YOU!
WELL, IF YOU DON'T LIKE IT, FEEL FREE TO GET OUT!
I WILL! I'M GETTING OUT RIGHT
OH MY GOSH!!!
SKY! F-FLYIN' CAR! M-- MOUNTAIN! STOP! STOP!!!
TOO LATE, MATE! BRACE YOURSELF!

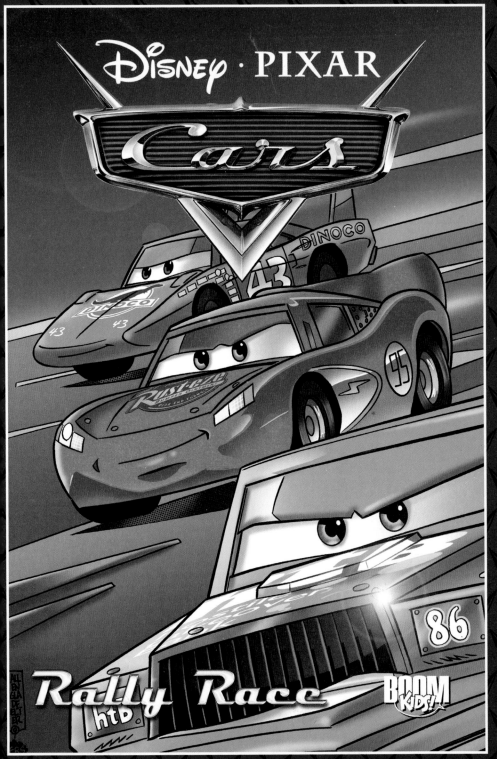

Disney · PIXAR

Cars

DINOCO

43

95

86

Rally Race
htD

BOOM Kids!

Lightning McQueen hosts a charity racing event
for a brand new car: Timmy! But when Chick
Hicks shows up, tempers flare and matters can
only be settled in the RALLY RACE!

CARS: RALLY RACE
DIAMOND CODE: FEB100767
SC $9.99 ISBN 9781608865178

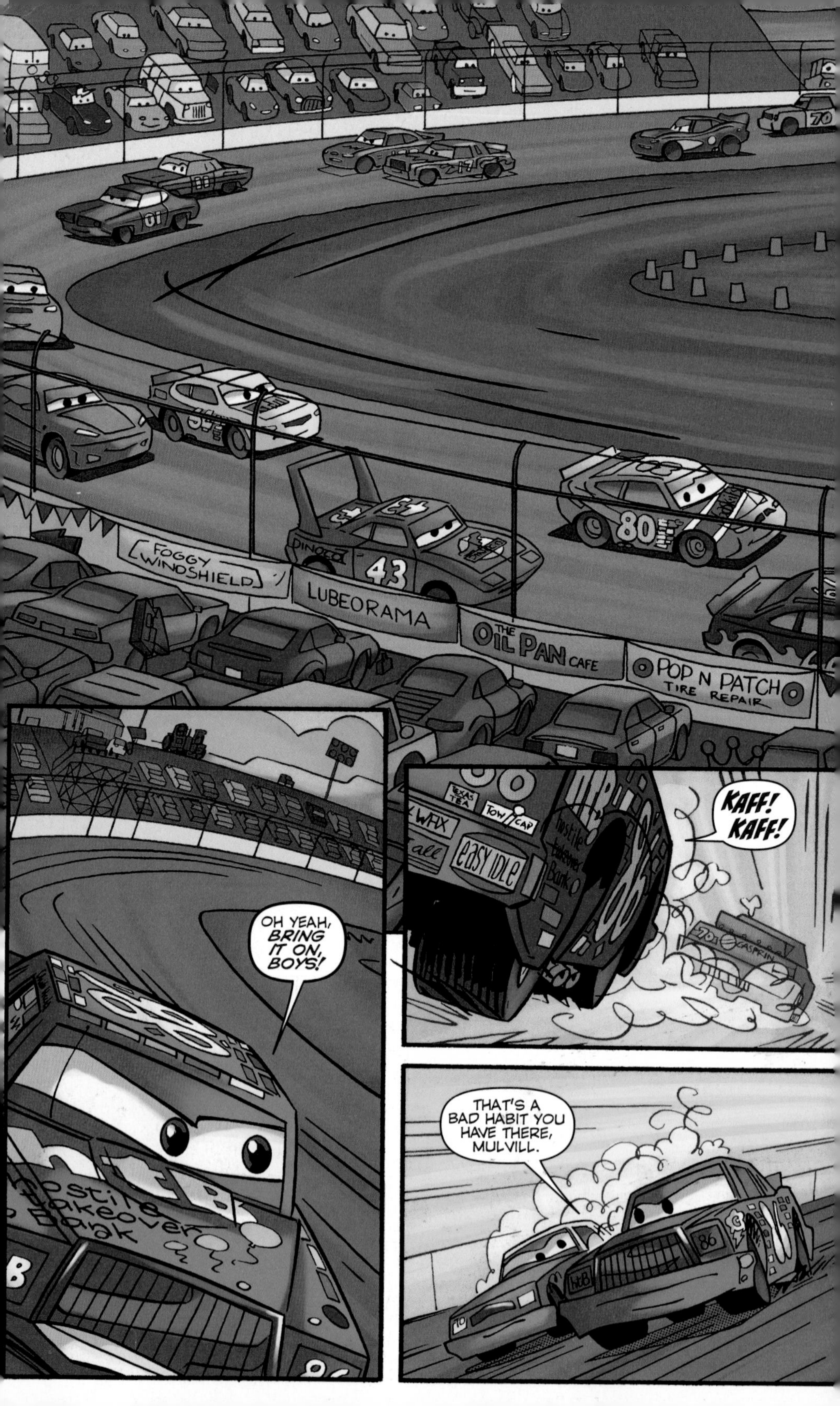

FOGGY WINDSHIELD
LUBEORAMA
THE OIL PAN CAFE
POP N PATCH TIRE REPAIR
OH YEAH, *BRING IT ON, BOYS!*
KAFF! KAFF!
THAT'S A BAD HABIT YOU HAVE THERE, MULVILL.

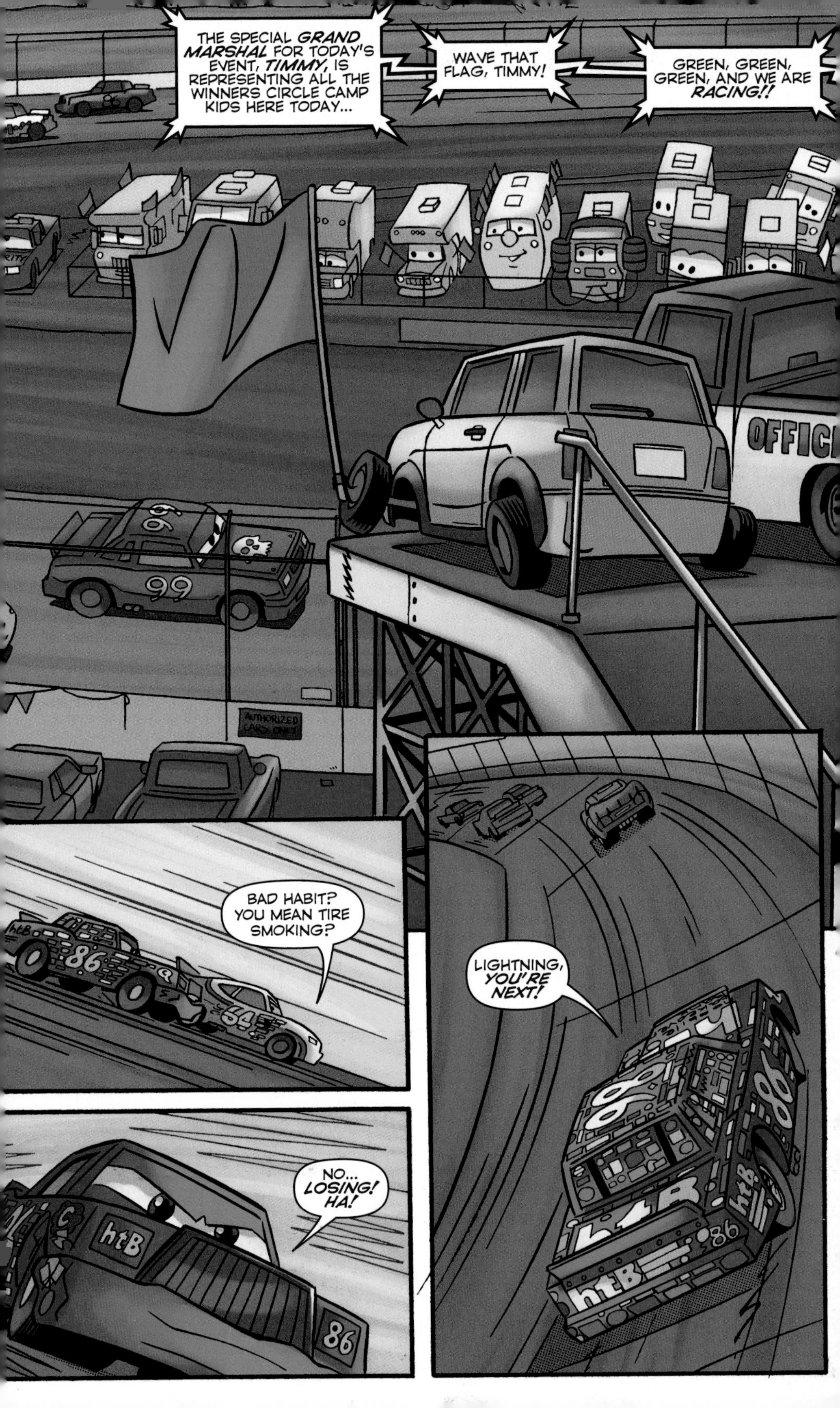

THE SPECIAL GRAND MARSHAL FOR TODAY'S EVENT, TIMMY, IS REPRESENTING ALL THE WINNERS CIRCLE CAMP KIDS HERE TODAY...
WAVE THAT FLAG, TIMMY!
GREEN, GREEN, GREEN, AND WE ARE RACING!!
OFFICI
AUTHORIZED CARS ONLY
BAD HABIT? YOU MEAN TIRE SMOKING?
NO... LOSING! HA!
LIGHTNING, YOU'RE NEXT!

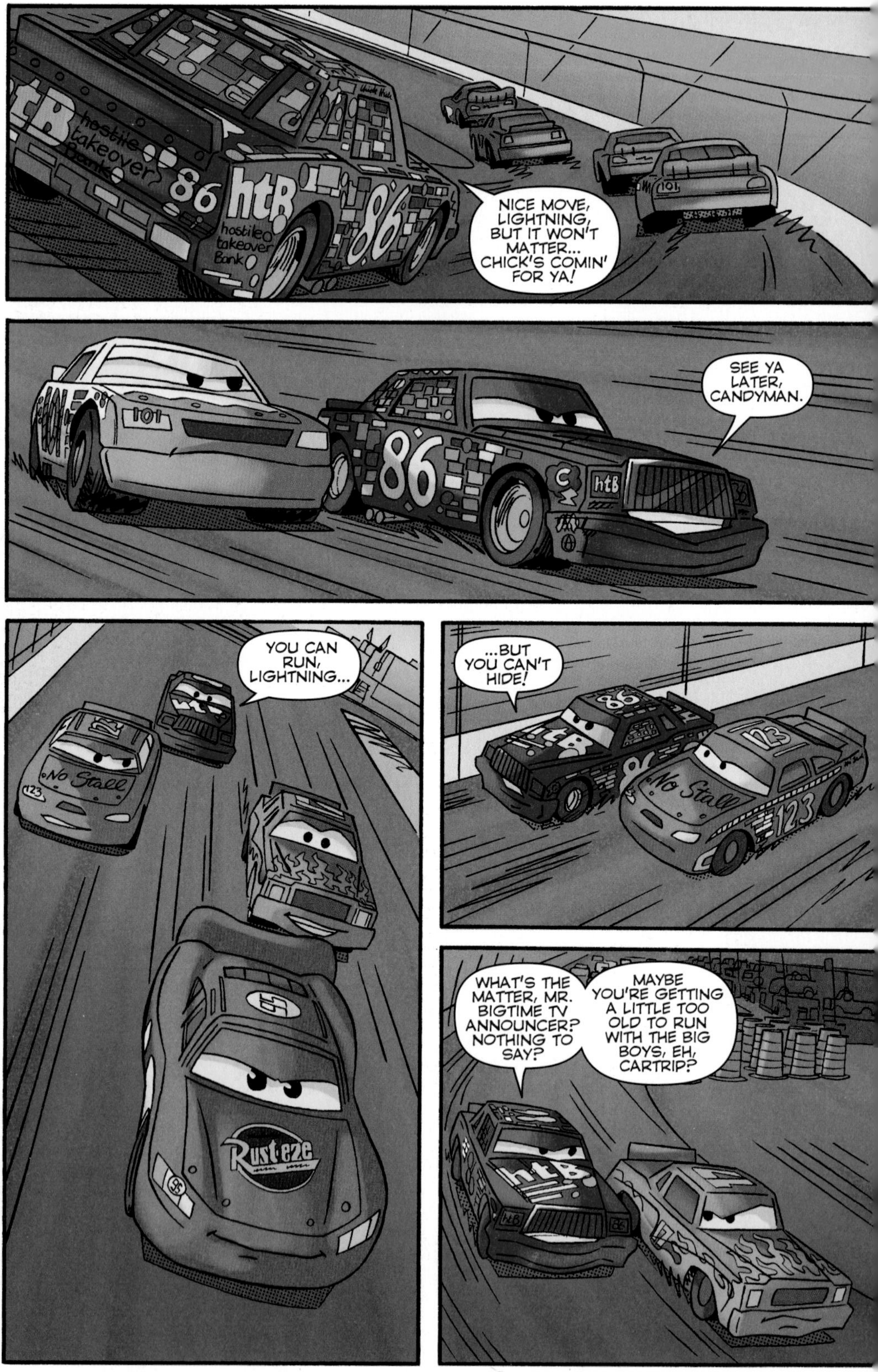
NICE MOVE, LIGHTNING, BUT IT WON'T MATTER... CHICK'S COMIN' FOR YA!
SEE YA LATER, CANDYMAN.
YOU CAN RUN, LIGHTNING...
...BUT YOU CAN'T HIDE!
WHAT'S THE MATTER, MR. BIGTIME TV ANNOUNCER? NOTHING TO SAY?
MAYBE YOU'RE GETTING A LITTLE TOO OLD TO RUN WITH THE BIG BOYS, EH, CARTRIP?

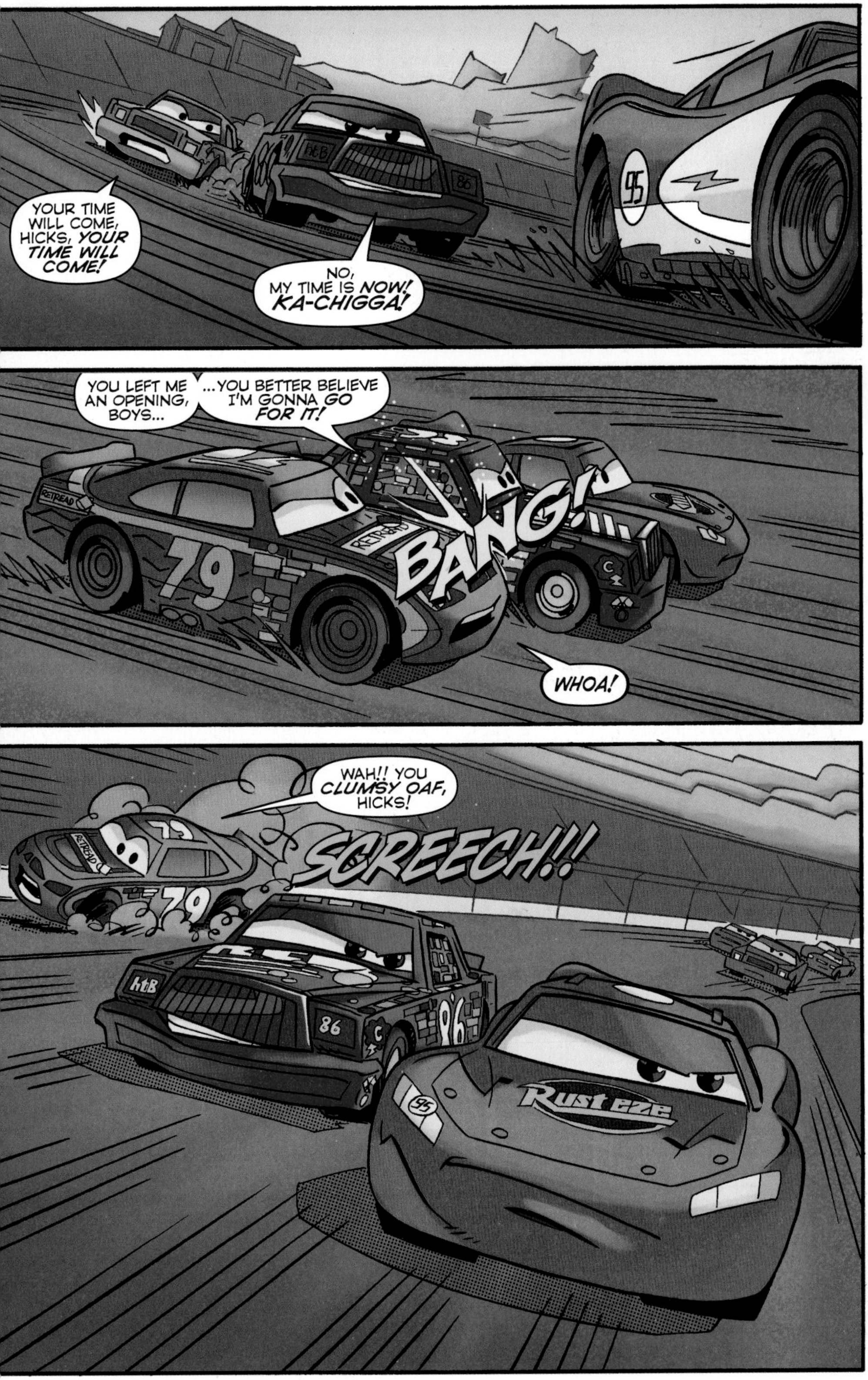
YOUR TIME WILL COME, HICKS, YOUR TIME WILL COME!
NO, MY TIME IS NOW! KA-CHIGGA!
YOU LEFT ME AN OPENING, BOYS...
...YOU BETTER BELIEVE I'M GONNA GO FOR IT!
BANG!
WHOA!
WAH!! YOU CLUMSY OAF, HICKS!
SCREECH!!
Rust eze

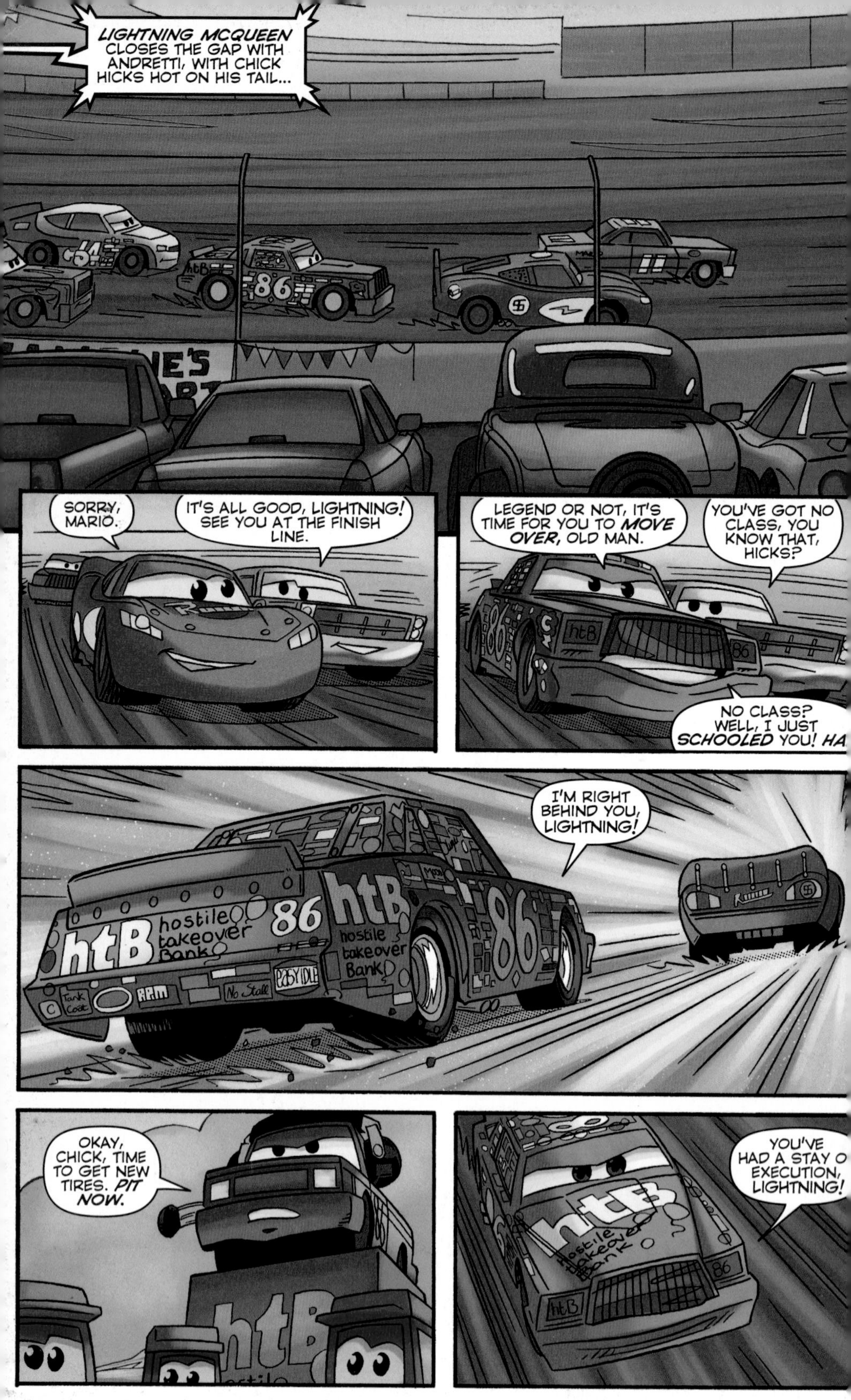
LIGHTNING MCQUEEN CLOSES THE GAP WITH ANDRETTI, WITH CHICK HICKS HOT ON HIS TAIL...
SORRY, MARIO.
IT'S ALL GOOD, LIGHTNING! SEE YOU AT THE FINISH LINE.
LEGEND OR NOT, IT'S TIME FOR YOU TO MOVE OVER, OLD MAN.
YOU'VE GOT NO CLASS, YOU KNOW THAT, HICKS?
NO CLASS? WELL, I JUST SCHOOLED YOU! HA
I'M RIGHT BEHIND YOU, LIGHTNING!
htB hostile takeover Bank
86
OKAY, CHICK, TIME TO GET NEW TIRES. PIT NOW.
YOU'VE HAD A STAY O EXECUTION, LIGHTNING!

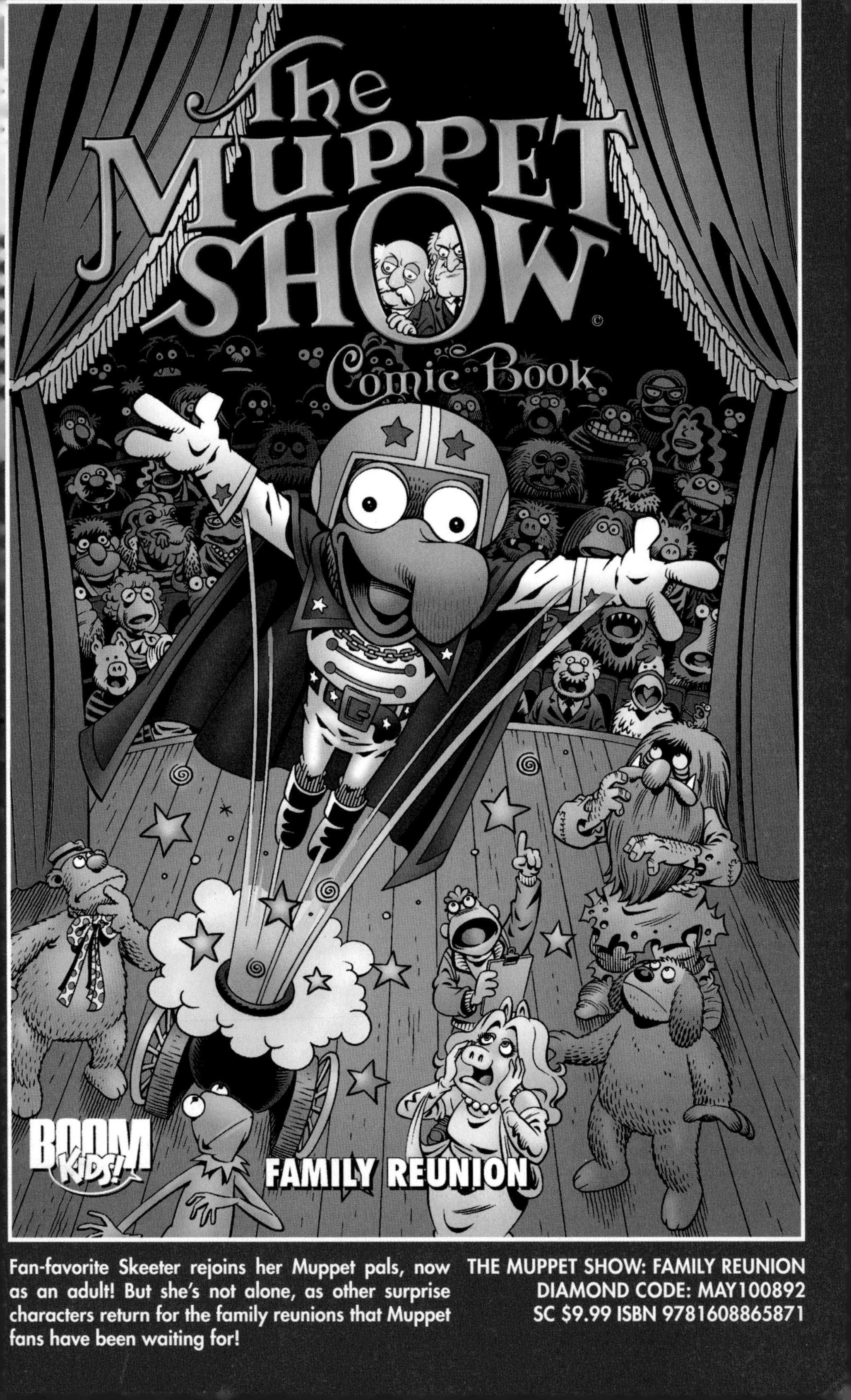
The Muppet Show
Comic Book
BOOM KIDS!
FAMILY REUNION

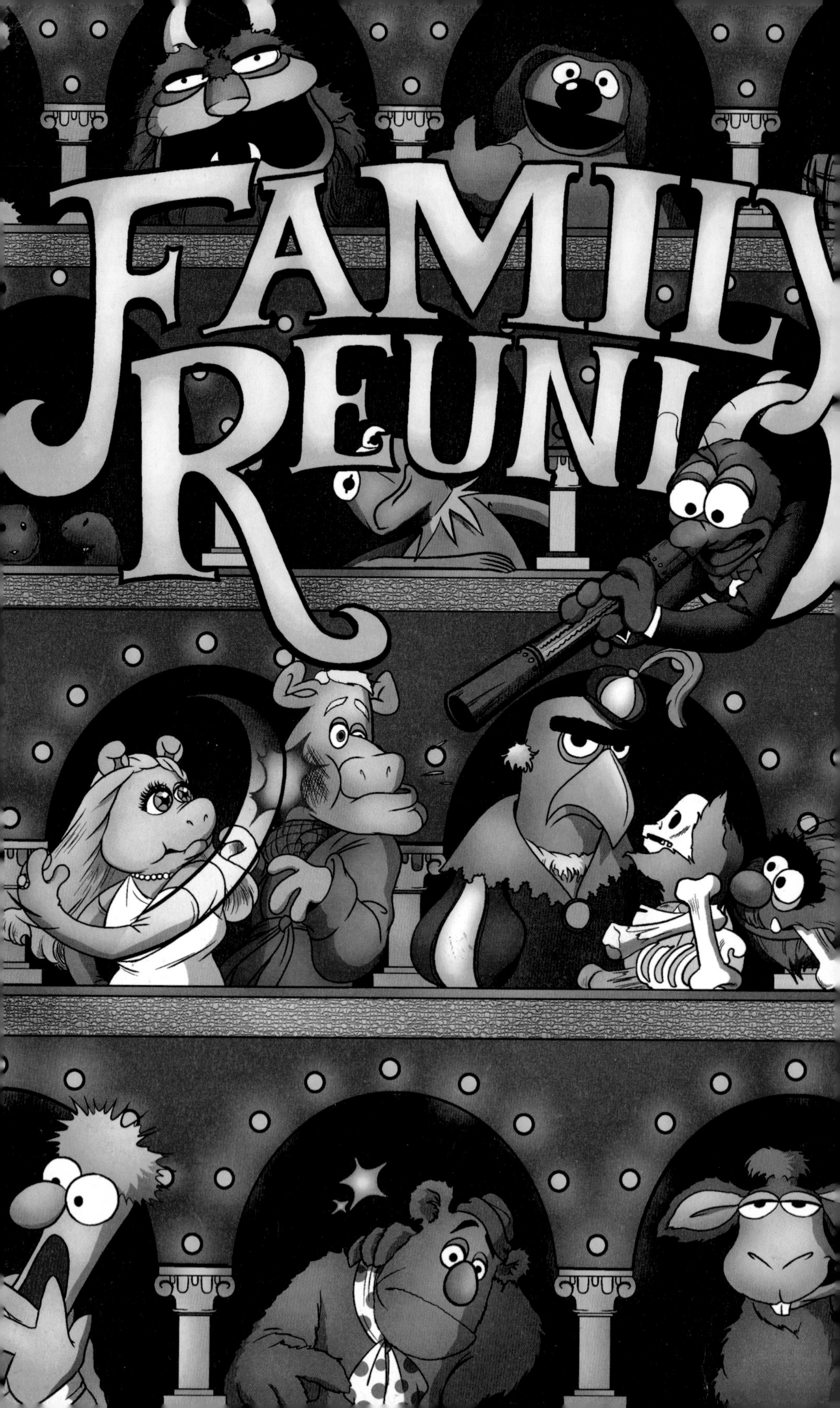
FAMILY REUNI

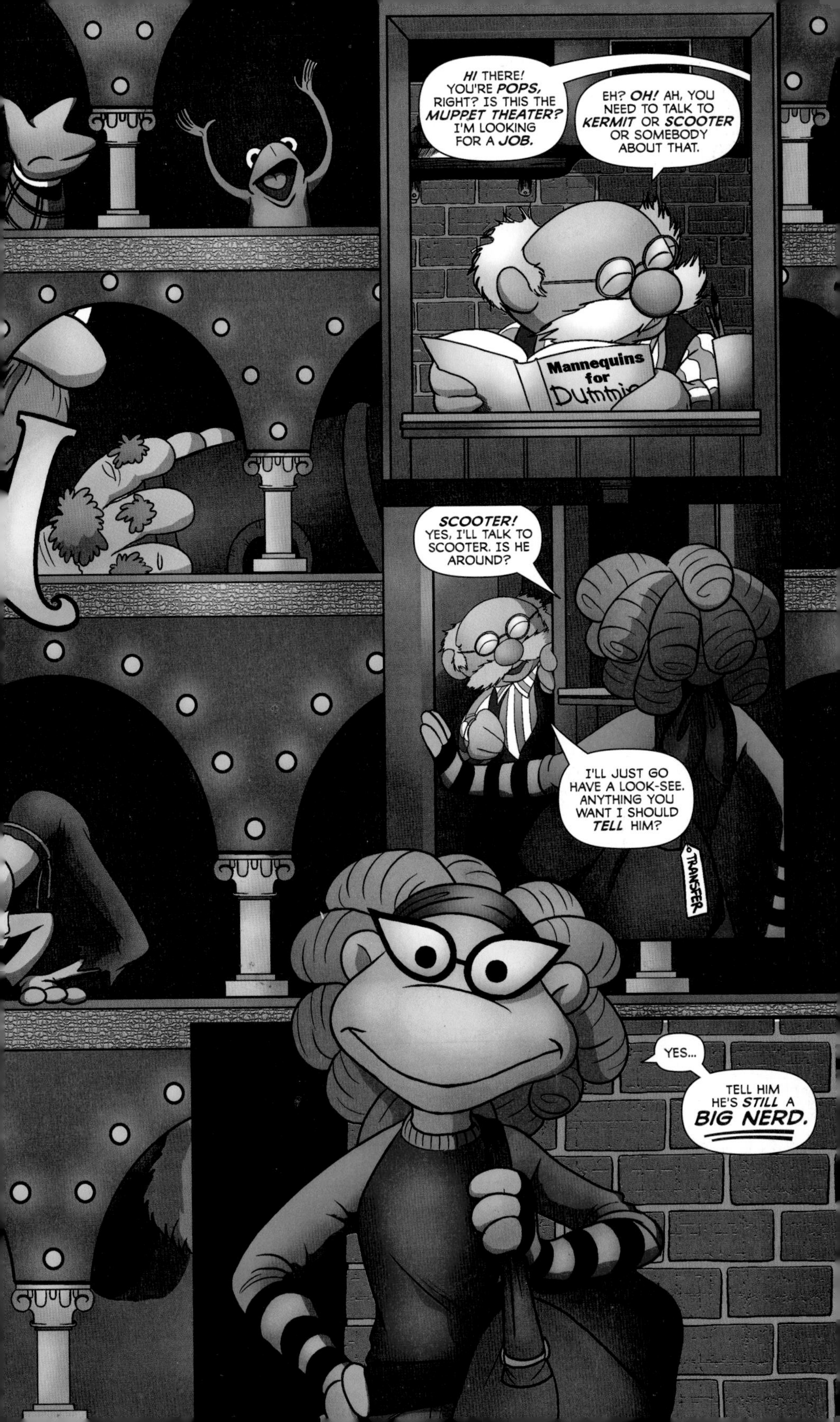
HI THERE! YOU'RE POPS, RIGHT? IS THIS THE MUPPET THEATER? I'M LOOKING FOR A JOB.
EH? OH! AH, YOU NEED TO TALK TO KERMIT OR SCOOTER OR SOMEBODY ABOUT THAT.
Mannequins for Dummies
SCOOTER! YES, I'LL TALK TO SCOOTER. IS HE AROUND?
I'LL JUST GO HAVE A LOOK-SEE. ANYTHING YOU WANT I SHOULD TELL HIM?
TRANSFER
YES...
TELL HIM HE'S STILL A BIG NERD.

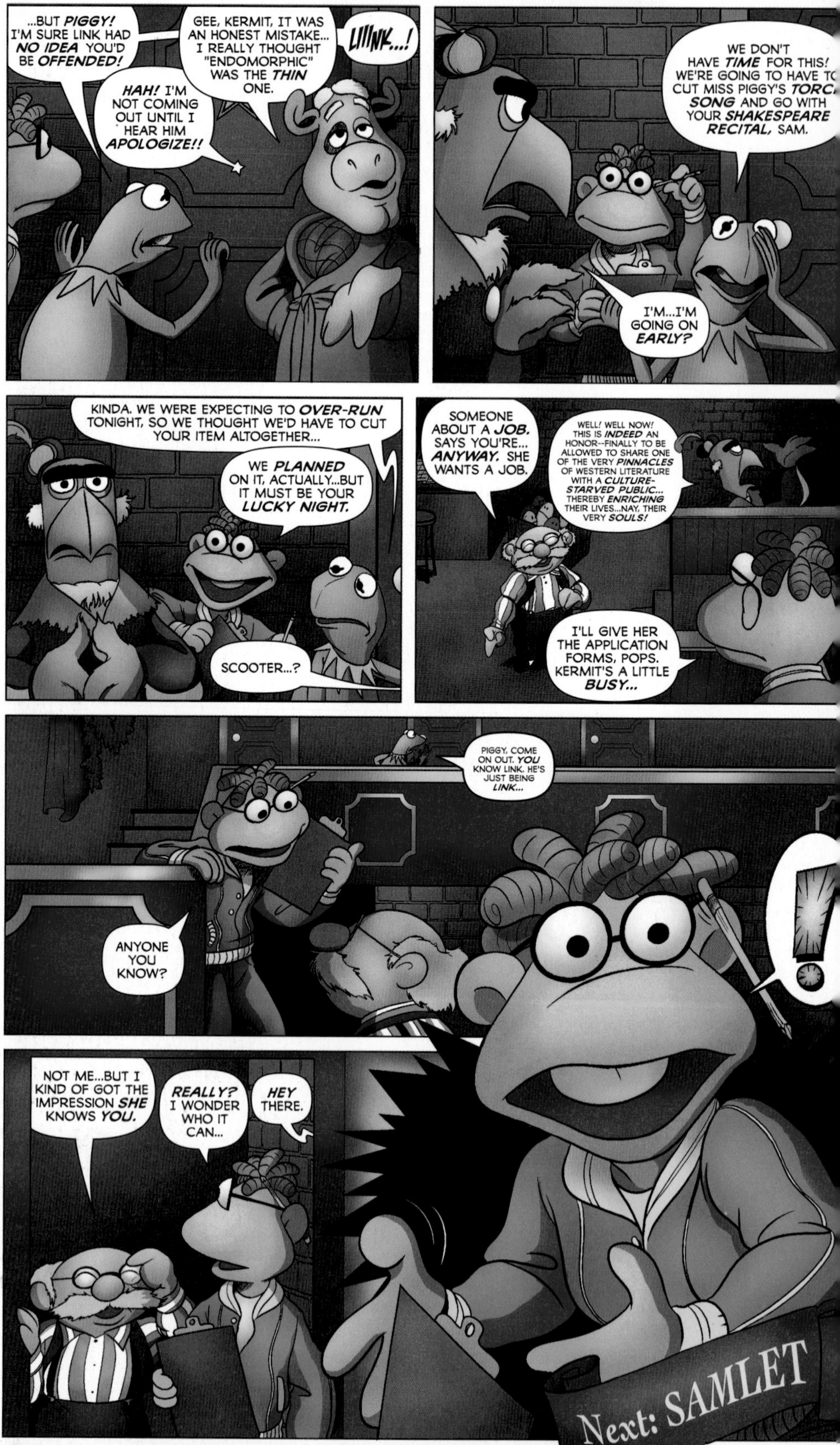
...BUT PIGGY! I'M SURE LINK HAD NO IDEA YOU'D BE OFFENDED!
HAH! I'M NOT COMING OUT UNTIL I HEAR HIM APOLOGIZE!!
GEE, KERMIT, IT WAS AN HONEST MISTAKE... I REALLY THOUGHT "ENDOMORPHIC" WAS THE THIN ONE.
LIIIINK...!
WE DON'T HAVE TIME FOR THIS! WE'RE GOING TO HAVE TO CUT MISS PIGGY'S TORCH SONG AND GO WITH YOUR SHAKESPEARE RECITAL, SAM.
I'M...I'M GOING ON EARLY?
KINDA. WE WERE EXPECTING TO OVER-RUN TONIGHT, SO WE THOUGHT WE'D HAVE TO CUT YOUR ITEM ALTOGETHER...
WE PLANNED ON IT, ACTUALLY...BUT IT MUST BE YOUR LUCKY NIGHT.
SCOOTER...?
SOMEONE ABOUT A JOB. SAYS YOU'RE... ANYWAY. SHE WANTS A JOB.
WELL! WELL NOW! THIS IS INDEED AN HONOR--FINALLY TO BE ALLOWED TO SHARE ONE OF THE VERY PINNACLES OF WESTERN LITERATURE WITH A CULTURE-STARVED PUBLIC... THEREBY ENRICHING THEIR LIVES...NAY, THEIR VERY SOULS!
I'LL GIVE HER THE APPLICATION FORMS, POPS. KERMIT'S A LITTLE BUSY...
PIGGY, COME ON OUT. YOU KNOW LINK. HE'S JUST BEING LINK...
ANYONE YOU KNOW?
!
NOT ME...BUT I KIND OF GOT THE IMPRESSION SHE KNOWS YOU.
REALLY? I WONDER WHO IT CAN...
HEY THERE.
Next: SAMLET

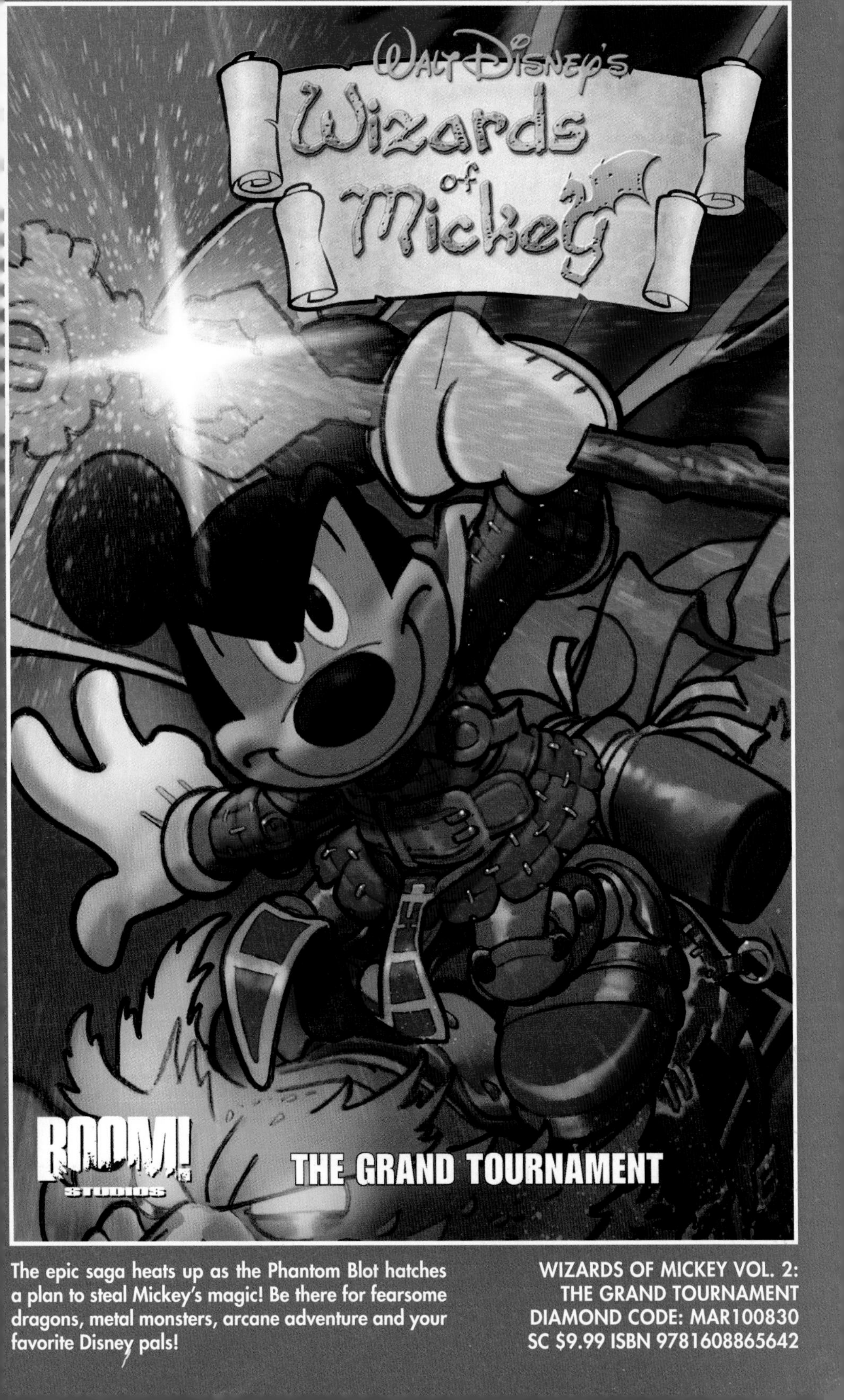
Walt Disney's
Wizards of Mickey
BOOM! STUDIOS
THE GRAND TOURNAMENT

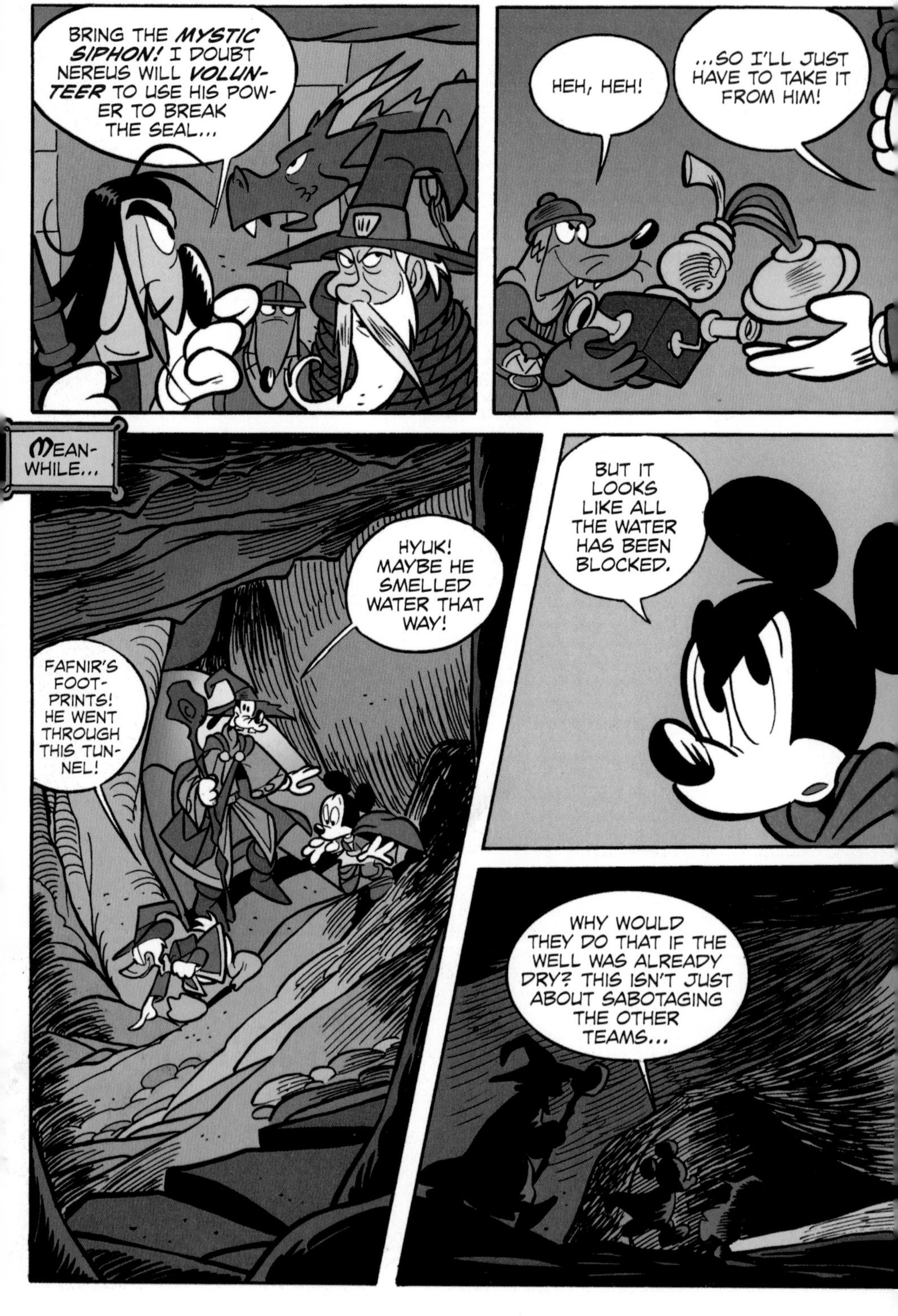
BRING THE *MYSTIC SIPHON!* I DOUBT NEREUS WILL *VOLUNTEER* TO USE HIS POWER TO BREAK THE SEAL...
HEH, HEH!
...SO I'LL JUST HAVE TO TAKE IT FROM HIM!
MEANWHILE...
FAFNIR'S FOOTPRINTS! HE WENT THROUGH THIS TUNNEL!
HYUK! MAYBE HE SMELLED WATER THAT WAY!
BUT IT LOOKS LIKE ALL THE WATER HAS BEEN BLOCKED.
WHY WOULD THEY DO THAT IF THE WELL WAS ALREADY DRY? THIS ISN'T JUST ABOUT SABOTAGING THE OTHER TEAMS...

"...SOMETHING FUNNY IS GOING ON HERE."

I KNOW JUST HOW TO GET RID OF THAT PESKY MOUSE! TAKE THE CLOAK OF INVISIBILITY...

...FOLLOW THOSE THREE UNTIL THEY GET TO THE BRIDGE...

AND WHEN THEY START TO CROSS, DESTROY IT!"

CRUNK

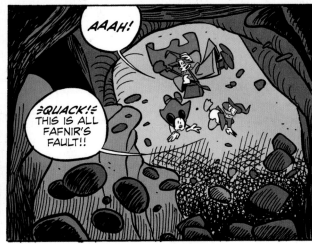

AAAH!

≠QUACK!≠ THIS IS ALL FAFNIR'S FAULT!!

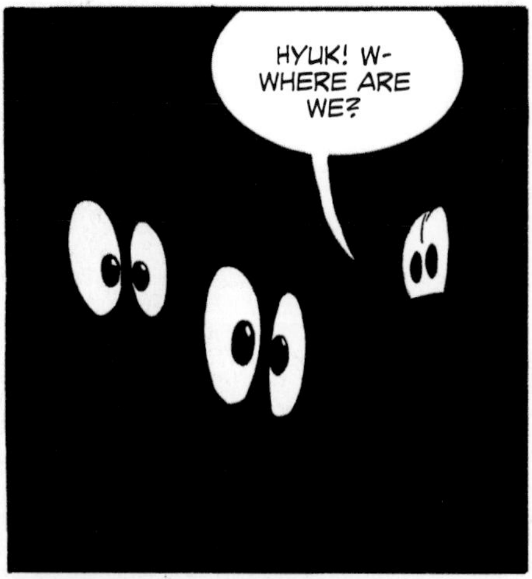
HYUK! W-WHERE ARE WE?

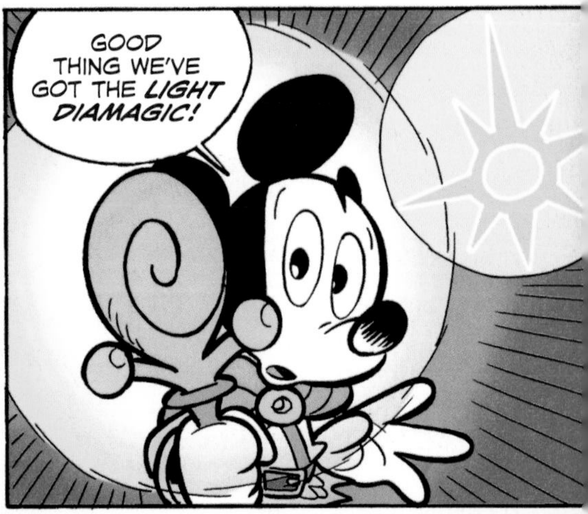
GOOD THING WE'VE GOT THE *LIGHT DIAMAGIC!*

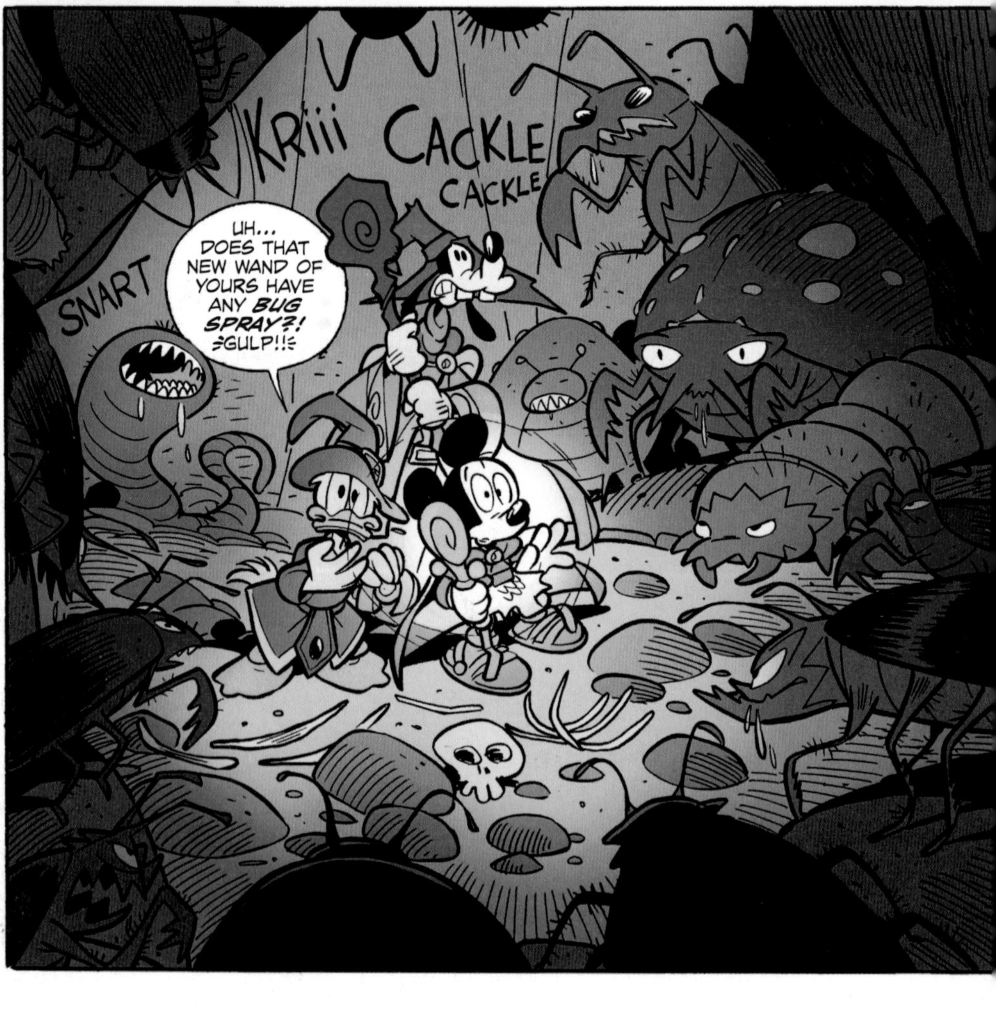
KRiii
CACKLE
CACKLE
SNART
UH... DOES THAT NEW WAND OF YOURS HAVE ANY *BUG SPRAY?!*
GULP!!

MONSTERS, INC.

LAUGH FACTORY

Someone is stealing comedy props from the other employees, making it hard for them to harvest the laughter they need to power Monstropolis...and all evidence points to Sulley's best friend, Mike Wazowski!

MONSTERS, INC.: LAUGH FACTORY
DIAMOND CODE: OCT090801
SC $9.99 ISBN 9781608865086
HC $24.99 ISBN 9781608865338

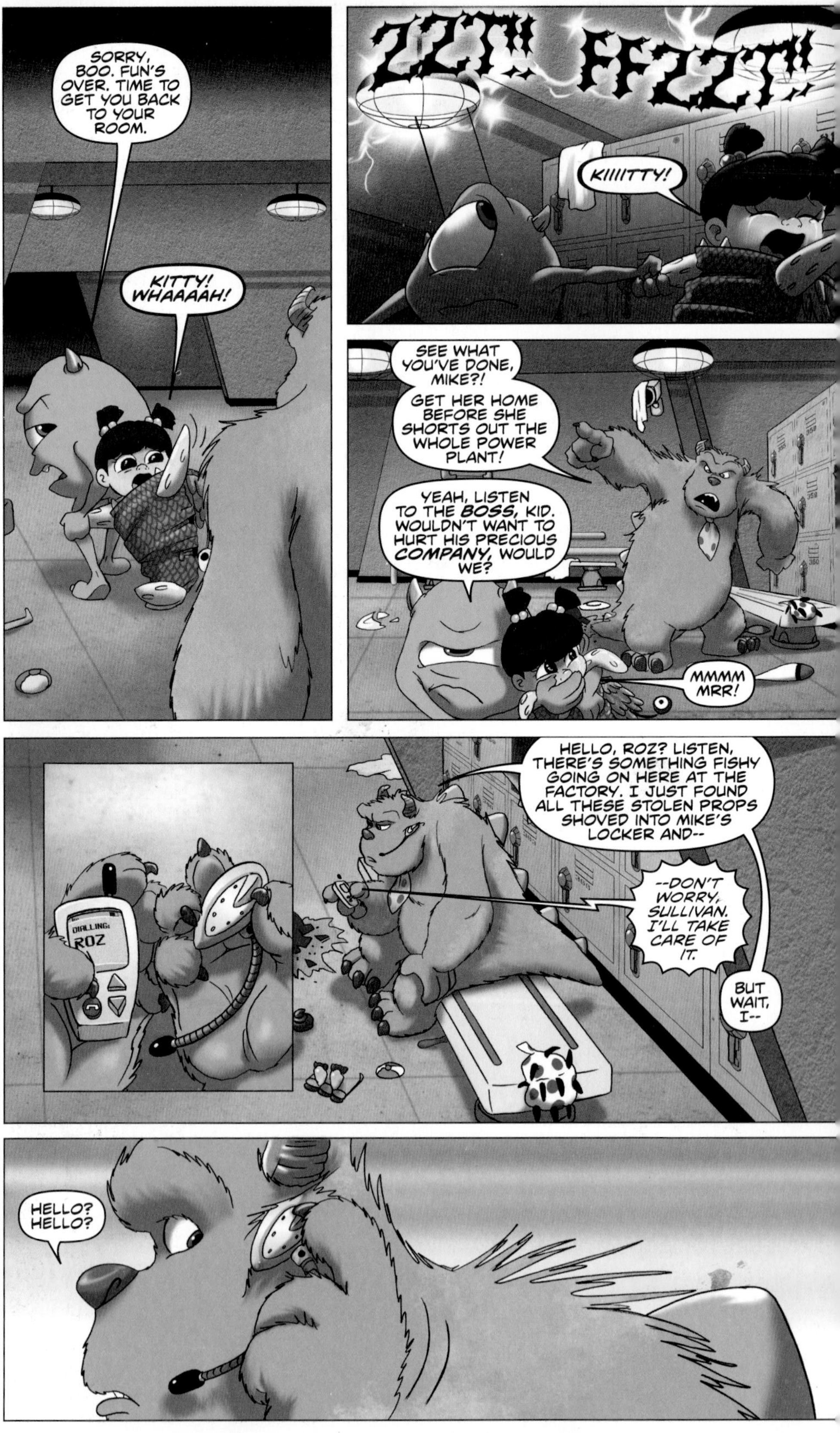
SORRY, BOO. FUN'S OVER. TIME TO GET YOU BACK TO YOUR ROOM.
KITTY! WHAAAAAH!
ZZZT!! FFZZZT!!
KIIIITTY!
SEE WHAT YOU'VE DONE, MIKE?!
GET HER HOME BEFORE SHE SHORTS OUT THE WHOLE POWER PLANT!
YEAH, LISTEN TO THE BOSS, KID. WOULDN'T WANT TO HURT HIS PRECIOUS COMPANY, WOULD WE?
MMMM MRR!
DIALLING: ROZ
HELLO, ROZ? LISTEN, THERE'S SOMETHING FISHY GOING ON HERE AT THE FACTORY. I JUST FOUND ALL THESE STOLEN PROPS SHOVED INTO MIKE'S LOCKER AND--
--DON'T WORRY, SULLIVAN. I'LL TAKE CARE OF IT.
BUT WAIT, I--
HELLO? HELLO?

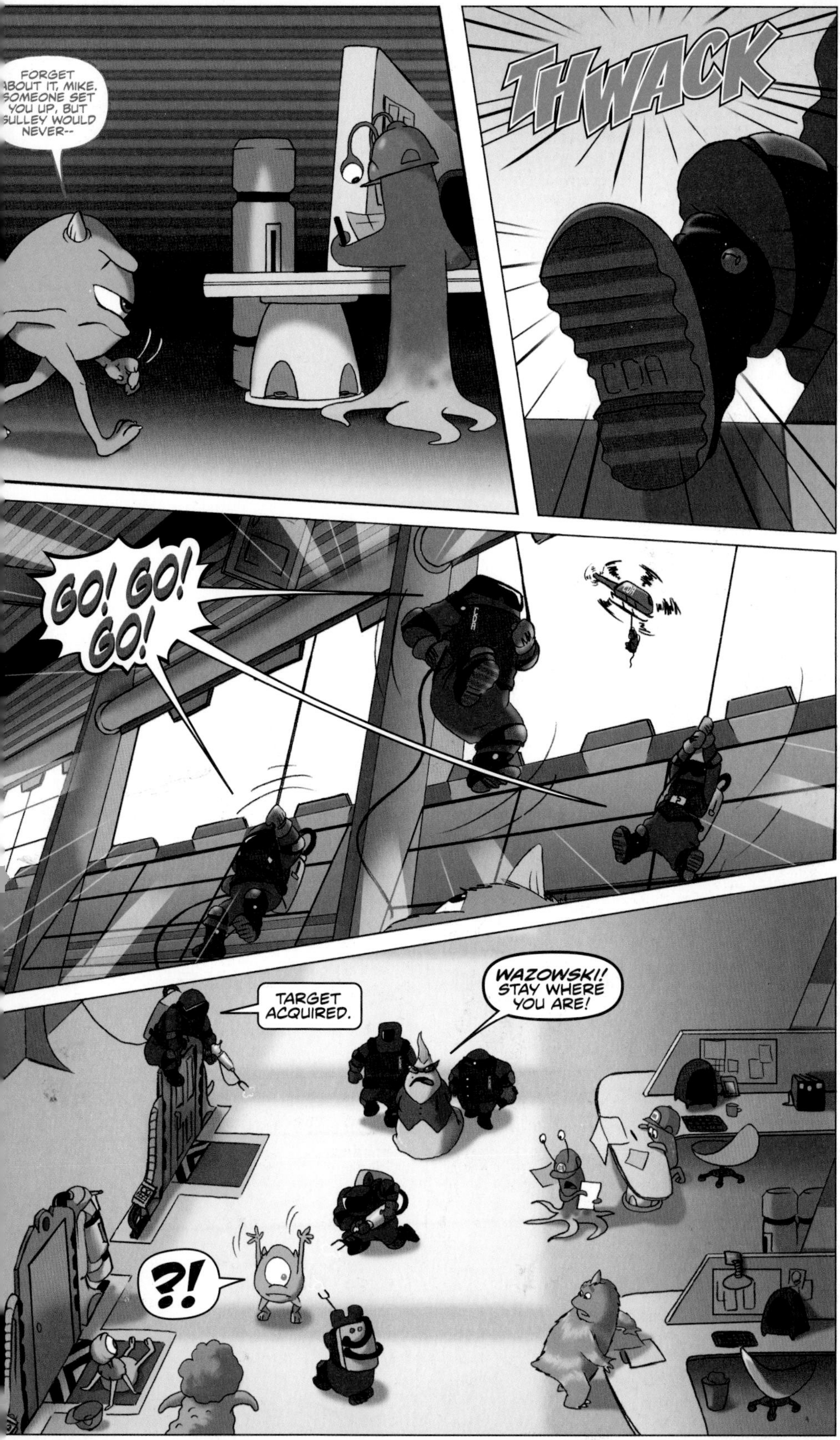

FORGET ABOUT IT, MIKE. SOMEONE SET YOU UP, BUT SULLEY WOULD NEVER--
THWACK
GO! GO! GO!
TARGET ACQUIRED.
WAZOWSKI! STAY WHERE YOU ARE!
?!

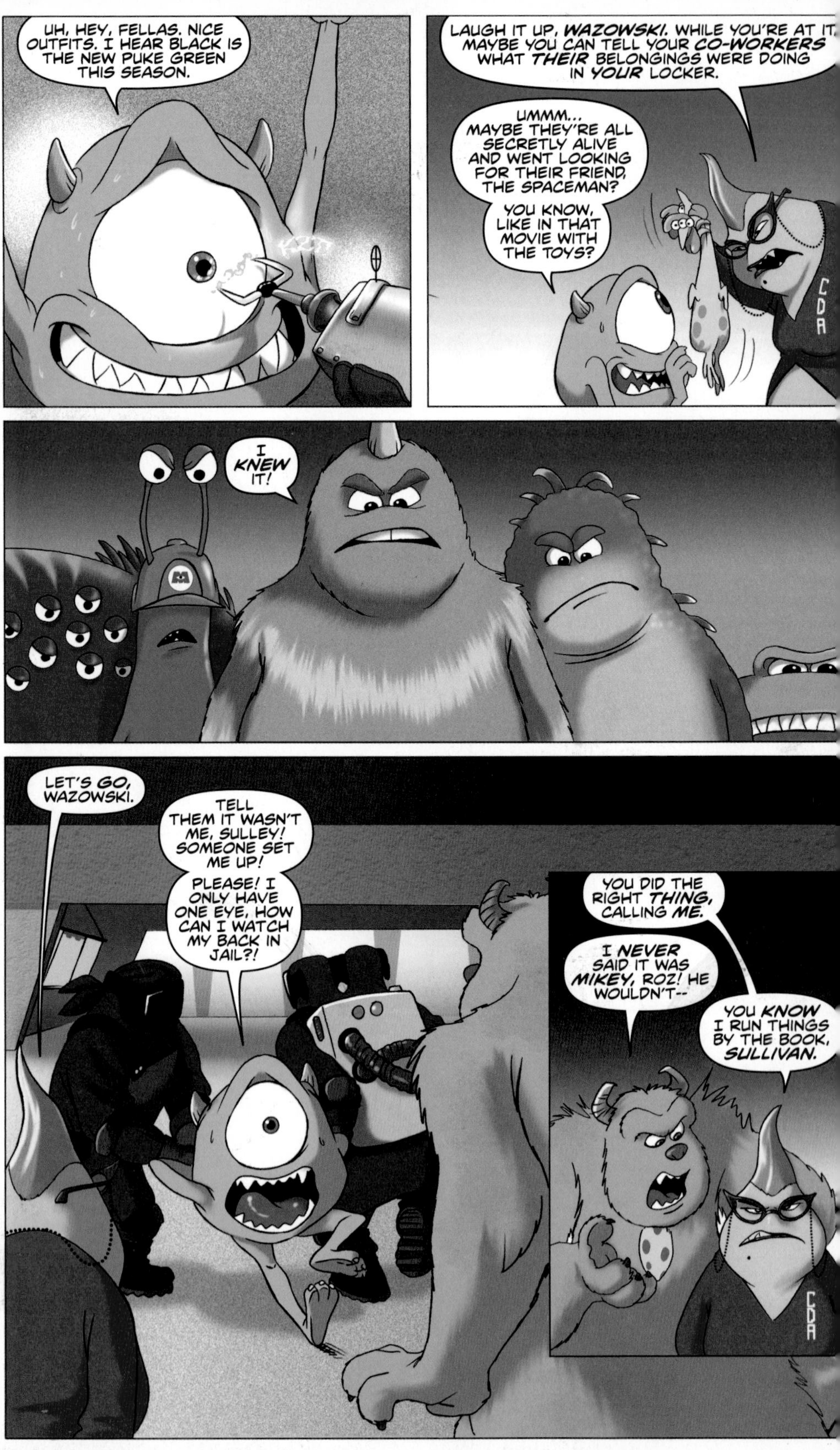
UH, HEY, FELLAS. NICE OUTFITS. I HEAR BLACK IS THE NEW PUKE GREEN THIS SEASON.
LAUGH IT UP, WAZOWSKI. WHILE YOU'RE AT IT, MAYBE YOU CAN TELL YOUR CO-WORKERS WHAT THEIR BELONGINGS WERE DOING IN YOUR LOCKER.
UMMM... MAYBE THEY'RE ALL SECRETLY ALIVE AND WENT LOOKING FOR THEIR FRIEND, THE SPACEMAN?
YOU KNOW, LIKE IN THAT MOVIE WITH THE TOYS?
CDA
I KNEW IT!
LET'S GO, WAZOWSKI.
TELL THEM IT WASN'T ME, SULLEY! SOMEONE SET ME UP!
PLEASE! I ONLY HAVE ONE EYE, HOW CAN I WATCH MY BACK IN JAIL?!
YOU DID THE RIGHT THING, CALLING ME.
I NEVER SAID IT WAS MIKEY, ROZ! HE WOULDN'T--
YOU KNOW I RUN THINGS BY THE BOOK, SULLIVAN.
CDA

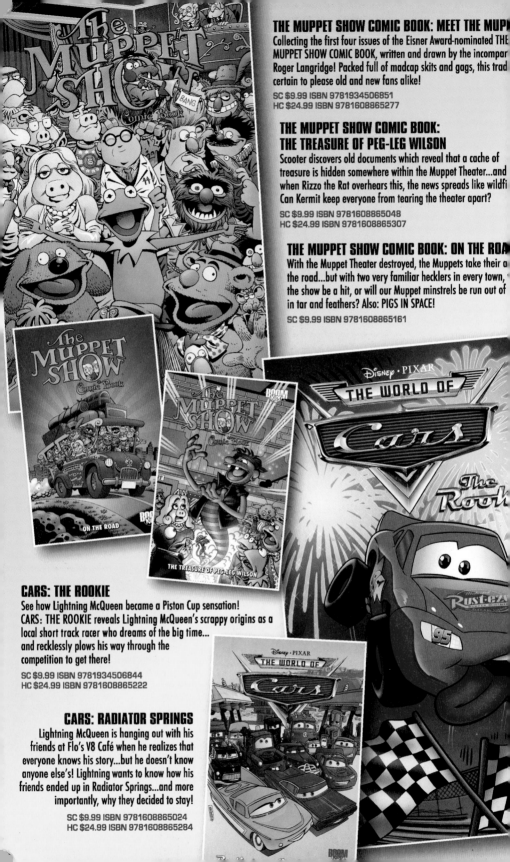

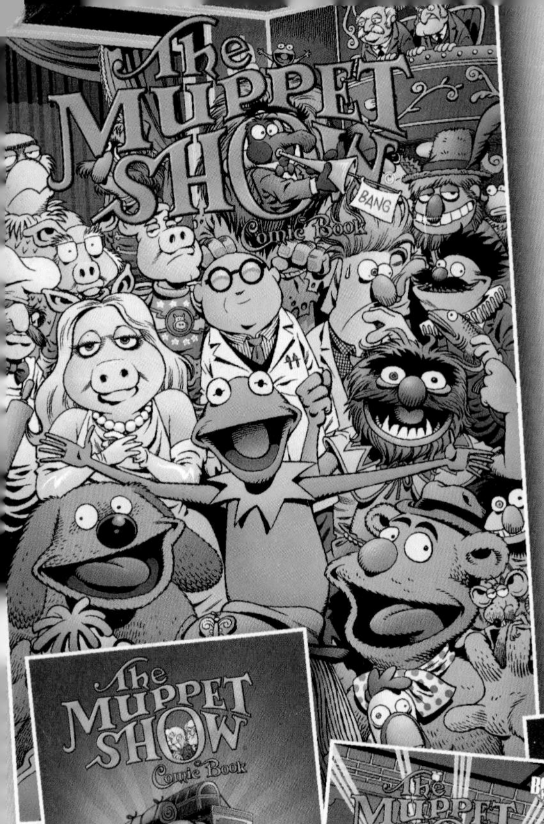
The Muppet Show Comic Book
BANG

THE MUPPET SHOW COMIC BOOK: MEET THE MUPP

Collecting the first four issues of the Eisner Award-nominated THE MUPPET SHOW COMIC BOOK, written and drawn by the incompar Roger Langridge! Packed full of madcap skits and gags, this trad certain to please old and new fans alike!

SC $9.99 ISBN 9781934506851
HC $24.99 ISBN 9781608865277

THE MUPPET SHOW COMIC BOOK: THE TREASURE OF PEG-LEG WILSON

Scooter discovers old documents which reveal that a cache of treasure is hidden somewhere within the Muppet Theater...and when Rizzo the Rat overhears this, the news spreads like wildfi Can Kermit keep everyone from tearing the theater apart?

SC $9.99 ISBN 9781608865048
HC $24.99 ISBN 9781608865307

THE MUPPET SHOW COMIC BOOK: ON THE ROA

With the Muppet Theater destroyed, the Muppets take their a the road...but with two very familiar hecklers in every town, the show be a hit, or will our Muppet minstrels be run out of in tar and feathers? Also: PIGS IN SPACE!

SC $9.99 ISBN 9781608865161

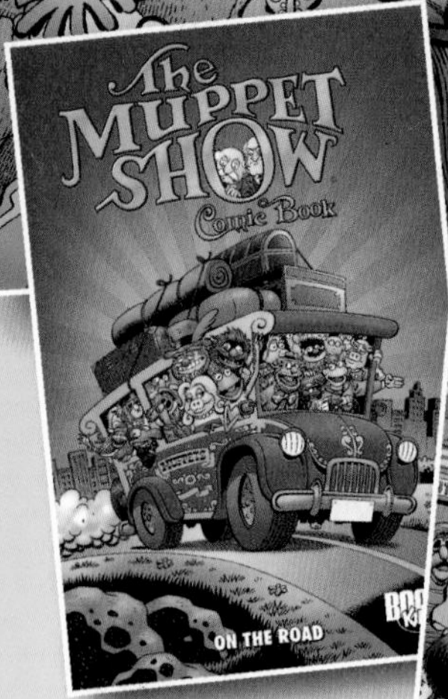
The Muppet Show Comic Book
ON THE ROAD

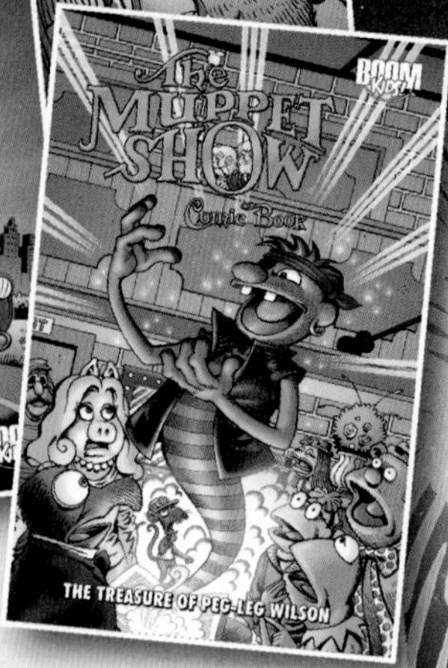
The Muppet Show Comic Book
BOOM KIDS!
THE TREASURE OF PEG-LEG WILSON

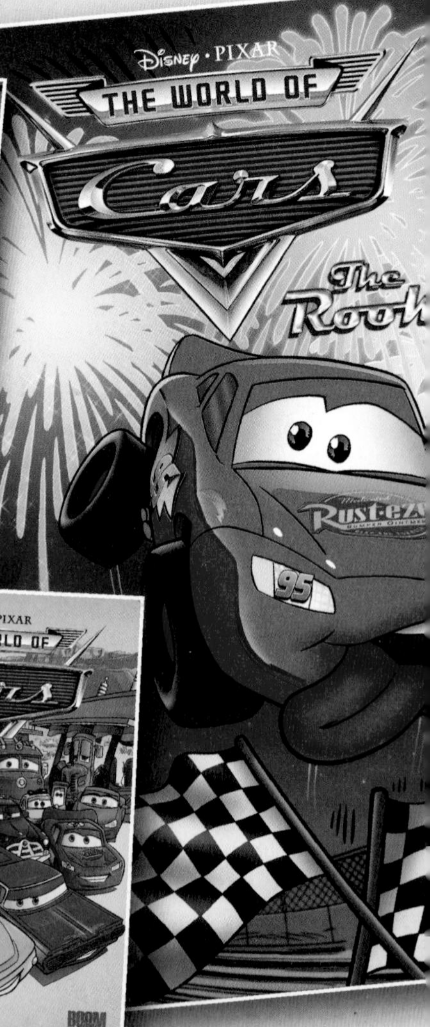
Disney · PIXAR
THE WORLD OF
Cars
The Rook
Rust-eze
95

CARS: THE ROOKIE

See how Lightning McQueen became a Piston Cup sensation! CARS: THE ROOKIE reveals Lightning McQueen's scrappy origins as a local short track racer who dreams of the big time... and recklessly plows his way through the competition to get there!

SC $9.99 ISBN 9781934506844
HC $24.99 ISBN 9781608865222

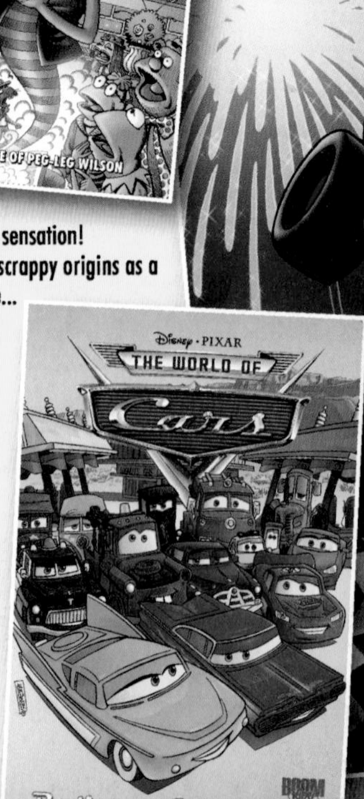
Disney · PIXAR
THE WORLD OF
Cars

CARS: RADIATOR SPRINGS

Lightning McQueen is hanging out with his friends at Flo's V8 Café when he realizes that everyone knows his story...but he doesn't know anyone else's! Lightning wants to know how his friends ended up in Radiator Springs...and more importantly, why they decided to stay!

SC $9.99 ISBN 9781608865024
HC $24.99 ISBN 9781608865284

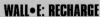

WALL•E: RECHARGE

e WALL•E becomes the hardworking robot we know and love, he he few remaining robots take care of the trash compacting while e collects interesting junk. But when these robots start breaking wn, WALL•E must adjust his priorities...or else Earth is doomed!

SC $9.99 ISBN 9781608865123
HC $24.99 ISBN 9781608865543

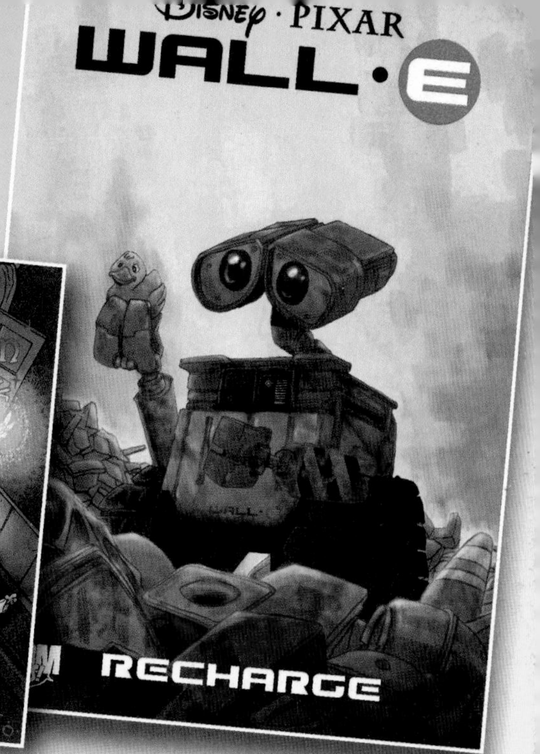
DISNEY · PIXAR
WALL·E
RECHARGE

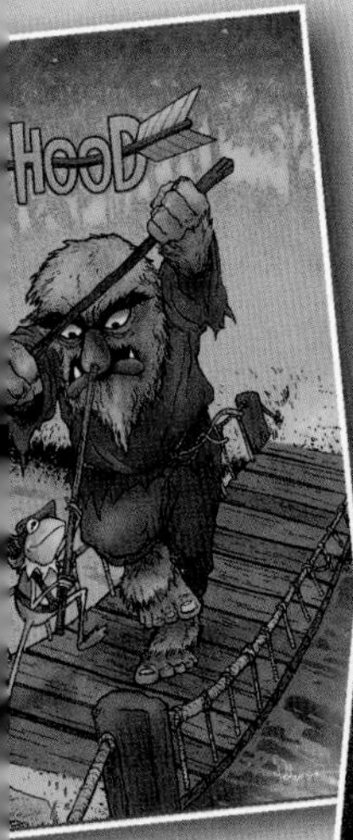
Hood

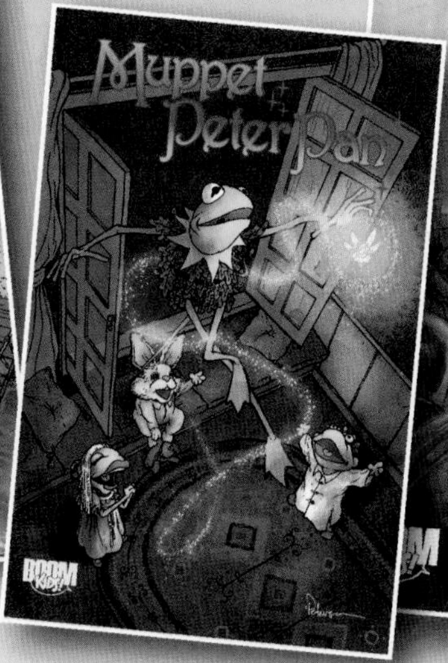
Muppet
Peter Pan

PET ROBIN HOOD

uppets tell the Robin Hood legend for laughs, and it's the reader who will be merry! Hood (Kermit the Frog) joins with the Merry Men, Sherwood Forest's infamous gang of outlaws, to take on the Sheriff of Nottingham (Sam the Eagle)!

.99 ISBN 9781934506790
4.99 ISBN 9781608865260

MUPPET PETER PAN

When Peter Pan (Kermit) whisks Wendy (Janice) and her brothers to Neverswamp, the adventure begins! With Captain Hook (Gonzo) out for revenge for the loss of his hand, can even the magic of Piggytink (Miss Piggy) save Wendy and her brothers?

SC $9.99 ISBN 9781608865079
HC $24.99 ISBN 9781608865314

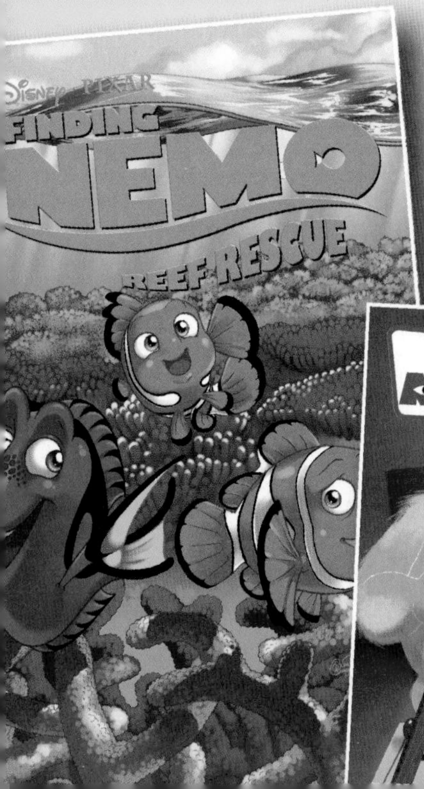
FINDING
NEMO
REEF RESCUE

FINDING NEMO: REEF RESCUE

Nemo, Dory and Marlin have become local heroes, and are recruited to embark on an all-new adventure in this exciting collection! The reef is mysteriously dying and no one knows why. So Nemo and his friends must travel the great blue sea to save their home!

SC $9.99 ISBN 9781934506882
HC $24.99 ISBN 9781608865246

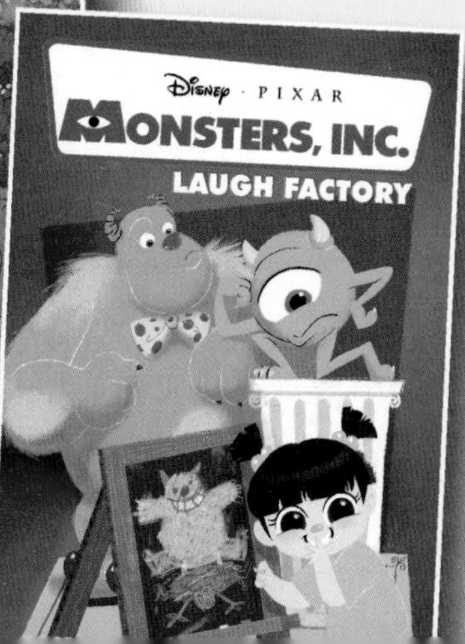
Disney · PIXAR
MONSTERS, INC.
LAUGH FACTORY

MONSTERS, INC.: LAUGH FACTORY

Someone is stealing comedy props from the other employees, making it difficult for them to harvest the laughter they need to power Monstropolis...and all evidence points to Sulley's best friend Mike Wazowski!

SC $9.99 ISBN 9781608865086
HC $24.99 ISBN 9781608865338

DISNEY'S HERO SQUAD: ULTRAHEROES VOL. 1: SAVE THE WORLD

It's an all-star cast of your favorite Disney characters, as you have never seen them before. Join Donald Duck, Goofy, Daisy, and even Mickey himself as they defend the fate of the planet as the one and only Ultraheroes!

SC $9.99 ISBN 9781608865437
HC $24.99 ISBN 9781608865529

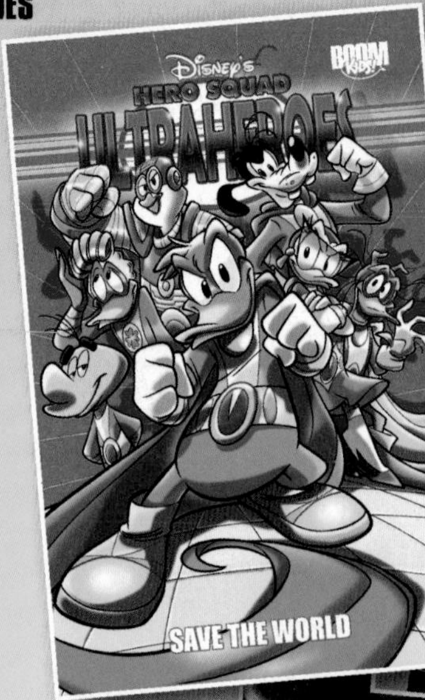
Disney's
HERO SQUAD
ULTRAHEROES
BOOM KIDS!
SAVE THE WORLD

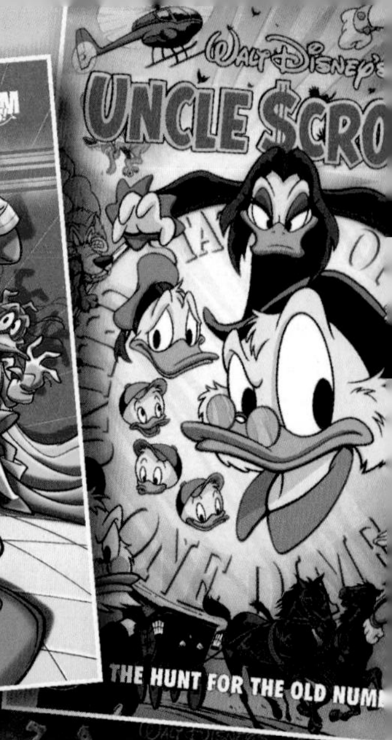
Walt Disney's
UNCLE $CRO
THE HUNT FOR THE OLD NUM

UNCLE SCROOGE: THE HUNT FOR THE OLD NUMBER ONE

Join Donald Duck's favorite penny-pinching Uncle Scrooge as he, Donald himself and Huey, Dewey, and Louie embark on a globe-spanning trek to recover treasure and save Scrooge's "number one dime" from the treacherous Magica De Spell.

SC $9.99 ISBN 9781608865475
HC $24.99 ISBN 9781608865536

WIZARDS OF MICKEY VOL. 1: MOUSE MAGIC

Your favorite Disney characters star in this magical fantasy epic! Student of the great wizard Nereus, Mickey allies himself with Donald and teammate Goofy, in a quest to find a magical crown that will give him mastery over all spells!

SC $9.99 ISBN 9781608865413
HC $24.99 ISBN 9781608865505

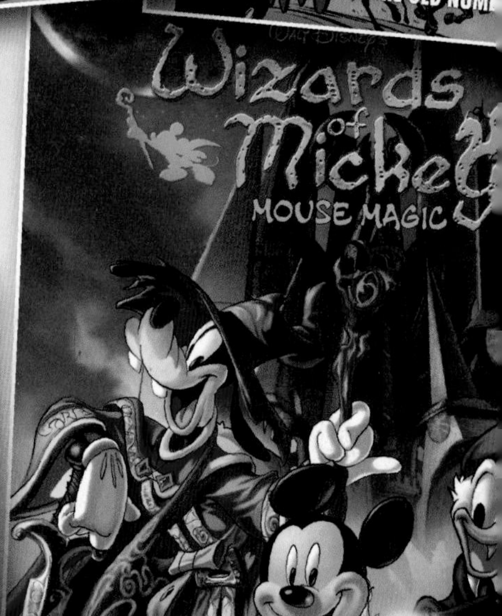
Wizards of Mickey
MOUSE MAGIC
BOOM! STUDIOS

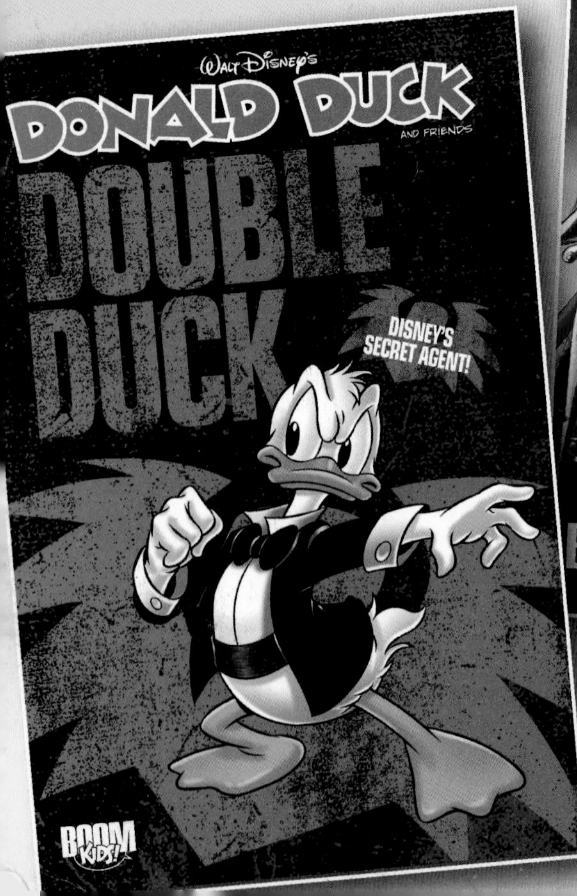
Walt Disney's
DONALD DUCK
AND FRIENDS
DOUBLE DUCK
DISNEY'S SECRET AGENT!
BOOM KIDS!

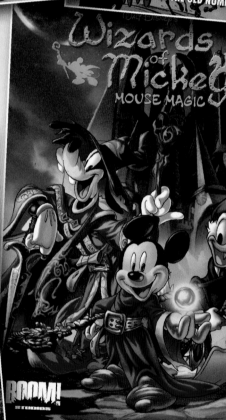

DONALD DUCK AND FRIENDS: DOUBLE DUCK VOL. 1

Donald Duck as a secret agent? Villainous fiends bew the world of super sleuthing and espionage will never the same! This is Donald Duck like you've never seen

SC $9.99 ISBN 9781608865451
HC $24.99 ISBN 9781608865512

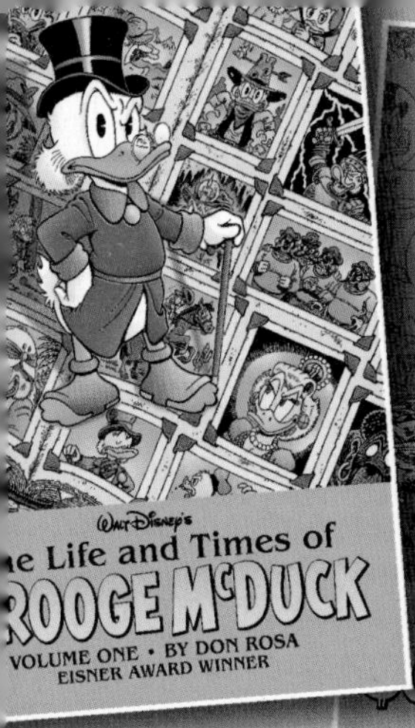
Walt Disney's
e Life and Times of
ROOGE McDUCK
VOLUME ONE • BY DON ROSA
EISNER AWARD WINNER

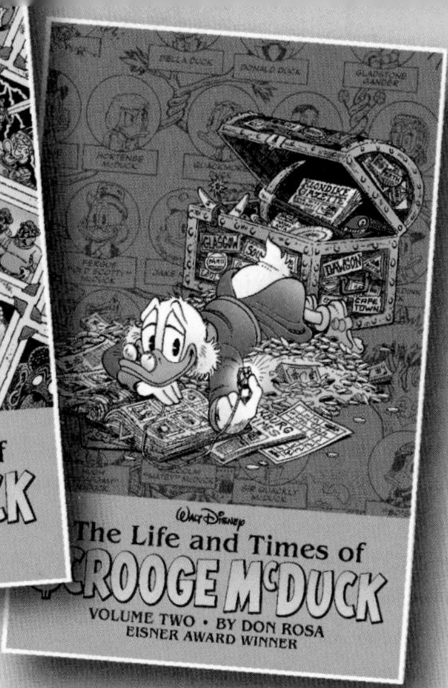
Walt Disney
The Life and Times of
SCROOGE McDUCK
VOLUME TWO • BY DON ROSA
EISNER AWARD WINNER

THE LIFE AND TIMES OF SCROOGE McDUCK VOL. 1

BOOM Kids! proudly collects the first half of THE LIFE AND TIMES OF SCROOGE MCDUCK in a gorgeous hardcover collection – featuring smyth sewn binding, a gold-on-gold foil-stamped case wrap, and a bookmark ribbon! These stories, written and drawn by legendary cartoonist Don Rosa, chronicle Scrooge McDuck's fascinating life.

HC $24.99 ISBN 9781608865383

THE LIFE AND TIMES OF SCROOGE McDUCK VOL. 2

BOOM Kids! proudly presents volume two of THE LIFE AND TIMES OF SCROOGE MCDUCK in a gorgeous hardcover collection in a beautiful, deluxe package featuring smyth sewn binding and a foil-stamped case wrap! These stories, written and drawn by legendary cartoonist Don Rosa, chronicle Scrooge McDuck's fascinating life.

HC $24.99 ISBN 9781608865420

MICKEY MOUSE CLASSICS: MOUSE TAILS

Mickey Mouse as he was meant to be seen! Solving mysteries, fighting off pirates, and nerally saving the day! These classic stories prise a "Greatest Hits" series for the mouse, including a story produced by seminal Disney creator Carl Barks!

HC $24.99 ISBN 9781608865390

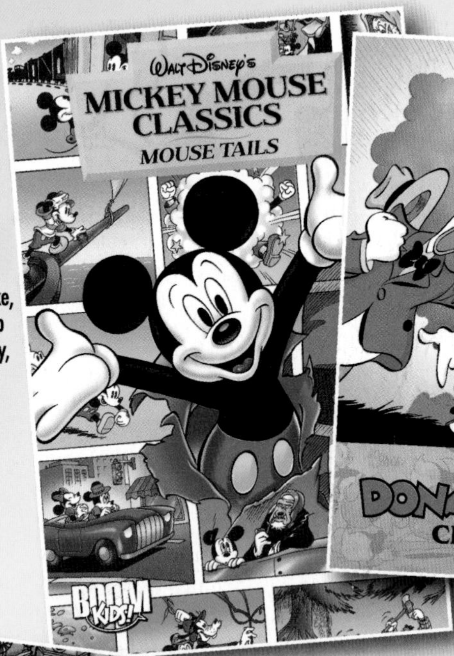
Walt Disney's
MICKEY MOUSE
CLASSICS
MOUSE TAILS
BOOM KIDS!

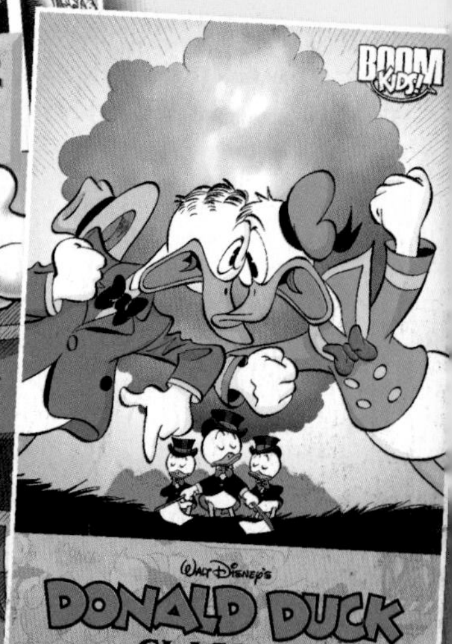
BOOM KIDS!
Walt Disney's
DONALD DUCK
CLASSICS
QUACK UP

ALD DUCK CLASSICS: QUACK UP

her it's finding gold, journeying to the Klondike, hting ghosts, Donald will always have the help much more prepared nephews – Huey, Dewey, ouie – by his side. Featuring some of the best d Duck stories Carl Barks ever produced!

24.99 ISBN 9781608865406

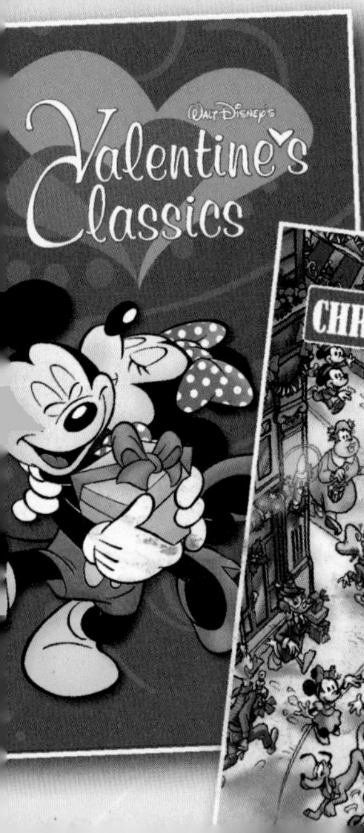
Walt Disney's
Valentine's
Classics

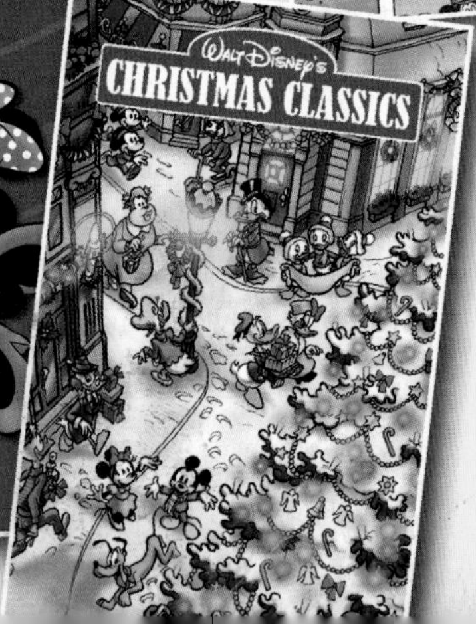
Walt Disney's
CHRISTMAS CLASSICS

WALT DISNEY'S VALENTINE'S CLASSICS

Love is in the air for Mickey Mouse, Donald Duck and the rest of the gang. But will Cupid's arrows cause happiness or heartache? Find out in this collection of classic stories featuring work by Carl Barks, Floyd Gottfredson, Daan Jippes, Romano Scarpa and Al Taliaferro.

HC $24.99 ISBN 9781608865499

WALT DISNEY'S CHRISTMAS CLASSICS

BOOM Kids! has raided the Disney publishing archives and searched every nook and cranny to find the best and the greatest Christmas stories from Disney's vast comic book publishing history for this "best of" compilation.

HC $24.99 ISBN 9781608865482

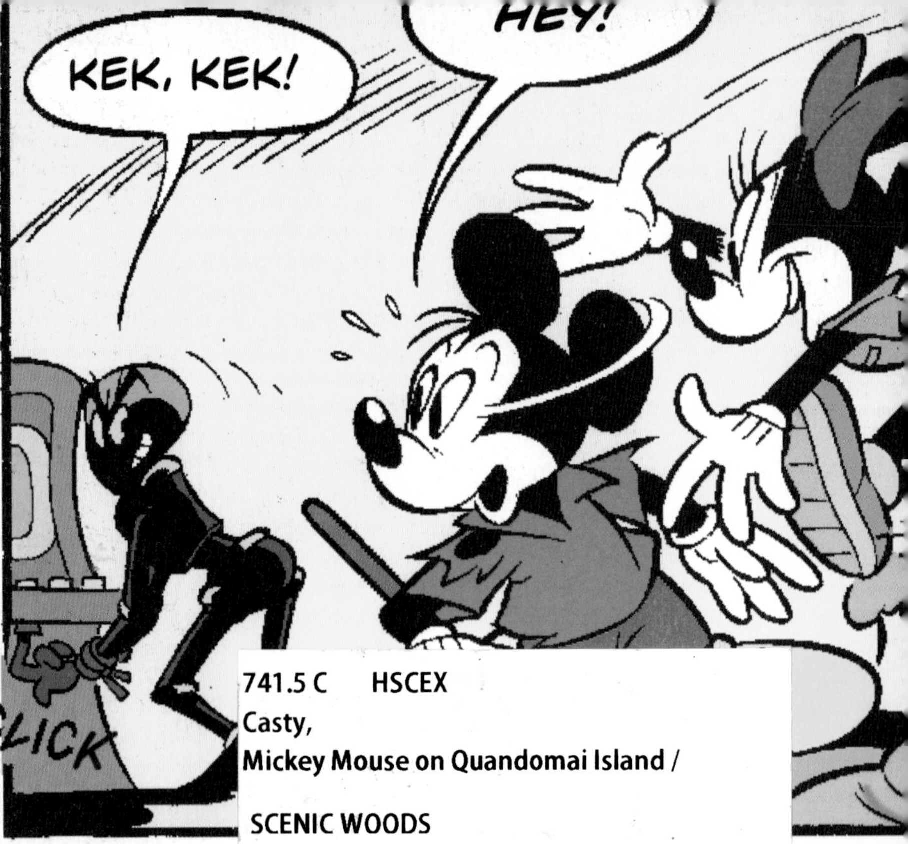
KEK, KEK!
HEY!
CLICK

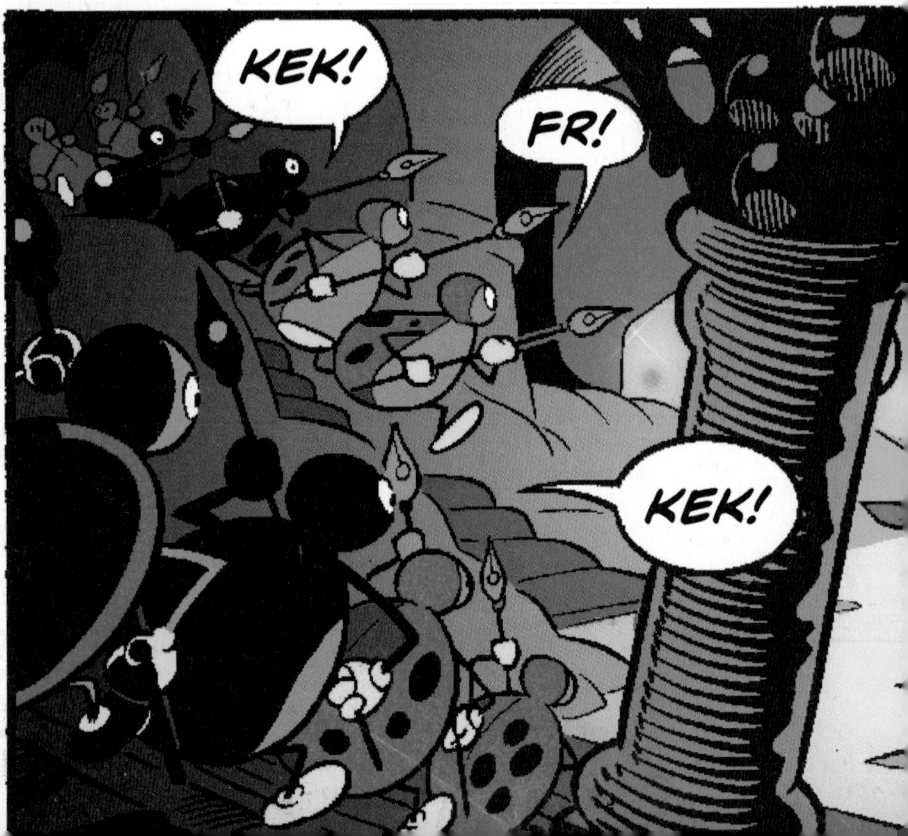
KEK!
FR!
KEK!